CAMBRIDGE LIBRARY COLLECTION

Books of enduring scholarly value

British and Irish History, Seventeenth and Eighteenth Centuries

The books in this series focus on the British Isles in the early modern period, as interpreted by eighteenth- and nineteenth-century historians, and show the shift to 'scientific' historiography. Several of them are devoted exclusively to the history of Ireland, while others cover topics including economic history, foreign and colonial policy, agriculture and the industrial revolution. There are also works in political thought and social theory, which address subjects such as human rights, the role of women, and criminal justice.

The Rural Economy of Glocestershire

William Marshall (1745–1818), from farming stock, became a farmer and then estate manager and land agent after several years spent conducting business in the West Indies. A pioneer of scientific methods of farming, he published widely on best practice, and was also known for his geographical surveys of agriculture. This two-volume 1789 work covers the county of Gloucestershire, but also includes dairy management in north Wiltshire and the orchards and fruit products of Herefordshire. A hands-on reporter, Marshall stayed in the vale of Gloucester to learn the art of cheese-making, and then spent a year in various locations studying local farming practice. Volume 2 covers the Cotswold Hills and the vale of Berkeley, with detailed descriptions of dairy farming in these areas. A section is devoted to Herefordshire, its orchards, and the manufacturing processes and marketing of its famous 'fruit liquors', cider and perry.

Cambridge University Press has long been a pioneer in the reissuing of out-of-print titles from its own backlist, producing digital reprints of books that are still sought after by scholars and students but could not be reprinted economically using traditional technology. The Cambridge Library Collection extends this activity to a wider range of books which are still of importance to researchers and professionals, either for the source material they contain, or as landmarks in the history of their academic discipline.

Drawing from the world-renowned collections in the Cambridge University Library and other partner libraries, and guided by the advice of experts in each subject area, Cambridge University Press is using state-of-the-art scanning machines in its own Printing House to capture the content of each book selected for inclusion. The files are processed to give a consistently clear, crisp image, and the books finished to the high quality standard for which the Press is recognised around the world. The latest print-on-demand technology ensures that the books will remain available indefinitely, and that orders for single or multiple copies can quickly be supplied.

The Cambridge Library Collection brings back to life books of enduring scholarly value (including out-of-copyright works originally issued by other publishers) across a wide range of disciplines in the humanities and social sciences and in science and technology.

The Rural Economy of Glocestershire

*Including its Dairy, together with the
Dairy Management of North Wiltshire,
and the Management of Orchards
and Fruit Liquor, in Herefordshire*

VOLUME 2

WILLIAM MARSHALL

CAMBRIDGE
UNIVERSITY PRESS

University Printing House, Cambridge, CB2 8BS, United Kingdom

Cambridge University Press is part of the University of Cambridge.
It furthers the University's mission by disseminating knowledge in the pursuit of
education, learning and research at the highest international levels of excellence.

www.cambridge.org
Information on this title: www.cambridge.org/9781108078818

© in this compilation Cambridge University Press 2015

This edition first published 1789
This digitally printed version 2015

ISBN 978-1-108-07881-8 Paperback

THE

RURAL ECONOMY

OF

GLOCESTERSHIRE;

INCLUDING ITS

D A I R Y:

TOGETHER WITH THE

DAIRY MANAGEMENT

OF

NORTH WILTSHIRE;

AND THE

MANAGEMENT

OF

ORCHARDS and FRUIT LIQUOR,

IN

HEREFORDSHIRE.

———————

By Mr. MARSHALL.

———————

IN TWO VOLUMES.
VOL. II.

———————

GLOCESTER:
Printed by R. Raikes,
For G. Nicol, Pall-Mall, London.
M. DCC. LXXXIX.

CONTENTS

TO THE

SECOND VOLUME.

NORTH

THE

THE

RURAL ECONOMY

OF

GLOCESTERSHIRE, &c.

IN YORKSHIRE, the more immediate vicinity of the STATION, affording an ample fupply of important information, the EXCURSIONS were neceffarily few, and fhort. Here, on the contrary, the diftrict of the STATION being lefs fertile in ufeful ideas on the fubject of thefe regifters, the excurfions have been more numerous, and made with greater deliberation.

VOL. II.   B   In

In the prefent inftance, EXCURSIONS were in a degree neceffary. The diftrict of the STATION, though evidently the beft I could have chofen for the general purpofe, was not in itfelf equal to it. The fubject DAIRY-MA-NAGEMENT muft have been left in a ftate of ob-fcurity had not the practices of the VALE OF BERKELEY, and NORTH-WILTSHIRE, been ad-ded to that of the VALE OF GLOCESTER ; nor could the fubject FRUIT-LIQUOR have been fully explained, without the practice of HEREFORDSHIRE.

The COTSWOLDS, having no immediate al-liance to the diftrict of the ftation, with regard to rural practice, might certainly have paffed as an INTERMEDIATE DISTRICT But viewing them as the fecond tract of calcarious hill which the ifland poffeffes ; and feeing the fpi-rit of improvement which has been of late years diffufed over them ; confidering, at the fame time, the near connexion they have with the diftrict of the ftation, in regard to contigu-ity of fituation ; and that I might not have them a fecond time within my reach,—it
would

would have been wrong to have neglected so
fair an opportunity; especially as I foresaw
that, with a little exertion, I should, nevertheless, be able to compass the other objects
I had in view.

The following account, of the rural practice of these hills, is offered as the produce of
an EXCURSION; not as that of a TWELVE
MONTH'S RESIDENCE. In May, 1788, I spent
a week in the center of the district; and have
been, at other times, over different parts of
it. My first object was to gain an adequate
knowledge of the district, and its general management as they appeared to the eye at the
times of survey: the next, to take a deliberate
view of the largest and best managed farm it
contains: the last, to converse with professi-
onal men upon the subject: digesting the useful ideas, as they rose, in a systematized regis-
ter, previously opened for the purpose. All
I have to say farther is, that, since the account
has received its present form, it has been seen
and approved, by those who are best able to
form an adequate judgement of the subject.

It

It might be fufficient to mention the name of Mr. PEACEY of NORTHLEACH; a man whofe fuperior management has fpread his name and charaĉter over *this* diftriĉt *at leaft*: I will, however, add that of Mr. JOHN CRADDOCK of the fame place.

THE

THE

W O L D S

O F

GLOCESTERSHIRE.

THE SITUATION of the Cotswold Hills has been given. Their outlines is irregular. Their extent, from Broadway Hill to near Tetbury, thirty miles; — from Birdlip Hill to Burford about twenty miles: containing upward of 300 square miles, or about 200,000 acres.

The surface billowy: the ftyle of hill fomewhat fimilar to that of the wolds of Yorkfhire; but lefs magnificent: the vallies are narrower, and the hills, efpecially toward the weftern margin, fharper; more in the mountain ftyle, than thofe of the Yorkfhire

wolds.

wolds. As fubjects of RURAL ORNAMENT, they are of courfe fufceptible of great beauty.

The CLIMATURE of the Cotfwold hills, when we confider their natural elevation and their prefent nakednefs, is unufually mild. I found vernal vegetation, in May, nearly as forward in the center of this highland diftrict, as in the richer warmer lands in the neighbourhood of Glocefter.

It is however remarked by men of obfervation, that thefe hills vary much as to their natural warmth. Spring fnows are obferved to pafs off fome of them much quicker than others. This is an evidence that climature depends on *foil*, or on fomething which is beneath the foil, rather than on what is generally termed *air*. The atmofpherical air is in almoft continual circulation, and cannot be liable, in the diftance of a few furlongs, or perhaps a few yards, to any other fpecific difference than that which is communicated by the foil over which it circulates, or upon which it it may chance to reft. Hence (by the way) the infalubrity of air ftagnant on ungenial foils: and hence, perhaps, the infalubrity of eafterly winds; which, travelling over an extenfive

tract

tract of continent—*land*—and having in its paffage received the communications of foils lefs genial (to our acquired habits at leaft) than our own,—become, here, injurious; not only to the animal, but to the vegetable kingdom.

In WATER, the Cotfwold hills, confidering their height, are fingularly happy. Almoft every dip has its rill, and every valley its brook. The fides of the hills abound with fprings ; and even on the higheft fwells, water generally lies within the reach of a pump. Benefits, thofe, with which few hill countries are bleffed.

The SOIL, generally, a calcarious loam: moftly mixt with gravel and fmall ftones : provincially " ftone brafh." But the foil varies much: in fome places it inclines to a lightifh loam, (a kind of foil common on cultivated hills.) In others—and moft generally—it is of a binding tenacious quality; baking with drought, and clinging to the feet in wet weather. And in fome places, efpecially on the hangs of hills, it is of a ftrong clayey nature. It may in general be called tolerable TURNEP AND BARLEY LAND. Here and there, but not often I apprehend, it comes within the idea of

WHEAT

WHEAT LAND. The *depth* of foil little:—four
to fix inches:—five inches may, I apprehend,
be confidered as the full depth, on a par of the
Cotfwold hills.

The SUBSOIL moft prevalent is a *calcarious
rubble*: namely, fmall ftones mixt with a grey
crumbly mould, full of efflorefcent matter. In
fome places a *calcarious rock* rifes to the foil:
and in others, a ftrong *loamy earth* intervenes
between the foil and the rubble.

The SUBSTRUCTURE, or natural MATERI-
ALS of which thefe hills are compofed, can only
be gueft at. Stone is found almoft everywhere
near the furface. Fine quarries of calcarious
granate are worked as freeftone, for troughs
and for building materials. Beds of clay are
here and there found ; and a fine jam of clay
marl has lately been difcovered. From thefe
circumftances, and from the fides of the hills
abounding with fprings, it feems probable that
the matter of which thefe hills are compofed is
an irregular mixture of *retentive earth* and *rock*.

ROADS are made acrofs thefe hills with fingular facility. Pits are dug by the fide of
them, and the ftones wheeled on, in barrows.
The materials, however, are more plentiful
than

than durable: prefently grinding down under heavy carriage. But the repairs are equally eafy as the forming.

This method of making and repairing roads is a great faving of team-labour; but it has its evil attendants. The pits are unfightly; and though not very deep, are neverthelefs dangerous. But the greateft evil which ftrikes me is that of their deftroying the SIDE ROADS, which every wide lane ought to have, for fummer travelling. Were a fmall fhare of attention paid to the fide flips in this and many other diftricts, the REPAIRABLE ROAD would lie in a ftate of difufe fix months in the year. It appears extraordinary that the fuperintendants of road fhould continue blind to this improvement. A very confiderable proportion of the expence which is at prefent beftowed on the roads of this kingdom might, I am fully convinced, be faved by a due attention to the wafte grounds on the fides of them.

INCLOSURE. Thirty years ago, this diftrict lay almoft entirely in an open ftate;— namely in arable common field, fheep-walk, and cow-down. At prefent, it may be faid

to

to be in a ftate of inclofure; though fome few townfhips yet remain open.

The difficulties of inclofure were not, in this cafe, numerous, or great. The fheep walks and cowdowns were all of them ftinted by "yard lands" in the arable fields: there was not, perhaps, one unftinted common on thefe hills. A circumftance fomewhat fingular. It is not, however, the only remarkable circumftance belonging to the Cotfwold townfhips. They were, formerly, many of them, or all of them, occupied by leafehold *tenants* for three lives renewable. A fpecies of *tenancy* I have not met with before. Many of thefe leafeholds had fallen in. The removal of thofe which remained, was the main obftacle of inclofure.

The effects of thefe inclofures, notwithftanding the land was appropriate in the open ftate, were very beneficial. The *arable* land in the open ftate was of little value. The improvement of this has been at leaft three fold. This improvement has been chiefly affected by turneps and the cultivated graffes. In the open ftate, fheep were only *bred:* now

the

the Cotſwold ſheep may rank among the firſt in Smithfield market.

Under the Cotſwold incloſures, the tithes of the reſpective townſhips were ſet out, in land: a circumſtance which aided much in the improvements which have taken place. The proportion was unuſually high: in ſome caſes, one fifth of the arable, and one ninth of the graſs lands of the townſhip: but the privilege of laying down ſo intolerable a burden, as that of tithes, in an arable country, can ſcarcely be purchaſed too dear.

PRODUCE. This is, in the ſtrict ſenſe of the phraſe, an *arable country*. Corn, turneps, and cultivated herbage, occupy, perhaps, nine tenths of its ſurface. Some little *ſheepwalk* and *cowdown* ſtill remain; and the bottoms and ſides of ſome of the deeper vallies are in a ſtate of *meadow*;—provincially " Engliſh graſs." There are alſo ſome patches of *woodland* ſcattered among theſe hills: one of them (in Chedworth) large—a thouſand acres.— But in general the country is bare, much too bare, of wood. A circumſtance, which thoſe who have no property in it can only regret.

But

But utility and ornament call equally loud on thofe who have, to cover its prefent naked-nefs. What a lovely paffage of hill country lies above Dowdfwell. Almoft every other part of thefe hills is capable of being rendered equally beautiful.

Viewing the Cotfwold hills as a fubject of RURAL ECONOMY, it will be proper to confider feparately the following particulars.

I. ESTATES.
II. MANAGEMENT OF ESTATES.
III. FARM BUILDINGS.
IV. DRINKING POOLS.
V. FENCES.
VI. WOODLANDS.
VII. PLANTATIONS.
VIII. FARMS.
IX. FARMERS.
X. WORKMEN.
XI. BEASTS OF LABOUR.
XII. IMPLEMENTS.
XIII. MANAGEMENT OF FARMS.
XIV. COURSE OF HUS-BANDRY.
XV. SOIL AND MANAGE-MENT.

XVI. MANURE AND MA-NAGEMENT.
XVII. HARVESTING.
XVIII. FARMYARD MA-NAGEMENT.
XIX. MARKETS.
XX. WHEAT.
XXI. BARLEY.
XXII. TURNEPS.
XXIII. CULTIVATED HER-BAGE.
XXIV. NATURAL GRASS-LAND.
XXV. HORSES.
XXVI. CATTLE.
XXVII. SHEEP.
XXVIII. SWINE.
XXIX. RABBITS.
XXX. LIST OF RATES.

I. ESTATES. Landed property is here in a few hands. Eftates moftly large. The yeomanry inconfiderable. The CHEDWORTH and the SHERBORNE eftates ftretch acrofs the

center

center of thefe hills, and include no inconfiderable part of them. Lord BATHURST has
fome eftate about his refidence near Cirencefter. Several gentlemen have likewife refi-
dencies, and confiderable eftates belonging to
them, in different parts of the diftrict. The
off eftates, I believe, are not numerous nor
great. The Cotfwolds are, or might be
made, a delightful land to *refide* in.

TENURES. Moftly *feefimple*. Some *Col-
lege leafehold*, of 21 years renewable. Little
or no *copyhold*.

II. MANAGEMENT OF ESTATES.

1. MANOR COURTS. Before the inclofures
took place, courts were held; chiefly for the
regulation of the ftinted grafs lands, and the
well ordering of the leafehold tenants. But
commons being done away, and the leafehold
tenancy becoming extinct, with the inclofure,
the manor courts have, in confequence, fallen
into difufe. A circumftance, which the country may have reafon to regret.

2. TENANCY. Notwithftanding the inclofures, and the fubfequent improvements
requifite

requifire to be made, the principal part of the tenants remain *at will*.

This might be ufed as an argument, that *leafes* are unneceffary to fpirited improvements. But it is proper to be known, that the more ftriking improvements have been made under *leafe*; and that the ordinary improvements, which have been made by tenants at will, have been made under *confidence* in the landlord.

The diabolical fpirit of over-renting has not yet got poffeffion of the owners of thefe hills; and as the eyes of men of landed property begin to open on the folly of deranging their eftates by exceffive rents, which they find can only be temporary, the neceffary confidence between landlords and tenants at will, may ftill remain unbroken on the Cotfwold hills: neverthelefs, in a country where faintfoin is the farmer's fheet anchor, it is well underftood, and is indeed felfevident, that leafes are effential to fpirited improvement. For though a general fpirit of oppreffion may not take place, *mifunderftandings* cannot always be avoided. A leafehold tenant improves with a degree of *certainty*, which gives vigour to
his

his efforts: a tenant at will, with a degree of *hazard*, which damps every intention as it rifes; and totally difcourages him from attempting the HIGHER STAGES OF IMPROVEMENT.

Moft of the *larger* farms, I underftand, are under leafes of feven, fourteen or twenty one years. Fourteen years appear to be a fatisfactory term.

3. RENT,—of the open townfhips 2s. 6d. to 5s. an acre, fubject to tithe: of the inclofed lands 6s. to 12s. an acre, tithe free.

4. RECEIVING. The times and mode vary on different eftates. The prevailing times are midfummer and Chriftmas; giving the tenants nine months credit.

5. REMOVALS. Chiefly Ladyday. Fortunately for the country, the bufinefs of removal feems to be little underftood. If the farm be let in time, the oncoming tenant fows wheat and fpring crops; if not, they probably go unfown; the outgoing tenant quitting every· thing at Ladyday; except, perhaps, the barns, which he occupies till Midfummer. How much more beneficial to an eftate and the community, when the out-

going

going tenant continues to cultivate the farm, until the day of removal; the landlord, or incoming tenant, allowing him the eſtimated value of the crops, herbage, and fallows, which are left. (See NORF: ECON: i. 79.)

6. COVENANTS. *Buildings* are erected and repaired by the landlord. *Fences* kept up by tenant, who is generally allowed to lop and crop *hedge timber* (if any upon his farm) and to fell *wheat ſtraw*; even in the center of the hills.

III. FARM BUILDINGS. 1. MATERIALS.

The WALLING MATERIALS are invariably *ſtone*. TIMBER, chiefly *oak*. COVERING, *ſlate*.— FLOORING, *ſtone, oak, deal*.

Rough ſtones for ordinary building are uſually raiſed by the perch of wall. The price 5d. to 8d. a perch of 16½ ſquare feet (that is a perch long and one foot deep) for a wall 24 inches thick. This is an unuſual, but an accurate mode of raiſing them. The variation of price is cauſed by the nature of the quarry.

The price of oak timber in the ſtick 1s. to 15d. a foot. Plenty to be had at this price. A ſtriking evidence, that a ſmall quantity of woodland

woodland is fufficient to fupply the *inland* demand for timber. The carriage, however, is to be added to the above price.

The flates (of a ftone-colour) are raifed in different parts of thefe hills. The price upon the roof—plaiftering beneath included—about 26s. a fquare (of 100 fquare feet).

Farm kitchens and lower rooms, in general, are laid with dreffed ftone. The price upon the ground complete 4½d. a foot.

CEMENT. Lime is exceffively dear; and fand not to be had, I believe, at any price; neverthelefs an excellent mortar is here prepared at a moderate expence.

Invention is feldom more fuccefsful, than when neceffity prompts it. The fcrapings of the public roads; namely levigated limeftone, impregnated more or lefs with the dung and urine of the animals travelling upon them; are found to be an excellent bafis for cement. For ordinary walls the fcrapings, alone, are frequently ufed. And from what I can learn, the proportion for the beft building is not more than one part lime to three of fcrapings. Neverthelefs I found mortar, which had not lain in the walls more than ten years, of a

VOL. II.　　　C　　　ftonelike

ftonelike tenacity: much firmer than the ordinary ftone of this country: probably much
harder than either of the ftones, from which
the bafis or the lime was made.   Similar
fcrapings might be collected in any diftrict,
where limeftone is ufed as a material of roads.

The method of PREPARING this CEMENT is
fimply that of collecting the roadfcrapings,
flaking the lime, mixing them intimately
together, and, as the mafs is worked over,
carefully picking out the ftones, or other
foulnefs which may have been collected.—
This, for ftonework, is found fufficient: for
brickwork, however, it might be neceffary,
that the materials fhould pafs through a fkreen
or fieve; previous to their being made up.

The price of lime, here, 8d. a bufhel of
eight gallons, level.   The price of coals about
30s. a ton.   The kilns fmall, *with funnel tops*;
to carry off the fmoke, and, it is faid, to give
a more regular draught.

2. FARMERIES.   I found nothing ftrikingly
new in the buildings and farm yards of the
Cotfwold Hills: except that I here met with
another GRANARY OVER A BARN FLOOR*;—
the

* See YORKS: ECON: i, 132.

the height about ten feet (juſt out of the reach
of the flail); and with two inſtances of GRA-
NARIES OVER PITCH-ROOF PORCHES; a new
idea, and a very good one. The corn is
hoiſted up by tackle; and ſhot down through
canvas tunnels into bags placed below.

The ſize of BARNS, in this country, is above
par. In height, above any I have obſerved.
Fifty two by twenty feet in the clear, and
ſixteen to twenty feet high to the plate, is
eſteemed a good barn. This ſize admits of
four bays of ten feet each, with a floor in the
middle. There are ſome remains of old mo-
naſtery barns, of great ſize, in this diſtrict.—
The height of modern barns may have ariſen
from obſerving in thoſe that " one foot below
the beams is worth two above."

BARN FLOORS are of a good ſize: 12 to
14 by 18 to 20 feet. The beſt of *oak:* ſome
of *ſtone:* but a ſpecies of *earthen floor* which
is made, here, is thought to be ſuperior to
floors of ſtone, or any other material, except
found oak plank. The ſuperior excellency
of theſe floors is owing in part to the materials of which they are made; and in part to
the method of making.

The

The materials are the calcarious earth of the fubfoil ;—a kind of ordinary gravel which is found in different parts of thefe hills ; and the chippings of freeftone (calcarious granate) from the freeftone quarries ; in equal quantities.

The method of making is on a principle peculiar perhaps to thefe hills. Earthen barn-floors, are made, in other places, with *wet* materials ;—a kind of mortar; which, as it dries, is liable to crack ; and requires fome months, after it is made, to dry it hard enough for ufe. On the contrary, the materials, in the practice under notice, are worked *dry*: they of courfe do not crack ; and are ready for ufe as foon as they are finifhed. The materials, mixed together, are fifted twice over. The firft time through a wide fieve, to catch the ftones and larger gravel ; which are thrown to the bottom of the floor. The next, through a finer fieve, to feparate the more earthy parts from the finer gravel, which is fpread upon the ftones; and upon this the more earthy parts ; making the whole about a foot thick ; and trimming down the different layers clofely and firmly upon each other. The furface being

ing levelled, it is beaten with a flat wooden beetle, made as the gardener's turf beater; until the furface become hard as ftone, and rings at every ftroke like metal. If properly made, they are faid to laft a length of years: being equally proof againft the flail and the broom.

Thefe materials, it is true, cannot be had in many diftricts; but the principle of making barn floors with DRY MATERIALS being known, other fubftances than thefe which are here in ufe, may be found to anfwer the fame purpofe.

YARD FENCES: invariably of ftone: fome of them of due height; but in general too low.

HOUSE WATER: *wells* being on thefe hills of moderate depth, *cifterns* are not neceffary:

IV. DRINKING POOLS. Where *fheep* is the prevailing ftock, FIELD WATER is lefs wanted, than it is where *cattle* abound. Neverthelefs fheep, in a dry feafon, will drink freely and frequently, when they have water to go to; and I have feen no country in which

they

they are fo affiduoufly fupplied with it, as they
are in this diftrict.

Where fprings rife on the aclivities of hills,
STONE TROUGHS are placed to catch it as it
rifes, or as it trickles down the fide of the
hill. Troughs are likewife frequently fet
acrofs rills. They make excellent drinking
places for all kinds of ftock.

In fituations deftitute of natural furface water, ARTIFICIAL POOLS are formed fomewhat
in the Yorkfhire manner. *   The ufe of lime,
however, is not known: but the nature of the
fubfoil of thefe hills being fimilar to that of
lime, worms may be lefs mifchievous in this
than in a fat non-calcarious fubfoil. The quantity of *clay* ufed here is much greater than in
Yorkfhire. Three coats ; each of them nearly
as thick as the fingle coat of Yorkfhire. But
they have much lefs labour beftowed upon
them ; only one beating each. The three coats
are nearly a foot thick when finifhed. The
clay is generally covered with *gravel*; on which
is fet a PAVEMENT ! A mode of finifhing
of which I had conceived a high idea in theory: and which is here proved to be good in
practice.

* See YORK: ECON: vol. i. p. 146.

pra&ice. * The ftones are fet edgeway ; but
in the inftance, I have feen, they are too fmall ;
efpecially near the brim ; and in general perhaps the *run* is not fufficiently attended to.
But pools, here, are principally intended for
fheep.

Artificial pools have now been made in this
manner thirty years ; and few (if any) failures
have yet, I underftand, happened.

The form of thefe pools is general.y fquare.
One fourteen yards fquare coft in manual labour 18l. Befides the carriage of ninety loads
of clay, two miles: together about 30l. But
this was made by the day, and no requifite expence fpared: the common price, by the grofs,
is 2s. 6d. a fquare yard ; meafuring the pavement when finifhed,

V. FIELD FENCES. LIVE HEDGES and
WALLS: the latter much the mo ftfrequent.
In fome few fpots, where good ftones are not
found in plenty near the furface, whitethorn is
planted, and thrives well. But live hedges
                                                  are

---

* It is proper to add, that, at the time I wrote the article
referred to above, I was an entire ftranger to the pra&ice of
forming pools on the Cotfwold hills.

C 4

are expenfive to raife. Ditches cannot be funk. Two guard fences are requifite; and materials fcarce. On the contrary, walls are raifed at a fmall expence, and are fences immediately. This alone can apologize for their frequency. The country in general is ftill to the eye as *naked* and is almoft as deftitute of *fhelter,* as it was before the inclofures took place. There is one inftance, and I believe only one, of planting whitethorn under the walls. A practice which ought to be encouraged. The wall and the live hedge, together, will be a much better fhelter than either of them, alone. The climature of the bleaker fwells would by this means be rendered much more genial, than it is at prefent.

The dimenfions of the Cotfwold FENCE-WALL is 26 inches at the bafe; 18 inches at the coping; and 4½ feet high, exclufive of a coping of flat ftones, where thefe are to be had. Sometimes a " comb" o f ftones fet edgeways is ufed as a finifh to the top.

The line of the intended fence being drawn, and the foundation cut out, quarries are dug by the fide of it, the ftones are wheeled in barrows, and the wall built by a gauge, by *mafons.* If the wall be fet upon the foil; the turf is li-

able

able to rot partially, and throw down the fence.

The coft of a wall thus made, and of thefe dimenfions, is eight to ten pounds a furlong, or about 10d. a yard. A penny a yard is the common price for walling; the raifing and wheeling, 8d. to 10d. a yard.

TEMPORARY FENCES—bar hurdles and ha-zle hedges.

VI. WOODLANDS. One extenfive woodland near the center of thefe hills: chiefly in a ftate of *wood:* namely timber and coppice wood mixed. The timber chiefly oak: the underwood afh and hazle: the former ufed for hurdles;—the latter for temporary hedges and fuel.

VII. PLANTATIONS. Unfortunately for the Cotfwold hills, a fpirit of planting has never been generally diffufed among them. Something has been done about Guiting and Dowdefwell. And an anceftor of Lord Sher-borne laid out and planted a new park, near his refidence at Sherborne. And Lord Bathurft's grounds near Cirencefter are well known.

known. But thefe have all been done with a view to ornament, merely. The propagation of wood *for the ufe of eſtates* appears not to have taken place; excepting ſome ſmall ASHEN COPPICES, which have been made, and ſtill I fee continue to be made, in the vallies, for hurdle ſtuff. Farms, in general, may be ſaid to be totally deſtitute of wood. Coals are fetcht 20 to 30 miles by land carriage; and faggot wood perhaps 8 or 10 miles. Not a pole upon the farm to aſſiſt in making a temporary fence, nor perhaps even a handful of bruſhwood to kindle the fire. Straw, I am afraid, is here conſidered as an article of fuel: a circumſtance which reflects no credit on the owners of landed eſtates.

It ſtrikes me forcibly that the corners and aſperities of every eſtate ought to be cut off, and the angles filled up with COPPICE WOOD: and that the more central farms ought each of them ·to have its SKREEN COPPICES; ſufficiently extenſive to admit of a plot being filled every year, for the uſe of the farm, and the cottagers of the townſhip it lies in.

In winter, the poor, on theſe ſhelterleſs hills, muſt be in a wretched ſtate as to FUEL.

There

There are few hill countries which do not afford either wood, coals, peat, or at leaft turf; but here ftraw may be faid to be the only fuel the country at prefent produces. Fortunately for the farmers ftone walls will not readily burn.

Few countries are fo well adapted to the propagation of woodland as this. Wall is of all other the beft plantation fence ; and here it is raifed at an eafy expence. Mark out the intended fite: cleanfe it by a turnep or a whole fummer fallow: wall is round: dibblè in acorns, beech mafts, afh keys, hazle nuts, or other feeds of wood beft adapted to the purpofe intended: cleanfe during the firft three or four years: and fell at the age beft fuited to the ware required.

For the minutiæ of the propagation of woodland from feeds, fee PLANTING and ORNAMENTAL GARDENING, a practical treatife, page 506.

VIII. FARMS. It is needlefs to fay that the Cotfwold farms are ftrictly ARABLE: though moft of them, efpecially on the eaftern margin, have more or lefs grafsland belonging

to

to them; but, in almoſt any inſtance, it is inconſiderable, comparatively with the arable land.

he SIZE of farms, moſtly large: from 200 to 1000 acres each. There is one inſtance of a tenant occupying near 2000 acres. Five hundred acres may be conſidered as a middle-ſized farm.

With reſpect to PLAN, the Cotſwold farms are in general without regularity. The houſes ſtand moſtly in villages. Even in the incloſed townſhips there are few central farmeries. One exception, however, on Lord Sherborne's eſtate, requires to be noticed. In this inſtace, five hundred acres are laid out *at preſent* in nine incloſures; with a commodious drift way acroſs the middle; and with a farmery, and a large artificial drinking pool near its center. Altogether perhaps as well laid out as the nature of it would admit. But no wonder:—it was planned by its intended occupier;—a *profeſſional* man; and one who in truth ſtands among the firſt of the profeſſion.

IX. FARMERS.

IX. FARMERS, The Cotſwolds, like other large-farm diſtricts, abound with intelligent, reſpectable farmers.

X. WORKMEN. LABOURERS are remarkably numerous for the nature of the country; and their wages as remarkably low. A ſhilling a day, no beer, in autumn, winter, and ſpring. Fourteen pence in hay time; except for mowing 18d.; and 2s. a day, for five weeks certain, in harveſt. Women in autumn and ſpring 6d. in hay time 7d. in harveſt 1s. No beer; except what is given voluntarily.

SERVANTS' wages are likewiſe low: ten pounds the higheſt. Second men ſo low as five or ſix pounds. The ſtanding food of farmers' ſervants, here, is bacon: with which they are allowed vegetables: a ſalutary accompaniment, which theſe moſt uſeful members of ſociety are, perhaps through a miſtaken policy, debarred from, in ſome diſtricts.

XI. BEASTS OF LABOUR. *Horſes* and *oxen.* The proportion, I fear, more than two to one.

OXEN,

Oxen, however, are in good eftimation; and, what is ftill more pleafing, they are growing in the efteem of moft farmers; and their number, in confequence, annually en-creafing. They are all worked in harnefs, at length, alone. The collar and hames being ufed as for horfes; not reverfed, as in moft cafes they are for oxen. They appear to be perfectly handy, and work, either at plow or cart, in a manner which fhews that, although horfes may in fome cafes be *convenient*, and in moft cafes *pleafurable to the driver*, they are by no means *neceffary* to hufbandry.

The BREEDS *of* WORKING OXEN, on thefe hills, are thofe of Glocefterfhire, Hereford-fhire, and South Wales (a variety of the mid-dlehorned breed). They are ufually bought in at four years old, and worked till fix; when they are either fold to graziers, or fatted on the premifes. There are inftances of their being worked to twelve or fourteen years old. But few work well to that age. They are found to grow heavy and inactive. Every thing, however, depends on breed: and, by due attention, a breed of oxen might, with-out doubt, be obtained, which would work

well

well, and fat kindly, at twelve or fourteen years old.

The FOOD OF WORKING OXEN is ftraw in winter; hay in fpring; and raygrafs, with other cultivated graffes, in fummer. They are feldom worked in winter, while at ftraw; except to keep them in a degree of exercife, and enure the young ones to harnefs. In early fpring, when they are firft put to the plow; they have ordinary hay or " faintfoin or raygrafs ftraw:" which, after *corn ftraw*, and before the dry winds of March have rendered them dry and harfh, are eaten with fufficient appetite. As fpring advances, better hay is afforded them.

From the time they are put to hay in the fpring, until they are thrown up to ftraw in autumn, oxen which are kept folely for work, are generally in harnefs fix days in the week. They are moftly ufed in plowing.

A MOVEABLE HARNESS-HOUSE—a wooden cabin with a fledge bottom—is drawn from pafture to pafture, or from place to place, as circumftances may require; by which means no time or labour is loft, either by the oxen, or their drivers. Five oxen are a team.

The

The HORSES worked on thefe hills are of the heavy-heeled kind; but, in general, lighter than they are in many other diftriĉts. Men of penetration, here, begin to fee the folly of fending elephants to plow: it would, indeed, be equally wife to fend horfes to battle with caftles on their backs. The horfe, which feems to be growing into eftimation as a plow horfe, at leaft, is a kind of ftrong coach horfe; the beft breed for the purpofe this kingdom is poffeffed of.

Five horfes are confidered as a team; and are the prevailing plow team of the country; except for ftirring turnep fallows;—during which operation fome few plow teams of four horfes each are feen.

A particularity in the manner of FEEDING CART HORSES with corn, here, is noticeable. In the ordinary practice of other diftriĉts, it is the cuftom for each carter to feed his own team. But here, one man, the " head car- ter," corns the whole ftable. This may be a means of preventing pilfering. Indeed, the feeder being confidered as a confidential man, is feldom allowanced. Another advantage in this cafe is, that only one confidential fervant

is

is requifite; whereas, when every man has the fole care of his own horfes, more or lefs confidence is obliged to be placed in each.

A circumftance, occurring in this diftrict, relative to the TREATMENT of FARM HORSES, is entitled to notice. The idea is not new to me; but I have not met with an incident, before, fufficiently authentic to warrant its being mentioned.

In the livery ftables in London, HE-GOATS are kept, for the purpofe of preferving the health of the horfes, which ftand in them.—Many carriers keep them in their ftables for the fame purpofe; and I have fomewhere met with an inftance of farmers doing the fame; particularly as a prevention of the *ftaggers:* but I have always confidered it as one of thofe popular *charms,* of which *wonderful* effects are related in every country. Nor have I yet any *proof* to the contrary: all I have at prefent to produce is *ftrong evidence:.* I give it, however, on fuch authority as no one, who know the author, will difpute.

About fixteen years ago, Mr. William Peacey, of Northleach, loft feveral horfes in the ftaggers. He was advifed by a friend,

VOL. II. D whofe

whofe experience had led him to believe, that
he had benefited much by what he recommended,—to keep a he-goat in his ftables.—
He got one, and had not for many years another inftance of the diforder. While the goat
lived, his horfes were free from the ftaggers ;
but the goat dying, his horfes again became
afflicted with this alarming diforder. He procured another goat (which is ftill living) and
has not fince had an inftance of the ftaggers.
He has feldom lefs than twenty horfes in his
ftables.

I do not mean to *recommend*, in general
terms, the keeping of goats in farm ftables.
But if this terrible difeafe can be prevented
at fo trifling an expence, what farmer in his
fenfes would be in want of a goat ? In the
midland counties, three years ago, many
farmers loft all their beft horfes in the ftaggers. Lofs, to the amount of feveral thoufand pounds was fuftained in Staffordfhire
alone.

I dwell the longer on this incident, as it
appears to me probable, that the influence
of the goat is not merely that of a charm.
The ftaggers appears evidently to be a *ner-*
vous

vous diforder. Odours are found in many
cafes, I believe, to act beneficially on the human nerves ; and, poffibly, the ftrong fcent
of the goat may have a fimilar effect on thofe
of the horfe. The fubject is certainly entitled
to enquiry.

XII. IMPLEMENTS. The Cotfwold
WAGGON has been mentioned. The vale
waggons are faid to be copied from it ; and
every country might profit by its introduction.

The Cotfwold PLOW is of the old long heavy
conftruction ; with a fingle wheel. It is
fteady, and makes good work, if properly
ufed; but requires great draught.——Five
horfes or five oxen; never, I believe, lefs
than four. Soil, which is at once tenacious
and ftoney, requires, no doubt, a fteady plow,
and a ftrong team: neverthelefs, I am of
opinion, that there is at prefent a wafte of
team labour upon thefe hills. The double
plow of Warwickfhire is, perhaps, the moft
likely to effect an improvement. The Norfolk plow has been introduced; I faw two or
three of them at work in one piece of turnep
ground; where they made good work; but

they

they are unfit for the Cotſwold ſoil; except in the fallowing ſeaſon. The Yorkſhire plow would work much better in it. The Turn-wreſt plow is certainly wanted on the " ſide-land" farms.

But a multiplicity of implements incurs an expence, which few farmers are willing to pay. Yet if any department of huſbandry requires the eſpecial attention of the *arable* farmer, it is that of working his land at as eaſy an ex-pence as poſſible. If the Cotſwold farmers object to two ſets of plows, let them endeavour to improve their own.

XIII. MANAGEMENT OF FARMS.

The primary OBJECT of the Cotſwold huſ-bandry is SHEEP. *Cattle* are ſecondary, and comparatively few in number. *Horſes* and *ſwine* are ſubordinate; being kept merely for the uſe of the farm.

The *marketable crops* are BARLEY and WHEAT. The *ſubordinate crops*, raiſed for the ſupport of the live ſtock, are *turneps, oats, peas, vetches* (vicia ſativa) *tares* (ervum hirſu-tum!) *ſaintfoin*, other *cultivated graſſes, natural graſsland*.

The

The great art of farming in a hill country lies in guarding againſt dry ſeaſons; and, of courſe, in proportioning the ſtock and the ſubordinate crops, in ſuch a manner, as always to have a ſufficient ſtore of dry food before hand; and *room* enough, at leaſt, in the paſture grounds. To overſtock any farm is bad management: to overſtock a hill farm is unpardonable.

XIV. COURSE OF HUSBANDRY.

The Cotſwold farmers have either fallen into the Norfolk ſyſtem of aration, or have ſtruck one out ſimilar to it. The prevailing practice, in the incloſed townſhips, is to divide the arable land into ſeven parts. One for ſaintfoin; the other ſix for the following crops.

Turneps,	Graſſes,
Barley,	Wheat,
Graſſes,	Oats, peas, &c.

Conſidering the profitableneſs of ſaintfoin, in any ſeaſon, and its being in a manner proof againſt a dry one; and conſidering at the ſame time the diſpoſition of the ſoil of theſe hills to produce it,—a ſeventh of the arable land may ſeem too ſmall a proportion for this almoſt

D 3   ineſtimable

ineftimable crop. But a fourth would, perhaps, be too great a fhare. It, therefore,
feems neceffary, that the round of annual crops
fhould be altered, or that the whole fhould
remain under the prefent regulation *.

XV. SOIL AND MANAGEMENT.

The soil has been fufficiently defcribed.—
We, therefore, proceed to its MANAGEMENT.

1. BREAKING-UP. During the inclofure,
a greater or lefs quantity of old turf was, probably, broken up, in moft townfhips. But,
at prefent, the only fubject of this operation
is faintfoin ley.

The invariable method of breaking up old
turf, on thefe hills, is, by SODBURNING FOR
TURNEPS. Except in fome few cafes, in
which landlords, for want of due information

on

---

* The ANCIENT COURSE of the common fields of thefe
hills was fingular. Each townfhip was divided into two
fields; for " crop and fallow,"—alternately: one year
wheat and barley, the next a whole year's fallow : except
a fmall part of each townfhip, which was ufed as a kind
of every year's land; for growing a few peas, oats, or
other fubordinate crop.

on the fubject, debar their tenants from be-
nefiting by this excellent practice*.   In thefe
cafes, the turf is broken up with the plow,
for oats, peas, &c. and got into tilth, next
year, for turneps.

The art of fodburning—provincially " paring and burning"—or " breaft-plowing"—
is well conducted; and the benefits arifing
from it feem to be, in general, well underftood.   The great difficulty, here, is in get-
ting turf tough enough to handle, and rough
enough to burn.   Temporary leys, and even
ftubble, are not unfrequently pared; and, if
unfit for burning, the parings, when duly
digefted, plowed under with the feed plowing of the fucceeding crop.   This is found
to be nearly as cheap as two plowings; and,
in many refpects, preferable.

This practice is new to me.   It feems ad-
mirably adapted as a preparation for fowing on
one plowing.   The furface weeds are effectually cut off; and, by lying fome time on the
furface, become a fit nutriment to the infant
crop.   In plowing, the fod naturally falls to
the

* See YORK: ECON: i, 304.

D 4

the bottom of the furrow; and not only prevents the feed from running down too low, and
thereby being buried too deep, but forms a
proper nidus for it to fall in. The infant plants,
inftead of having the living weeds to ftruggle
with (which is the cafe when the whole furrow
is fown, as in moft cafes it ought to be, while
frefh) find in them, when digefted, a friendly
affiftance: while the toughnefs of the furrows
being done away, by the operation, they become obedient to the harrow: the furface is, of
courfe, rendered fine, and the feed duly covered.

The Cotfwold labourers are expert and in-
defatigable in the work of " breaft plowing"
—the moft flavifh work of hufbandry. The
paring, burning and fpreading has been done
for 15s. an acre! from 15 to 20s. the common price; *notwithftanding the ftoninefs of the
foil.* In fome diftricts the paring, alone,
would coft as much. Paring for plowing under is fometimes got done in winter, a leifure
feafon, fo low as 5 to 7s. an acre. When fods
intended to be burnt have been caught in a
rainy feafon, as they are liable to be in every
country, and have grown to the ground by lying

ing a length of time upon it, they have been
turned back again, for half a crown an acre.
An admirable operation, this, when it can be
done at fo low an expence.

Sods are all burnt in fmall heaps, about a
rod apart ; the unburnt pieces are collected
and burnt together in frefh heaps. Not a piece
of raw fod the fize of the hand to be feen.
Sometimes the afhes are fpread prefently after
burning; but more generally, I apprehend,
they are fuffered to ftand in heaps, until barley feed time be done ; when they are fpread
among the grafs and weeds which have rifen,
and the land plowed the firft time for turneps.

2. TILLAGE. The Cotfwold farmers are
fparing of tillage: in the ordinary courfe of
hufbandry, they never plow more than once
for any crop; except turneps ; and for this,
in the common practice of the country, feldom more than three times. So that in the
eftablifhed round they have fix crops for fix
plowings.

There are men, however, who do not limit
the number of their turnep-fallow plowings ;
but continue ftirring until the weeds be overcome, and the foil be brought into a proper
ftate

ftate of tilth ; and they find their account in it,
I faw a piece of clover, fucceeding, in courfe,
a turnep fallow of feven plowings ; and it was
worth any other two pieces of equal fize I faw
in the country. This, and the other crops of
the courfe, will, in all probability, pay ten fold
for the extra plowings.

It would certainly be eligible in any large
occupier to have a fet of light two-horfe plows,
for the purpofe of ftirring his fallows. He
would with them give his fallows five plowings, with the fame expence he now gives
them three The price of the Yorkfkire plow
complete is not thirty fhillings * : if men could
be got to hold them properly, a fet of thefe
plows would earn their coft doubly the firft
feafon.

With the prefent extravagant plow team,
farmers, in general, cannot *afford* to keep their
lands in fufficient tilth. The ordinary price of
plowing is 8s. an acre. Each plowing now
cofts them, perhaps, as much as the rent of
their land.

The Cotfwold farmers are fingular in their
ideas refpecting a leading principle of tillage.
They

* See YORK: ECON: vol. i. p. 277.

They endeavour to plow, for a crop, when the foil is *wet* ; and to work even their *fallows*, when they are *moift*. They argue that if they plow their fallows dry, they lofe their foil, which gets fhallower every ftirring. This is, probably, owing to the nature of the foil, and the nature of their team. The foil is moftly of a binding quality. Five horfes following each other, in the fame track, render it, in dry weather, as firm, and almoft as hard, as a pavement. In the next ftirring, the fhare refufes to lay hold of it ; and, in this operation, another layer of foil is trodden down. Two horfes drawing abreaft would not produce this effect.

It may be faid to be the univerfal opinion of farmers throughout the kingdom, that fallows moft efpecially ought to be plowed when they are *dry*. I never met with the moft diftant intimation, before, that plowing them when *wet*, or even *moift*, was anyway eligible ; excepting two incidents which occured in my own practice ; in which plowing fallows *very wet*, was apparently deftructive of couchgrafs. *

The

The intention, however, of the practice under notice, is not that of deftroying weeds, but of affifting the crop: nevertheless, it is obfervable, that, notwithftanding the fmall quantity of tillage which the lands of thefe hills receive, they are far from being remarkably foul ;—nor do they appear to the eye ftrikingly deficient in tilth. Their productivenefs, however, is not equal to their general appearance: and, *perhaps*, working the land while wet is at once injurious to the weeds and the crops which follow.

One objection will probably be made to this general pofition. It is obferved, in many countries, that wheat never fucceeds better than when the feed plowing is given while the foil is wet. But may not the advantage, in this cafe, arife from the prevention of weeds, rather than from any immediate benefit to the crop ?

Thefe reflections, however, are offered with the greateft diffidence. The PRINCIPLES OF TILLAGE may be faid to be as little known, now, as they appear to have been in the day of Hefiod. Much, no doubt, depends on fituation and fpecific quality of foil: neverthelefs,

lefs, it is not probable, that a practice fo clofely connected with an important procefs of nature, as is that of adapting the foil to the purpofes of vegetation, fhould be entirely deftitute
of GENERAL PRINCIPLES. Every glimmering
of light, tho' faint, ought, therefore, to be collected, in order to endeavour to elucidate
this important fubject, and raife it from its
prefent obfcurity.

Another inftance of practice refpecting fallows is entitled to particular attention. It requires no comment: its eligibility is evident
at fight; and its eftablifhment as a practice is
likely to reflect much credit on the fpirited
management of thefe hills. For although it
may be faid to be, as yet, the practice of one
individual only,—this individual is at the head
of his profeffion; in a country which abounds
with intelligent hufbandmen; and there can
be no doubt of a practice fo obvioufly eligible
being extended.

I have myfelf WEEDED a fallow, to prevent
the weeds from feeding before the plows could
be at leifure to turn them under; but never
had an idea of the HOING OF FALLOWS, until

til I faw the operation in practice, upon the Cotfwold hills.

It has hitherto been chiefly applied to beds of the *common corn thiftle*; and with ftriking fuccefs. I walked over a piece of wheat after a thiftley fallow; without perceiving a thiftle in it. Though it had neither been hoed nor weeded. It was in effect *weeded in the fallow*.

The operation is performed fome days, or perhaps a few weeks, before plowing.—the hoe taking off the top, fomewhat beneath the crown, the root has frefh fhoots to make: while thefe fhoots are yet in a tender ftate, the plow fevers the root below. By thefe means the plants, if not deftroyed, receive a check which they do not readily recover.

The work is done by women, boys and girls, with full-fized turnep hoes. The operation requires no dexterity, nor is it by any means tedious. There are no plants to fet out; nor any crop to hinder. When the ground is gone over, the hoers return to the fide they began upon, and go over it a fecond time, to cut up fuch as have been miffed, in the firft time going over.

The

The fame excellent manager fpuds up thiftles, and other perennial weeds, in his raygrafs leys, previous to their being plowed for wheat ; and with a fimilar effect. His wheats feldom or ever want weeding. It is always better management to PREVENT WEEDS, than to DESTROY THEM IN THE CROP.

XVI. MANURES and MANAGE-MENT. The MANURES principally in ufe are *dung*, *fheepfold*, and *afhes* procured by fod-burning. A bed of a fpecies of blue *marl* has lately been difcovered, and its effect proved on grafsland.

The effect of *dung* on the Cotfwold foil is extraordinary. There is an inftance produced of its lafting near fifty years ! Its effect is evident in a piece of wheat now growing (May 1788) on a patch, lately common field land, which now makes part of an inclofure.

But this extraordinary effect is on land which lies at a great diftance from the dung yard ; and is perhaps no more than an incident, (ftriking in thofe days) of the efficacy of a *new* manure,—even of dung,—on land which has not been accuftomed to it. It is well known that

that the dung of *sheep* (the sheepfold) is singularly beneficial to land which has not been folded upon; and there seems to be no reason why the dung of *horses* and *cattle* should not be similar in their effects. The duration is the only thing extraordinary. The retentive nature of the soil is the only probable cause of it. Had not the fact been well authenticated by a most intelligent husbandman *, who has personal knowledge of the circumstance, and has probably seen every crop which has grown upon the land since the circumstance took place, I should not have thought it an object of notice.

MANURING. In the established course of husbandry, the manure is wholly applied to the turnep crop. And for this seldom more is set on than ten loads of dung an acre.

XVII. HARVESTING. The harvest is got in chiefly without foreign assistance: (except some few reapers from the forest of Wichwood): a remarkable circumstance in a wold country. Wheat is invariably reaped and set up in " shucks" *uncovered.* Barley
and

---

* Mr. John Craddock of Northleach.

and oats are mown outward, and harvefted in fwath. The work is principally done by harveftmen, hired for five weeks certain, at two fhillings a day, no board nor beer; except what is voluntarily given.

XVIII. FARMYARD MANAGEMENT. 1. BARN MANAGEMENT. Thrafh in the fouth-country manner. Winnow, in the common practice of the country, with the fail fan. Some few machine fans in the diftrict.

2. STRAWYARD MANAGEMENT. Store cattle go loofe in yards. The ftraw being given in moveable cribs: or in mangers formed againft the fences.

I met with an idea, here, that cattle may be fatiated with ftraw ; or, in other words, may be ferved with it in too great plenty. It has been obferved, that after a dry fummer, when ftraw is fcarce and the cattle have it dealt out to them regularly, they do better, than when, after a plentiful year, it is thrown before them in profufion from the thrafhing floor. Not through the fuperior quality of the ftraw in a

fcarce year; as thefe effects have been obferved to be produced from the fame ftraw.

This fubject is by no means uninterefting
to thofe who winter large quantities of cattle.
I have obferved in Yorkfhire, where cattle are
kept tied up, and of courfe are regularly fed,
that they in general do better at ftraw, than
cattle in the fouth of England where they go
loofe among a much greater plenty; but
whether it proceed from the warmth, from
their refting better, from the breed of cattle,
or from their being regularly fed and *eating
with an appetite*, I will not pretend to decide.

XIX. MARKETS. Smithfield, principally, for fheep and cattle. Glocefter for
barley. The country millers for wheat. It is
obfervable that in this diftrict; more particularly, I believe, in the manufacturing country, about Stroud;—the miller and the baker
center in the fame man. The mill and the
bakehoufe being covered by the fame roof.

XX. WHEAT. 1. The SPECIES principally " red lammas"—fome " cone" is grown;
but it is not fo prevalent here as in the vale.

A NEW

A NEW VARIETY of cone wheat has lately been raifed, from the mere circumftance of finding one grain in a parcel of feed. The body is remarkably long and large; but the quality, (as yet) is not good, or at leaft not fightly. I mention it merely to fhew that, by a little attention, new forts of corn may be readily raifed; even from a fingle grain.

2. SUCCESSION. Wheat generally fucceeds the fecond year's ley, once plowed. When land is very foul, it is fometimes fummerfallowed for wheat.

3. TILLAGE. Endeavour to begin plowing early in July; and let the land lie in rough furrow until fown.

4. SOWING. 1. *Time of fowing.* The Cotfwold hills are in a manner proverbial for the early fowing of wheat. Auguft and September are the principal months. The general rule is to begin plowing in July, and begin fowing the firft *wet weather* in Auguft. Wheat feed time therefore generally commences in wheat harveft. Scarcely a handful of new wheat is fown in the diftrict.

It is, however, feldom fown when more than one year old. There is, indeed a popu-

lar

lar idea (not altogether well founded however)
that wheat will not grow if more than that
age.

The Cotſwold farmers wiſh to ſee the
ground covered before Michaelmas. The
motives held out for this very early ſowing are,
that leſs ſeed is by this means requiſite ; and
that it is known from experience that early
ſown wheats do the beſt on the Cotſwold land.

This is another ſtriking evidence of the
wide difference in the cuſtoms of countries,
with reſpect to the time of ſowing wheat ; and
corroborates, ſtrongly, the idea of theſe cuſtoms being founded on EXPERIENCE ; not on
habit or *caprice*. The diſtricts which form the
two extremes are included within the ſame
county: lie contiguous to each other ! A
ſtone might be ſlung from the country which
ſows its wheat in Auguſt, into that which ſows
its wheat in December !

2. *Quantity of ſeed.* In Auguſt, the ordinary quantity is *ſix pecks* ; about fourteen
gallons;—in September *two buſhels* (9½ gallons each). But it has been found that *one
buſhel* ſown in Auguſt, provided the land be
clean and in heart, is abundantly ſufficient !

We

We may venture to fay that one third of the
feed wheat fown in moft other diftricts is faved
in this. A faving of fome importance when
wheat is dear.

3. *Covering.* " Dragged" and " harrowed":
that is harrowed with rough and fine harrows:
and what is peculiar, I believe, to the weft of
England, SHEEP are generally PENNED upon
the land, or at leaft DRIVEN repeatedly
over it, between the fowing and the coming
up. A practice which might perhaps be
found beneficial in other upland diftricts,

5. VEGETATING PROCESS. If wheat get
rank in autumn, it is efteemed good management to eat it down with fheep: not, however,
by a few kept long upon it; but by a large
flock, at once.

This is a new idea. The practic emay be
good. The great complaint againft the early
fowing of wheat is that of its being liable to get
winter-proud. EATING it off, in AUTUMN,
may give it a check, and prevent that evil confequence. Eating it *in Spring* is here confidered as pernicious.

Wheat is ufually *weeded* with fpud-hooks;
not hoed, as in the vale. One inftance, how-

ever, in which a thin crop, full of feed weeds,
was HOED IN AUTUMN with uncommon fuccefs, occurred in the practice of a fuperior
manager, in this diftrict: and others in which
wheat have been WEEDED IN AUTUMN, with
great advantage. Where wheat is fown very
early, as in this diftrict, and the land at the
fame time full of feed weeds, one or other of
thefe operations feems to be in a degree requifite.

6. HARVESTING. The method of har-
vefting has been mentioned.

I met with a well authenticated inftance,
here, of the good effect of *cutting* MILDEWED
WHEAT while *very green*. A fine piece of
wheat being lodged by heavy rains, and being
foon after perceived to be infected with the mildew, was cut, though ftill in a perfectly green
ftate: namely about three weeks before the
ufual time of cutting. It lay fpread abroad
upon the ftubble until it became dry enough
to prevent its caking in the fheaf; when it
was bound and fet up in fhucks. The refult
of this treatment was, the grain, though
fmall, was of a fine colour, and the heavieft
wheat which grew upon the fame farm that

feafon:

feafon ; owing no doubt to the thinnefs of its fkin. What appears much more remarkable the ftraw was perfectly bright ; not a fpeck upon it.

The idea of the judicious manager, in whofe practice this expedient took place, is, that cutting the crop, " as foon as it is ftruck, *kills* the mildew." And on this principle he practifes himfelf, and recommends in general terms, the cutting of mildewed wheat " as foon as it is ftruck." It is well underftood that the fap or nutriment, which is in the ftems of corn that is cut under-ripe, circulates to the ear, and fills the grain, in the fame, or in a fimilar manner, as it would have done, had the ftems remained upon their roots. Hence, the advantage of cutting mildewed wheat as foon as it is infected with the difeafe feems to be, that, by thus ftopping the dif-eafe, the nourifhment in the ftraw, paffes to the ear in a pure untainted ftate.

7. BARN MANAGEMENT. Wheat is moft of it kept in the rick over the winter ; and, when the markets are flat, frequently over the year. There is at this time (May 1788) more unthrafhed wheat on the wolds of Glo-

cefterfhire,

cefterfhire, than perhaps any other entire county is poffeffed of. The *ftrength* of the farmers,
and the practice of fowing old wheat, account
for it. In countries where new wheat is fown,
it is in fome degree neceffary to begin thrafhing immediately after harveft. In this country,
there is a fimilar neceffity for keeping wheat in
the ftraw over the winter. Wheat generally
bears the beft price in fummer. The Cotfwold
farmers experiencing annually, through the nature of their practice, the advantage of having wheat to difpofe of in fummer, endeavour
to keep all they can until that feafon: and, no
doubt, find their intereft in the practice.

8. MARKET FOR WHEAT. The millers of
the neighbourhood. The meafure nine gallons and a half, bare. The medium weight of
clean wheat, in a good feafon, 70lb.

9. THE PRODUCE OF WHEAT. Twelve to
twenty bufhels an acre. Two quarters of
wheat an acre may, perhaps, be taken, on a
par of years, as the medium produce of thefe
hills.

GENERAL OBSERVATION. The produce,
and the weight (confidering the meafure) are
both of them ftrong evidences againft the
Cotfwold

Cotfwold foil, as a matrice for wheat. It
ftrikes me forcibly, that too large a proportion of it is, at prefent, appropriated to this
crop. It is an error in the practice of moft
upland diftricts to grafp at too much wheat.
I know not a more common, nor a more
fatal error in hufbandry. The Cotfwold foil
is evidently adapted to *barley*; but very little
of it to *wheat*. Yet, in the ordinary courfe
of hufbandry, the number of acres refpectively occupied by each of thefe crops is
equal.

I do not mean to cavil at the Cotfwold
practice, which is, in many refpects, very
judicious; nor to dictate in pofitive terms to
the Cotfwold farmers: but I flatter myfelf
they will excufe my offering my fentiments on
this interefting fubject. I am clearly of opinion, that, inftead of the whole of the fecond
year's leys being indifcriminately plowed up
in July or Auguft for wheat,—fuch part of
them only as can, with an ordinary feafon, be
depended upon for a middling crop; fay twenty
bufhels an acre; fhould be fown with wheat.
The reft to be referved for barley: either to
be broken up after harveft, winter plowed,
and

and fown in early fpring; or, if this fhould
interfere too much with the prefent fpring
crops, attempt to fow barley in autumn; (I
have reafon to believe, from my own experience, that it will ftand the winter perfectly
well*) or, if this cannot be done with certainty, leave out the oat crop, or otherwife
alter the prefent fyftem of management, in
fuch manner, as to render it convenient to
fow a greater proportion of barley, and a fmaller fhare of wheat.

XXI. BARLEY. 1. Species. The
common long-eared barley.

2. Time of sowing. The latter end of
March, and the beginning of April: a fortnight before, and a fortnight after, Lady day.

3. Quantity of seed. Three bufhels
an acre. This, the meafure and the time of
fowing being confidered, is an extraordinary
quantity of feed. But land which is naturally
inclined to tenacity, is out of tilth, and fown
with barley on one plowing, may, unlefs the
feafon prove uncommonly kind, require it.

4. Harvesting

* See MIN : OF AGRI : date, 2 Feb : 1776

4. HARVESTING. Cocked with corn forks and at prefent raked with drag-rakes ; an implement but lately introduced, here.

5. BARN MANAGEMENT. Moftly thrafhed in winter. Sometimes kept over the year, on account of price ; or as a fource of fodder, in cafe of a dry feafon.

6. MARKET. Glocefter: where it is bought chiefly by the Briftol factors. *Mea-fure* the fame as wheat. Weight 60lb.

7. PRODUCE. Twenty bufhels to four quarters an acre. Three quarters are deemed a fair crop.

GENERAL OBSERVATION. This is a low produce ; and may feem to militate againft the practice I have juft recommended. It muft be obferved, however, that this produce is from land deficient in tillage ; and that barley delights in a fine pulverous tilth. It muft alfo be confidered that wheat in this country occupies the foil perhaps upwards of twelve months ; barley not more than fix ; and that the feedage of the leys in the wane of fummer are loft by the wheat crop. Other arguments offer themfelves in favor of the propofed alteration ; but it was, perhaps, enough in me to intimate,

mate, what appears to be an improvement ; and I may, perhaps, already have faid too much.

XXII. TURNEPS. 1. Species. Various—-white—-red—green-—round and long-rooted. The Norfolk white-loaf feems to be in the beft efteem.

2. Succession. In the eftablifhed courfe, turneps.fucceed oats, &c. ; or faintfoin ley, when this is broken up by fodburning

3. Tillage. The *ftubbles* are broken up in winter ; and have, after barley feed time, two, or perhaps three more plowings. Some collect the root weeds into heaps and burn them ; others leave them on the furface to wither. The *fodburnt ground* is, in the common practice of the diftrict, rice-balked, or half-plowed, as foon as barley-fowing is done ; and the balks croffed by the feed-plowing. But fome good farmers object to this management ; rather choofing to give it two clean plowings, fleet, and acrofs each other. While others judge one plowing to be beft. Confidering the price of plowing and the fparing hand with which it is applied in this diftrict, it

is

is to me a matter of furprize how two plowings fhould, in this cafe, become cuftomary.

4. MANURE. Upon the *ftubble ground*,
about ten loads of dung is confidered as a tolerable dreffing. The *fodburnt land* has nothing but the afhes.

5. SOWING. *Time of fowing.* Begin the
latter end of May, and continue fowing until
Auguft.

The quantity of feed; one to two pounds.

6. HOING. Good farmers, and farmers in
general, I believe, hoe twice. There are,
neverthelefs, fome few men, ftill left, who do
not think that even one hoing is neceffary.—
The price of the two hoings 6s. an acre: four
for the firft, two for the fecond: the land all
ftirred the firft time over. This, confidering
the ftoney quality of the foil, is extraordinarily
cheap.

7. EXPENDITURE OF TURNEPS. They are
all fed off with fheep, as they ftand upon the
ground: beginning upon them about Michaelmas: moftly fatting fheep without fol-
lowers. Give them a frefh " hitch " every
day: and if hurdles can be had in fufficient
plenty, leave three or four fhifts of the eaten
ground

ground open, for the fheep to fall back upon;
for it is found that, in three or four days, they
will return to the fcraps and pick them up in
preference to thofe, which have been recently
made. This is a minutia of practice, which
is not univerfally attended to; but if it be
right, in any country, to eat off turneps upon
the ground, with *one* flock of fheep, this circumftance is certainly worthy of attention.

Another minutia of practice, which does
the attention of the Cotfwold farmers (thofe,
at leaft, who obferve it) very great credit is,
that of " FOLDING UP-HILL :" beginning upon
the lower parts of the field or piece to be fed
off, and proceeding upward; not upon the
higher parts and proceeding downward.—
Sheep have a natural propenfity to lodge upon
high ground : if this be fed off firft, and left
open as in the above practice, no fooner have
they fatisfied themfelves, on the lower
grounds, than they return to the hill to lodge:
on the contrary, if the lower parts be eaten
off firft, and the fold carried ftill higher every
move, they follow the hurdles: confequently,
every part becomes evenly trodden and equally
manured.

XIII. CUL-

XIII. CULTIVATED HERBAGE.

In diftricts, in which natural grafsland is
fcarce, the CULTIVATION of HERBAGE becomes
a primary object of attention; and nowhere
do we fee it fo affiduoufly attended to as on
thefe hills. The two principal fpecies——
SAINTFOIN and RAYGRASS—are here cultivated with fuperior fkill.

1. SAINTFOIN. The entire wolds are productive of this princely herb. The calcarious
rubble, which has been mentioned as forming
the fubfoil, is in fome places two or three feet
deep; and the rock, below, moftly open. The
roots have been traced, in ftone quarries, to
ten, fome will fay twenty feet deep. Here
the faintfoin flourifhes luxuriantly. But in
other places the rock rifes, in flat horizontal
feams, to near the furface: there the faintfoin
is weaker, and goes off fooner. It is faid to
have been cultivated upon thefe hills upwards
of one hundred and fifty years.

The

The culture of faintfoin requires, in this place, to be regiftered in detail, under the following heads:

1. Succeffion
2. Sowing
3. Management while young
4. After management
5. Expenditure of hay
6. Expenditure of aftergrafs
7. Its duration on thefe hills
8. Recroping the Cotfwold lands with faintfoin

1. *Succeffion.* In the eftablifhed practice, faintfoin is generally fown with barley after turneps.

But it has lately been difcovered, in one of thofe INCIDENTS of practice, to which every farmer ought to be attentive *, that it is more eligible to fow it with oats after wheat: that is, when the foil is foul!——even with couchgrafs!

Saintfoin, fown on a foil which is clean and in tilth, is liable, on the Cotfwold hills, to be choaked with " bents" *(bromus mollis)* which,
                                        feeding

---

* See EXPERIMENTS AND OBSERVATIONS. &c. p. 1.

feeding before faintfoin is cut, annually en-
creafes. The weaker plants of faintfoin are, by
this means, fmothered or kept under, and the
quality of the hay proportionally injured.

In laying down land, which had been inclofed from intermixed common field, and
which was, of courfe, in various ftates as to
tilth and foulnefs, it was obferved, in more
inftances than one, that where the land happened to be foul, the bents were few, while
that which was clean and fine, at the time of
fowing, was, in a few years, overrun with
them.

This incident was caught at; not, however,
by flovens, for the purpofe of faving trouble
or expence; but by men, whofe activity and
fpirit, in matters of hufbandry, are indifpu-
table. Saintfoin has now been repeatedly
fown, on a large fcale, on foil worn out and
fouled by a fucceffion of corn crops: and the
event has been invariably what the incidents
pointed out. The couch occupying the furface prevents the bents from gaining a footing;
while the faintfoin, feeding in the fubfoil, has
little occafion for the furface.

It has ever ſtruck me, that ſaintfoin ought
to be ſown when the ſoil is *poor*; that is, out of
heart as to manure; in order that it may be
induced to ſtrike downward, and feed below;
as well as to prevent the graſſes and weeds
from luxuriating above, to its annoyance:
but I had no conception of its being able to
work its way in a bed of couch. The plants
are, it ſeems, checked during the firſt two or
three years; but, at length, the couch dwind-
ling, or in its nature growing weak for want
of the ground being ſtirred, the ſaintfoin gains
full poſſeſſion: and although it may be then
thiner than ſaintfoin ſown on a clean ſurface,
this is thought to be no diſadvantage to its pro-
ductiveneſs. It is allowed, however, that
the land, on breaking up ſaintfoin cultivated
in this manner, is ſtill foul. But even this
circumſtance has its attendant advantage, in
this country; it affords an eligible turf for
ſodburning; and although this operation may
not clean it thoroughly, it is to be remem-
bered, that its foulneſs was cauſed by a ſuc-
ceſſion of corn crops, previous to the ſowing
of the ſaintfoin; and that had it not been ſown,
the

the foil would have required a fallow to cleanfe it.

Neverthelefs, upon the whole, it does not ftrike me as a practice to be univerfally recommended to the cultivators of faintfoin :—circumftances vary in different diftricts; and the fame judicious cultivator, who has ftruck out, and indeed may be faid to have eftablifhed, this novel practice, has found, that the bents may, in a clean foil, be overcome by handweeding, the firft and fecond years; for although every bent may not be extirpated, the furface afterward becomes too ftale for the feeds to ftrike in; and it appears to me more than probable, that the expence of handweeding is not equivalent to the lofs of produce, by the new practice, in the crops of the three firft years.

My obfervations are the fuller on this fubject, as it appears to me interefting; and, notwithftanding the practice, which has been ftruck out, may be in fome refpects objectionable, it has already been adopted, by fome principal farmers; and will, probably, in a fhort time, become the prevailing practice of the Cotfwold hills.

2. *Sowing*

2. *Sowing faintfoin. The time of fowing faint-foin*, here, is the middle of March; or from that time to the latter end of the month.

The quantity of feed is proportioned to the ftate of the foil. A foul foil requires more feed than one which is clean: from one bufhel to three bufhels an acre. The advocates for thin faintfoin think a bufhel of feed fufficient; provided the foil be clean.

This is another interefting particular, in the cultivation of faintfoin. It is remarked by men of obfervation, that where the plants of faintfoin ftand at fome diftance from each other, they grow taller, ftronger, and afford more herbage, than where they ftand thick upon the ground; in which cafe, the plants are not only weaker; but the crop is fhorter and lefs productive. The *ftrength* of the plants may, perhaps, be the only caufe of difference: a ftrong plant, in all probability, ftrikes deeper than a weak one; by which means its pafture is proportionally enlarged*.

3. *The*

PRICE OF SAINTFOIN SEED,—three to fix fhillings a bufhel,——four fhillings and fixpence a medium price. Chiefly raifed in the neighbourhood.

3. *The management of the faintfoin crop while young.* But if thin faintfoin be advantageous, why not fet out the plants, and keep them clean the fecond year, with the hoe? With this, and a fmall addition of handweeding, when the bents run up to head, thefe trouble-fome weeds might, perhaps, be wholly over-come.

4. *The after management of faintfoin.* It is invariably mown every year. If it be once fuffered to be eaten with ftock during the fummer feafon, its productivenefs is in a man-ner deftroyed; it is faid that it will not, in this country, ever afterward rife to the fithe.

It is a principle here laid down, by men, who feem to have paid fingular attention to the culture of this plant, *that it ought never to be eaten upon the ground when in a growing ftate.* They have reduced their ideas to ftill greater accuracy; they are clearly of opinion, that faintfoin cannot, on a par of feafons, be fed with *fafety* in more than two months of the year: namely the months of October and November: in a mild December, it will fre-quently make a fhoot; which being cropt is faid to be nearly fatal to the plant. Pafturing

F 3   in

in fpring is obferved to have a fimilar effect. Even mowing too early is confidered as very prejudicial: and what appears extraordinary, (being contrary to the general nature of plants) fuffering the plants of faintfoin to mature their feed is believed to prolong their duration!

It is well known, that cutting *trees* while in a ftate of growth, is injurious to their future progrefs; being, it is underftood, prejudicial to their roots: and cutting this ftrong, deep-rooting plant, in a fimilar ftate, may have a fimilar effect. If the injury be done to the root, and take place in the lower extremities of it, the damage, which follows, is eafily conceived; for whatever portion of the length of the root is deftroyed, in fuch proportion will the pafturage of the plant be contracted; and, until it has had fufficient time to re-extend its roots, in the fame ratio will be its produc-tivenefs. Thefe reflections are offered inci-dentally; in order to excite a fpirit of enquiry, which may lead to more accurate ideas con-cerning the nature of this moft ufeful plant.

5. *The expenditure of faintfoin hay* is chiefly on turnep-fheep and horfes. The *produce* one to two tons an acre

6. *The*

6. *The expenditure of the aftergrafs* is principally on lambs, which are newly weaned;
alfo on grown fheep, as well as on cattle;
but is feldom, I underftand, eaten with horfes.

7. *The duration of faintfoin* on the Cotfwold hills is fhort. Seldom more than ten
years: not even with the management above-
mentioned, on land which has never borne
faintfoin before. *This,* however, may be difficult to afcertain. It has been cultivated on
thefe hills, it feems, the major part of two
centuries. It is not likely, however, that
every patch fhould have been hit: the fhort-
nefs of its duration muft therefore be given to
the nature of the foil, or fubfoil.

8. *Recropping with faintfoin.* The general
idea feems to be, that land ought not to be re-
cropt with faintfoin under twenty years. But,
it is probable, that it cannot be cultivated,
with fuccefs, after fo fhort an interval. There
is an inftance of a piece of land on thefe hills
being cropt three times with faintfoin, within
memory; but the laft crop was of little value:
it went off in about three years. Therefore,
notwithftanding what has been faid above,
the prefent proportion of faintfoin ley to the

arable

arable crops may be fufficient. In the prefent
courfe of crops, each piece will come round
for faintfoin in feventy years: and it appears
doubtful whether, even after that interval of
reft, the fubftrata will be fufficiently recharged
to fend up ten more crops, equal to thofe at
leaft which it afforded the firft time. The food
of faintfoin it then contained might have been
fome thoufand years in forming.

2. RAYGRASS. Next to faintfoin, raygrafs
is here in the higheft efteem. I have obferved
no other diftrict in which it is fo well underftood, and fo judicioufly managed, as it is in
this. Not only the green herbage, but the
hay of raygrafs is here confidered as fuperiorly
nutritious. The greateft *proof* I have ever
met with in *grazing*, of any kind, was given
by bullocks finifhed with ordinary barley and
with raygrafs hay. I do not mean with the
ftraw of raygrafs, which had ftood to mature
its *grain*; but with the *herbage* of raygrafs,
cut in a ftate of fucculency, and properly
made into *hay*.

The Cotfwold farmers this year (1788) began cutting their raygrafs leys about the 22
May ! *while the fpikes were yet fhooting*: it is
true

true the feafon was then dry, and there was no
profpect of its improving; it neverthelefs was
allowed, by men who beft underftand its nature, to be fully fit for cutting ; and it is, I
underftand, every year cut in a fimilar ftate.

Men of obfervation affert that there are *two
fpecies* of raygrafs now in cultivation in this
diftrict: the one annual, the other perennial.
The former, the ordinary fort which is fold at
the fhops ; the latter, raifed on thefe hills.
This is a ftrong evidence of the advantage to
be expected from the cultivation of the *native*
raygrafs of a country. And every country
ought, without lofs of time, to fet about a work
which is fo eafy, and promifes fo much advantage. The fort here fpoken of, as an annual,
is probably *a worn out variety*; or one whofe
acquired habit is averfe to the Cotfwold foil.

3. TREFOIL. (Trifolium procumbens—
provincially "hop clover.") This is in good
efteem: and is frequently fown among raygrafs.
Its hay, *when well got*, is thought to be of a
fuperior quality.

4. WHITE CLOVFR. When *pafturage* is
the object, this is commonly fown among raygrafs ; but for *hay* trefoil alone is fown.

5. RED

5. RED CLOVER. It is obfervable, that, notwithftanding this plant has not been cultivated on thefe hills more, perhaps, than twenty or thirty years, its productivenefs is on the decline. In a country, however, productive of faintfoin, its lofs is the lefs to be regretted.

XXIV. GRASSLAND. The graffy vallies, which have been mentioned, are tolerably well herbaged ; but are very much over-run, in patches, with the red autumnal crocus—(*colchicum autumnale*) which in many places occupies, in effect, the entire furface ; and as yet no mode of extirpation has been hit upon.

Thefe vallies are applied indifferently to hay and pafturage ; but no dependence can be placed in them: in a moift feafon they will throw out good crops of grafs: but in a dry fummer they are of little value.

XXV. HORSES. Some cart horfes are bred on thefe hills. The mares are ufually worked until they drop their foals ; but not while they fuckle ; the foals being weaned early ;

early; while there is plenty of grafs upon the ground.

XXVI. CATTLE. A good many cattle are kept in this diftrict. Some Cows are kept in the vallies; and on the fkirts of the hills there are confiderable dairies.

THE SPECIES OF CATTLE are the Glocefter-fhire, the long-horned, and a mongrel breed between thofe two.

1. Cows. In the higher townfhips,— more particularly, perhaps, in the townfhip of Northleach,—cows are kept on " cow-downs" (old upland grafs) in the day, and foddered in yards, at nights, with weeds, rough grafs, or other herbage, mown in the byways and hedges. The craftsmen and farm labourers have each of them a cow: by this means they not only obtain a relief for their fa-milies; but acquire at the fame time habits of induftry. I mention this circumftance; as in all probability, this was, formerly, the prac-tice in moft open upland townfhips, through-out the kingdom.

2. GRAZING. The fatting of cattle is not the common practice of thefe hills; neverthe-

lefs

lefs they may boaſt of at leaſt one good grazier. * His practice is to buy in large Welch
bullocks, at Gloceſter, in autumn and winter. He gives them the run of the ſtraw yard
the firſt winter; and ſummers them on raygrafs
and clover leys,—as *companions* to his fatting
ſheep,—to eat off the bents of raygrafs; and
thereby not only give the ſheep a freer better
bite than they otherwiſe would have; but at
the ſame time turns to a valuable purpoſe that
which would otherwiſe (if not ſwept of with
the ſithe) remain an encumberance to the ſurface. The enſuing winter, they are finiſhed in
ſtalls, with hay and ſecondary barley. A new,
but an excellent practice.

His method of ſtall fatting merits particular
notice. His fatting cattle are all *tied up*;—
ſome in ſingle, ſome in double ſtalls. His rea-
ſon for this practice is not altogether that of
ſaving room; he is clearly of opinion that
they do better—fat faſter—than bullocks which
are kept in looſe ſtalls †. His reaſoning is
fair: beſides the indiſputable advantage of
their

* Mr. PEACEY. .
† See VALE OF GLOCESTER, Page 250.

their not being liable, in this cafe, to foul their
meat and water ; he holds out another which
is not fo obvious, but may neverthelefs perhaps be equally true: cattle which are tied up
are more *cadifh* (tamer—lefs wild) than thofe
which are kept in loofe ftalls. A loofe bullock
(fome loofe bullocks at leaft) when a ftranger
enters the fhed, or any difturbance happens in
it, will rife and fly into the yard for refuge ;
while a bullock which knows that he has not
the power of flight will lie ftill and chew his
cud. In the yards, loofe bullocks are equally
liable to difturbance ; and quietnefs is no
doubt effential to quick fatting.

Each bullock has two troughs ; a fmall one
for corn ; a large one for hay ; with a water
trough, which runs the whole length of the
fhed, and is covered by a board ; each bullock having a hole (large enough to admit the
nofe) to drink at. The water trough (a hollow tree) forms, as it were, a top rail to the par-
tition wall of the gangway. The others are
beneath it ; nearly level with the bed of the
ftall.

The *corn* is ground, and given to them,
mixt among *cut hay*, two or three times a day ;

beginning

beginning with about half a peck, and encreafing to about a peck a day.

The method of feeding with *hay*, which in
this inftance is practiced, does the practitioner
infinite credit. He feeds his bullocks with hay
as cart horfes are ufually fed with corn: giving
it to them *by handfuls at once*: never more at
a time than the two hands can grafp: continuing to feed them, in this manner, *until they
lie down*; or until they refufe to eat. Thus
they never have any hay to blow upon; (the
great objection againft *tying up* bullocks);
even at night, they have not a mouthful left
before them. The leading principle of this
practice is, that fatting cattle fhould never be
cloyed with food:—fhould always *eat with an
appetite*. In the morning they are fed with
the worft of the hay (if any difference) for being
then hungry, they eat it with an appetite.—
Thus the hay is eaten up clean; and the bullocks are preferved in a thriving habit; while
the extraordinary expence, where a number of
cattle are fatted at once, is inconfiderable. In
this cafe it is proper to appropriate a man's
time to their attendance, and he might as well
be employed in *feeding them by handfuls*, *until
they*

they lie down as in cloying them with arm-
fuls, and idling the reft of his time away.

XXVII. SHEEP. The Cotfwolds have
long been celebrated for their fheep; which
ftill remain the grand objeſt of the Cotfwold
hufbandry. They are, here, in their proper
element,

1. SPECIES. The prefent breed is a
polled, longwooled, middlefized fheep: a
breed which has been prevalent on thefe hills
time immemorial: it has been *improved*, but
has not been *changed*. Hence it is probable
that the popular idea of the Spaniards' having
originally procured their breed of fine-wooled
fheep from the Cotfwold hills has no foundation. The fpecific difference of the prefent
ftock from other breeds of long-wooled fheep,
is that of their being fuller behind, and lighter
forward, than moft other breeds. The Leicefterfhire rams, however, having now gained
a firm footing on thefe hills, will, of courfe, fill
up the fore quarter. · The prefent eftablifhed
breed will fat at two fheer—that is, at 3 years
old—to 25 lb. a quarter wedders; 20 lb ewes;
and

and cut from 7 to 9 lb of wool. Wedders generally run about three and a half to the tod.

2. Rearing. Before the inclofures took
place, the whole diftrict was ftocked with
breeding flocks; the yearlings being fold to
the graziers of Buckinghamfhire, and other
neighbouring counties. Still, moft farmers
rear their own ftock.

3. Folding. I met with nothing on thefe
hills which furprized me more than the almoft
total neglect of the fheep fold. The prefent
breed of fheep is not adapted to folding: their
legs are too fhort, and their wool too heavy.
If a farm have a fheep down belonging to it,
the hoggards (yearlings) and fometimes the
fharhogs (two years old) are folded on the arable land.

4. Fatting. The fharhogs are kept, at
head, in the *raygrafs* &c. *leys*, or at *vetches*,
during fummer, and are finifhed with *turneps*;
eaten off in the manner already defcribed;
and with *hay*; which is given to them within
the fold in bottomlefs racks, of a fimple porta-
ble conftruction. Two feet high, two feet
wide; and nine or ten feet long. The ftaves
9 inches from middle to middle:—the bottom

rail

rail a flab or other board. A man, by ftep-
ping into them, moves them with great facia-
lity.

XXVIII. SWINE. The SPECIES va-
rious: the old, long, white breed feems to be
in good efteem: the rind thin; and the individuals fat to a good fize.

Moftly *reared* upon the hills; each farmer
generally breeding his own ftock.

Fatted chiefly on peas: fome barley is given.

The *bacon* is moftly confumed on the farms:
being the principal food of farmers' fervants.

XXIX. RABBITS. Formerly it feems
there were fome warrens on thefe hills; but at
prefent there are few (if any) remaining. The
reafon given for plowing them up is, that the
rabbits were apt to break their bounds and
ftray over the country.

Much of the Cotfwold land appears to me
to be well adapted to rabbits; and where
ftone walls can be raifed at the reafonable expence which has been mentioned, the above
objection to them falls to the ground.

It

It ftrikes me, that in fome fituations, much of the expence of inclofing might have been faved ;—and the value of the eftates, containing fituations favorable to the pur-pofe, might have been increafed by the plant-ing of rabbit warrens. Some of the few town-fhips which ftill remain to be inclofed may profit by this mode of inclofure. See RURAL ECONOMY OF YORKSHIRE, article RABBITS.

XXX. LIST OF RATES. Raifing *building ftones* by the perch of 16½ fquare feet, 5d. to 8d. a perch.

Slates laid upon the roof, and plaftered be-neath, 26s. a fquare of 100 fquare feet.

Stone floors, 4½d. a foot, carriage and laying included.

Lime, 8d. the bufhel of 8 gallons level.

Oak timber in the ftick 1s. to 15d. a foot.

Afh timber 1s. a foot.

Journeyman mafon's wages 20d. a day, no beer.

Journeyman carpenter's 20d.

Blackfmith's work, for plow irons and other heavy work 4½d. a lb. (Coals dear).

Farm

Farm labourers--by the day--1s. in autumn, winter and fpring—14d. in hay time—18d. for mowing—2s. for five weeks certain in harveft. No beer by agreement.

Women, 6d. in the fpring—7d. in hay time, 1s. in harveft.

Men fervants wages—8 to 10l.

Second men—5 to 7l.

Maid fervant's wages about 4l.

Hire of a team (5 horfes, carriage, man and boy) 12 to 14s. a day.

Price of plowing by the acre 8s.   Plowing for and harrowing in wheat 10s. 6d. an acre: the cuftomary charge between outgoing and incoming tenant, when wheat is fown and left upon the ground.

Hoing turneps:—6s. an acre for two hoings, is the cuftomary price:

Mowing " Englifh grafs" by the acre 20d.

Mowing faintfoin—according to the crop.

Mowing raygrafs and clover—14d. an acre.

Mowing corn 1s. to 14d. an acre.

Reaping wheat 5 to 7s. an acre.

Thrafhing wheat 4d. a bufhel (generally cut early) An inftance of giving 8d. a bufhel for thrafhing wheat, fee page 54.

fee page 54.

G 2   *Thrafhing*

Thrashing barley 14d. to 20d. a quarter.

Size of bushel 9½ gallons, barely.

Keep of strawyard cattle 6d. to 1s. a-head, a week.

Price of fuel:

Coals by the ton 20 to 40s. according to the distance from water carriage—the price at Glocester 13s.—at Northleach (twenty miles distant mostly back carriage) 28s.

Wood by the chord 20s.

Faggots by the hundred 24s.

THE

THE

VALE

OF

BERKELEY.

THE OUTLINES of this charming plot
of country form the fegment of a circle, nearer
than any other regular figure. The Severn,
an irregular chord :—the hills to the fouth and
eaft, a curve, which the Painfwick and Matfon hills continue to the northern angle.

The EXTENT, from Auft cliff to the foot of
Matfon Hill, twenty five miles. The medium width of the diftrict has been eftimated
at four miles; but the narrownefs of its extremities, I apprehend, renders that too great a
medium width. Including the fkirts of the
hills, it may contain eighty fquare miles; or
about fifty thoufand acres.

The

The SURFACE of the vale of Berkeley is lefs uniform than that of the upper vale. The feet of the hills, in many places, ftretch a confiderable way toward the river; raifing the furface into inequalities. Other fwells rife fpontaneoufly in the area; efpecially toward the extremities. In the more central part of it, however, round the town of Berkeley, there is a confiderable extent of vale country. But the flatnefs even of this is brcken, and the eye relieved, by the rifing grounds of Berkeley Park, which form a hillock near its center.

The SOIL, whether it lie on the flat, or is fpread over the fwells, is almoft uniformly rich. The more level parts are invariably covered with a deep fat loam; excepting a plot immediately above Berkley, which is clayey, cold, and lefs productive. The foils of fome of the higher fwells, too, are of a cold clayey nature. But in every part there appears, evidently, a *native unctuoufnefs* of foil, which gives a degree of richnefs—*fatnefs* —to all its productions.

The SEVERN, here, as in the upper vale, is the common receptacle of SURFACE WA- TERS; which are collected by rivulets ftretch- ing

ing acrofs the flat, and winding among the
hills which back it. One of thefe rivulets
has been rendered NAVIGABLE to Stroud and
its neighbouthood: a navigation, which is now
under extention toward Lechlade; to join the
THAMES NAVIGATION; and thereby open a
communication between thefe two rivers.

Out of the rivulets COMMON SHORES are
funk; and well preferved; under a COMMIT-
TEE OF SHORES: an inqueft effentially neceffary to every vale country.

PRODUCE;—principally *grafs*. Excepting
fome common fields toward the upper angle,
there are not perhaps a thoufand acres of *arable* land within the diftrict. The area of the
vale is likewife in a manner free from *wood*:
but the fides of the hills—a calcarious foil—
are moftly hung with beech; which thrives
with uncommon vigour.

Placing this lovely paffage of country in the
light of ORNAMENT; and viewing it with a
picturefque eye; it appears with fingular advantages. But, to detail the views from every
hillock happily placed, would be foreign to
the prefent defign. Suffice it therefore, in
this place, to convey fome general idea of the

fcenery,

fcenery, in faying,—that the waters of the Severn, which here form a lengthened eftuary
rather than a river—(*yet winding with the ut-
moft eafe !*) are productive of infinite grandeur
whenever they mix in the view:—that the furface, even of the vale, is happily broken;
and *clad in perpetual verdure*: while the marginal hills not only command a near and diftinct
view of the vale with the Severn, as a *fore-
ground*; and rife high enough to catch the various *diftances* which furround it; but form,
among themfelves, fcenes of fuperlative
beauty: in general they are hung with beech of
the moft luxuriant growth; with cultivated
vallies winding every way among them. The
views from Stanchcomb Hill furpafs, in *grandeur*, *richnefs*, *variety* and *beauty* every other
circle of views I have feen.

Leaving, however, the hills and the fcenery
which hangs round them, until fome more
fuitable opportunity fhall offer itfelf, it will be
proper to defcend into the vale, and take a
view of it as a DAIRY COUNTRY;—under
which character, alone, I was led into it.

The objects of my attention have been
I. Eftates.
II. Farms.
III. Soils and management.
IV. Water.
V. Herbage and managemement.
VI. Cows, and management.
VII. Managemement of the dairy.

I. ESTATES and MANAGEMENT,
The EARL OF BERKELEY, whofe principal refidence is fituated near the center of the yale, is the owner of a very confiderable fhare of it. LORD DUCIE has an eftate in it. There are other off eftates, and a confiderable yeomanry: but what is extraordinary, confidering the advantages of the fituation, this vale contains few principal refidences.

The RENT of land in this diftrict is low, confidering its intrinfic quality. But it is fituated at a diftance from market: a circumftance which influences the rental value of land as much as the quality of the land itfelf. Immediately round the town of Berkeley, there is land lets from 50s. to 3l. an acre. But I believe there are few *farms* of any fize which are

rented

rented higher than 25s. Perhaps 20s. may be confidered as the medium rent of the diftrict. Some of the coldeft, leaft-productive parts are rented fo low as 10s. an acre.

The TENANCY, moftly *at will: leafes* are leaft wanted on grafsland farms.

REMOVALS. Ladyday is the univerfal time of removal in this grafsland dairy country. Mayday is objected againft; becaufe the outgoing tenant would, in this cafe, fpring feed the mowing grounds. This, however, might be guarded againft. Mayday is certainly the moft eligible time of removal, on grafsland eftates.

II. FARMS. The SIZE of farms has of late years increafed. This circumftance I have heard complained of; as increafing the the number of poor; and, in confequence, the poor's rate. Farms, at prefent, rife from fifty to two three or four hundred pounds a year.

The univerfal CHARACTERISTIC of farms, here, is *grafs*. There are many confiderable farms without an acre of *arable* or *wood land* upon them. Some, however, have patches
of

of arable land belonging to them. But it is,
in general, ufed in a manner fo unfkilful ;—
and when laid down to grafs, is laid down fo
fhamefully,—that landlords are fcarcely cen-
furable for keeping the prefent undue proportion of it in a ftate of grafs. Indeed, while
they remain fatisfied with the prefent rents,
the tenants may have no reafon to complain:
themfelves and the community are the lofers.
Were a due proportion of plowland permitted,
the tenants might, with judicious management, be enabled to pay a rent equivalent to
the intrinfic quality of the foil. At prefent,
the inconveniency of a want of ftraw muft be
great ; and the annual wafte of hay exceffive.

With refpect to the PLANNING and divifion of farms, no regular method of laying out
has, perhaps, ever been attempted ; nor have I
met, in theory, with any accurate ideas on the
fubject. There are grounds of all fizes ; lying in every fituation with refpect to the home-
ftall. It is, however, generally underftood,
that the cowgrounds ought to communicate
with the yard, for the conveniency of milking.
In the planning of thefe farms one important
circumftance, however, feems to have been
attended

attended to. The homeſtalls in general are
fituated on the farm ; not in villages, as they
too frequently are, in other diftricts.

The FARMERIES are very fimple ; and in
general very mean. A fmall, old, timber-
built dwelling-houfe, with a calfstage, a hovel to hold a cow occafionally, and a ſtable for
two or three horfes, are confidered as the only
requifites. If a cowſhed be added, the farmery is compleat. Were a due proportion of
the lands to be broken up and kept under
aration,—barns and other additional buildings
would be neceſſary. This may be confidered
as a *fubftantial* reafon for keeping them in their
prefent ſtate,

III. SOILS AND MANAGEMENT.

The prevailing SPECIES of foil has been mentioned as a deep rich clayey loam. The MA-
NAGEMENT is very fimple ; even the bufinefs
of *manuring* has been difpfenfed with, until of
late years. The cows were kept, without
litter, in yards and foddering grounds, and
the dung fuffered to wafte where it dropt, or
to be waſhed away by heavy rains.

The

The principal part, or the whole, of the lands of this vale appear to have been formerly under the PLOW; lying now in ridge-and-furrow; various as to height and depth. In one inſtance (at the foot of one of the hills) I obſerved the ridges, about a rod wide, laid round and high; with a ſlip, about a yard wide, lying flat between each of them. The ridges were covered with the fineſt turf, cloſely paſtured; while the intervals were ſtrong beds of ruſhes. The appearance, at ſome diſtance, was ſingular.

IV. WATER. The RIVULETS which croſs the vale afford a ſupply of water to the grounds which lie near them. But many of the cow grounds appear to be deficient in good watering places.

The art of POOL MAKING does not appear to have been, at any time, ſtudied, in theſe vales. The ſame deep, ſteep, narrow holes, which are obſervable in moſt old graſsland diſtricts, are common here. It is therefore probable, that the ſuperiority of Berkeley cheeſe does not ariſe from the quality of the w TER.

V. HER-

V. HERBAGE and MANAGEMENT.

As in the vale of Glocefter, RAYGRASS is the predominant *species*, fo in this vale the DOGS-TAIL (cynofurus criftatus) is prevalent; with a mixture of *raygrafs*; the *poes*, and *white clover* (trifolium repens.) In autumn, the furface of the founder, richer lands, is covered with one entire fleece of thefe excellent graffes; but chiefly of dogstail, ráygrafs, and the white trefoil;—the two former faccharine in a fuperior degree; and, in fome places, as highly coloured as rank wheat in the fpring.

In the richnefs of the foil, and the fuperior quality of the herbage, the fuperiority of the Berkeley cheefe may feem to be accounted for The fact, however, is, that, at prefent, the beft cheefe is made from the coldeft, leaft-productive foil; and from herbage of a defcription very different from that which is given above. I have feen cows grazing among *rufhes, fleabane,* (cineraria paluftris) *devilfbit* (fcabiofa fuccifa) *reftharrow* (ononis arvenfis fpinofa) and the whole tribe of weeds common to neglected cold land; with, however, an admixture of better herbage; neverthe-lefs, from thefe cows, Berkeley cheefe, of the

first

firft quality, was made. I was affured by an intelligent man, who has made a handfome fortune by cheefmaking, and who, having retired from the bufinefs, could have no motive for deceiving me,—that of two farms he occupied, one of them was well foiled and well herbaged;—the other unproductive, with herbage (I fpeak from my own obfervation) of the laft-given defcription; and that from the worft land he made, invariably, the beft cheefe.

It feems, indeed, to be a fact univerfally underftood, and fufficiently eftablifhed, that there is a ranknefs—an over-richnefs, — in the better lands of the vale, which renders them lefs fit for cheefmaking, than cooler lefs forcing foils: the cheefes made from them being liable to a fpecies of fermentation— provincially termed "heaving"—-a defect, which will be fpoken of in its proper place : more efpecially when thefe lands are ftill farther enriched by *manuring :* a practice, which has, of late years, encreafed.

Inftances are produced, in both vales, of the evil effect of MANURING COW GROUNDS: not only with *dung* ; but with other manures. In
the

the upper vale, *pond-mud*, for inftance, was
found to have a bad effect. In the lower vale,
a moft judicious dairywoman, fpeaking with
concern of the decline of Berkeley cheefe, accounted for it in this way. " Formerly people were ufed to think nothing of dung; but
now every body is fcraping all they can together; for fince the rents have been raifed they
could not live if they did not help their land."
The fact is, dung is found to give more grafs;
but injures the quality of the cheefe,—during
the firft, and fometimes the fecond, year after manuring: afterwards, the evil effect wears
out. Hence, judicious dairy farmers graze
(that is pafture with fatting cattle) or mow
(when they are permitted) the firft year after
manuring. A practice which ought to be
univerfal.

From any information which I have been
able to obtain in this diftrict, it does not appear that either a foil of fuperior richnefs, or
herbage of fuperior finenefs, is neceffary to
the production of cheefe of the firft quality.
It ought to be obferved, however, that the
infertility of the foils which are here fpoken of
as unproductive, may be owing more to the
retentivenefs

retentivenefs of the fubfoil, than to the intrinfic quality of the foil itfelf; which may partake
of the *unctuoufnefs* which has been mentioned ;
and which manifefts itfelf, evidently, in foils fituated on a better bafis. Neverthelefs, I do
not find any thing in this diftrict, which con-
tradicts the pofition, that cheefe of the firft
quality may, *under proper management*, be
produced in *many* other diftricts of the ifland.
Here, even on the fame farm,—a change of
pafture will fometimes require an alteration of
management. But, by attentive practice, the
proper management is hit upon, and good
cheefe made.

With refpect to the *age* of the herbage of
the Vale of Berkeley, I have met with nothing
fatisfactory: it may be fome centuries old.
But the excellency of its cheefe cannot be altogether owing to the age of its turf: other
diftricts have old grafslands: lands which have
probably never been in a ftate of aration.

In regard to the MANAGEMENT of GRASS-
LAND in this diftrict, little is to be learnt.
It refembles that of the upper vale. Hay is,
here, of too little value to be rigidly attended
to: and pafture grounds have little attention

paid them; except in one particular, which ought to be copied by every diftrict that has a pafture ground in it. The herbage of the cold, rough lands have of late years been very much improved by "fkimming":—that is by mowing off the weeds and ftale grafs, once or twice during the fummer;—a practice which cannot be fufficiently recommended. The rank deep-rooting weeds, which occupy the furface, and overfhadow the tender graffes, are by this means checked, and in time deftroyed; leaving the furface in the occupation of more profitable herbage.

VI. COWS AND MANAGEMENT.

The size of dairies has of courfe increafed with that of farms. A hundred cows are, neverthelefs, confidered as a very large dairy: there are few fo large. Forty or fifty cows are confidered as a dairy above the middle fize.

The species of cow, here, as in the upper vale, is indeterminate. *Glocefterfhire, north-country,* and a *mongrel breed,* between the two. Five years ago it was faid that the north country

country cows were lofing ground : and that
the old ftock were coming again into efteem.

I remember the obfervation of an experienced dairywoman in 1783 was, " that the
northcountry cows neither milk fo well nor
fat fo well as the true dark-brown Glocefterfhire breed." Neverthelefs I cannot perceive
that they have made any progrefs. On the
contrary the longhorned breed appear to have
increafed fince that time.

A man whofe knowledge of the rural affairs
of this diftrict, and of the feveral breeds of
cattle of this quarter of the ifland, is extenfive,
and whofe remarks are feldom fuperficial, fees
this recent increafe of the northern breed of
cows in a point of view which feems to have
efcaped the obfervation of others. He is of
opinion, that it has been effected by other circumftances than the comparative merits of the
two breeds of cows ; which, he thinks, has had
little or no influence in the change that has
been taking place. He attributes it to the advanced price of dairy produce, during a fucceffion of years laft paft. The DAIRY being
found, in this well foiled dairy country, to pay
better than BREEDING ; *this* of courfe declined:

and,

and, as the young ftock diminifhed, the quantity of vacant pafture encreafed: confequently·
an increafe of alien cows became doubly requifite. This increafe was not to be obtained
from the Glocefterfhire breed; nor could the
fupply be drawn from the kindred breeds of
the neighbouring diftricts; nor perhaps from
any other fource than that from which it has
been principally drawn: namely the north of
Staffordfhire;—where breeding is the principal object, and where the produce of the dairy
is of much lefs value than it is in the vales of
Glocefterfhire.

Certain it is, that on farms whofe grounds, by
foil and fituation, are wholly adapted to the
dairy, we fee the greateft proportion of north
country cows; while on thofe which have
rough or diftant grounds belonging to them,
adapted to breeding, the Glocefterfhire cows
ftill hold poffeffion;—and, *by thofe who have
them*, are ftill in the higheft efteem.

Impreffed with thefe ideas, the ingenious
author of thefe remarks is of opinion, that
fhould the dairy continue, for a length of
years in its *prefent* declining ftate; efpecially
if breeding fhould continue to pay fo well as it
has

has lately done ; the influx of alien cows will
be ftopped : their prices will no longer
be a temptation to the dealers, and their
places in the paftures will be occupied by
rearing ftock: not of the northcountry, but of
the Glocefterfhire breed.

Be this as it may, it is, I believe, a well
known fact, that the cheefe of this diftrict has
been falling off, in point of fuperior excellency,
fince about the time of the introduction of
northcountry cows; and an advocate for the
Glocefterfhire breed would of courfe argue,
that the northcountry cows are unfriendly to
cheefe. On the contrary, however, it is af-
ferted, by thofe who are the beft authority in
this cafe (the cheefe factors) that there are
dairies confifting wholly of northcountry cows,
which make cheefe of the firft quality. While
the advocates for the breed affert, that their
milk not only makes cheefe of a good quality,
but that it affords a greater proportion of curd,
than that of the Glocefterfhire breed.

Upon the whole, therefore, we have fufficient evidence, I think, to conclude, that the
fuperior excellency of the Berkeley cheefe is

not,

not, nor ever was, owing to the SPECIES OF
COW.

The cow MANAGEMENT, here, is similar to
that of the upper vale; except that a smaller
proportion are *bred* in this vale: the richer
lands having been considered, of late years at
least, as too good for breeding. On the skirts
of the hills and on the colder lands, there are,
neverthelefs, many breeding farms. The north
country fort are bought of the jobbers at Glocefter. As they fail in their milk, they are put
to fatting on the dairy farm, or fold to graziers.

A defect which has, it feems, lately crept
into the management of cows in this vale is
noticeable.—The cows, of many dairies, are
faid to come in too early in the fpring: their
milk is fpent before the autumnal flufh of grafs
fets in. The cool months of autumn are not
only favourable to the manufacture of cheefe ;
but the milk, of that feafon, is thought to yeild
a greater proportion of curd, than that of the
fummer months. I mention this as the obfervation of a man who is fingularly entitled to attention ; being intimately acquainted with
every department of the dairy management of
this

this country. But may not this deficiency of autumnal produce be in fome meafure owing to the nature of the longhorned cows ? which, though they afford a flufh of milk prefently after calving, are obferved (the higher bred ones at leaft) to lofe it much fooner than thofe of moft other breeds.

VII. MANAGEMENT OF THE DAIRY. It will be proper to remark, in this place, that the HUNDRED of BERKELEY, which forms a confiderable part of the diftrict now under furvey, has ever been celebrated for the fuperior quality of its cheefe. What, in the kingdom at large, is termed GLOCESTER CHEESE; particularly DOUBLE GLOCESTER; is, in Glocefterfhire, called " DOUBLE BERKE-LEY": not more on account of the fuperior quality of the cheefe of this diftrict; than be-caufe the principal part of the thick cheefe of Glocefterfhire is made within this hundred.

It will likewife be proper to apprize the reader, in this place, that the cheefe of this diftrict was in higher repute, fome fifteen or twenty years ago, than it is at prefent; as other-wife fome expreffions which occur would be

H 4   obfcure

obfcure. It muft, however, be underftood that there is no cheefe of the firft quality now made in the vale of Berkeley: all that is meant to be conveyed, and which is acknowledged by all parties concerned, is, that the cheefe of Berkeley hundred is not fo *uniformly excellent* as it was fome fifteen or twenty years ago.

In this cafe, as in that of the vale of Glocefter, on the fame fubject, it will be proper, before the OBJECTS be feparately examined, to take a view of

Managers	Utenfils
Dairyrooms	Milking.

The three laft, however, vary fo little from the defcription already given of thofe of the upper vale, that it is unneceffary to repeat the defcriptions here. Therefore, the only thing requifite, in this cafe, previous to an account of the particular objects, is fome account of the MANAGERS of the lower vale; efpecially thofe from whom I gained my information; and whofe practice I am about to regifter.

A fuperior dairywoman is fo highly fpoken of, and fo highly valued, in this diftrict, that one is led to imagine every thing depends

upon

upon MANAGEMENT. Inftances are mentioned of the fame farm, under different managers, having produced good and bad cheefe: even changing a dairy *maid* has been obferved to make a confiderable difference in the quality of the produce.

On the other hand, it has likewife been fre-quently feen that the fame managers ; the fame dairywoman, the fame affiftants, *and the fame cows*, which on one farm produced cheefe of the firft quality ; have not, on being transferred to another, been able, on their firft removal, (at leaft) to produce marketable cheefe. Indeed, it feems to be generally un-derftood throughout the two vales, that it is neceffary " to know the ground", by two or three years experience, before good cheefe can be made with any degree of certainty.

Thefe two circumftances tend to prove the fame fact : namely, that *very much* depends upon *management*.

I had an opportunity of feeing different dairies in the vale of Berkeley ; and of ob-ferving the practices of different dairywomen. But the dairy which principally engaged my attention was that of *Maberley*, (near Berkeley) whofe

whofe manager, Mrs. WADE, whether we confider her *education*, her natural abilities, or
her experience, ranks, moft defervedly, among
the firft dairywomen of the diftrict. Her mo-
ther was miftrefs of an hundred cows : herfelf
of forty or fifty ; during the laft twenty or
thirty years. What renders her practice, fingularly valuable, is that of its being the old
eftablifhed practice, which brought the Berkeley cheefe to its higheft degree of excellency;
unaltered, as that of moft dairies has been, by
modern deviations.

From this I was led to a modern dairy,
equally diftinguifhable : that of Mr. BIGLAND
of FROCESTER : the man moft capable of
giving me information, in every department
of the fubject I was inveftigating. As purchafer of, perhaps, half the cheefe which is
made in the vale of Berkeley, he is, of courfe,
intimately verfed in the quality of cheefe.—
As proprietor of a dairy of more than fifty
cows, the bufinefs of a dairy farm is familiar
to him. And, as a man of fcience, he has
paid more attention to the minutiæ of the art,
moft efpecially under confideration, than any
cther man I have converfed with on the
fubject.

subject. His ability of information, however,
was exceeded by his liberality in communicating it. He not only gave me free admit-
tance into his dairy; but led me over his warehoufes; and, in the moft difinterefted manner, made me acquainted with thegoodand
bad qualities of cheefes: of the defects they
are liable to, and the excellency they are capable of.

The OBJECTS of the dairy of this diftrict
are, in fpecies, the fame as thofe of the upper vale: namely

Calves	Whey butter
Milk butter	Swine.
Cheefe	

In the management of the two firft, I met
with nothing new or noticeable. The quantity of milk butter made here in fummer is
fmall. Every pound is plunder. CHEES-
MAKING was the object which led me into
the diftrict; and was the almoft only fubject
which engaged my attention. WHEY BUTTER
and SWINE will, neverthelefs, require to be
mentioned.

I. CHEESE.

I. CHEESE. The SPECIES of cheefe is, in refpect to *quality*, uniformly new milk— one meal—beft making. But, in regard to *fize*, the fpecies varies. It is either " double" or " fingle:" —— " thick" or " thin."— The thin cheefes, when marketable, weigh from nine to twelve pounds each : the thick, from fifteen to twenty five pounds. The *width* of the vats is for both fpecies the fame; namely about fifteen inches; the fize being varied altogether by *thicknefs*.

The requifite fübdivifions of the fubject, in this cafe, are the fame as in the upper vale.

1. Time of making
2. Quality of milk
3. Colouring
4. Rennets
5. Running
6. Management of curd
7. Management of cheefe
8. Difpofal
9. Produce.

1. THE SEASON OF MAKING. " *Thin cheefe*" is made from April to November : but the principal feafon for making " *thick cheefes*" is
during

during the months of May, June, and the
beginning of July. If made late in the fummer, they do not acquire a fufficient degree
of firmnefs, to be marketable the enfuing
fpring.

2. MILK. Here, as in the upper vale, the
milk is feldom genuine: it being, I believe,
a univerfal cuftom to "keep a little out."—
The practice has two conveniences attending
it: it brings in a little eafy-got ready money
to go to market with (while the tradefpeople
in return are furnifhed with better butter than
otherwife they might have) and the fkimmed
milk is found ufeful in lowering the too great
warmth of milk immediately from the cow.
If the proportion fkimmed be not great, the
crime committed is venial; the milk of this
country being much above par as to richnefs:
even lowered as it is, the cheefes made from
it will fometimes, in hot weather, exude an
oleaginous liquid which might be collected
in fpoonfuls, from their furfaces.

3. COLOURING. Colouring is here confidered as a thing of the firft importance in the
art of cheefmaking. A good material is
highly valued; but is not always to be eafily
come

come at by dairywomen; who, perhaps, have only one market to go to. For this reafon, it is here a pretty general practice for the cheefe-factor to furnifh the dairies, whofe cheefes he expects to purchafe, with colouring of the beft quality.

Thus we find the *crime* of colouring cheefe is not an act of darknefs, done clandeftinely by the dairywoman, to *deceive* the factor: but, on the contrary, an open, known department in the bufinefs of cheefmaking, to which the factor gives his affent and his affiftance. The dairywoman's motive is evidently that of obliging her *cuftomer* the *factor*. Should it be afked what can be the factor's motive for encouraging this adulteration of an article of human food,—the anfwer is evident: he can have no other than that of obliging *his* cuftomers, the *cheefemongers*; who as evidently encourage this abominable practice, for the bafe end of obliging *their* cuftomers,—the *confumers*.— The truth is, men in general prefer well coloured cheefe to that which is ill coloured; or, in other words, highly coloured cheefe is at prefent *fafhionable*. The cheefemongers knowing this, will not purchafe pale coloured cheefe
of

of the factors; and, for this reason, the factors object to a pale-coloured dairy of cheese.

In the infancy of the art, the colouring of cheese was a *crime*; because it was then done with an intent to *deceive*. But dairywomen, at present, have no such intention. They colour it, now, through a kind of necessity, and with intentions as innocent as those of other manufacturers who change the colour of their raw materials. If the eaters of cheese were to take it into their heads, to prefer black, blue, or red cheese, to that of a golden hue, I will venture to pass my word for the dairywomen, they would do their best endeavour to gratify them.

If, in the colouring of cheese, any pernicious substance be made use of, the consequences to the community may be of a serious nature. But whether the preparation of annotta, which is now in common use for that purpose, be pernicious or salubrious to the human frame, no man perhaps has ever attempted to ascertain: it may, for any thing the declaimers against it appear to know to the contrary, be the most salutary alterative human invention can devise. It may, however,

be

be deftructive to human health ; and its medical qualities ought certainly to be enquired into.*

It appears by obfervations, fufficiently accurate, that one ounce, averdupois, of this preparation will colour, fufficiently, more than two hundred pounds of cheefe. The number of grains in one ounce averdupois are 437½. So that each pound of cheefe, *moderately coloured*, contains two grains of the preparation.

Few men, perhaps, eat more than a pound of cheefe a day each: (I fpeak of men whofe principal food is cheefe). It ought without difpute to be enquired into, whether two grains of that preparation, taken daily, is or is not injurious to the human frame. As to the fmall quantity which is eaten by men in general, on a ftomach already cloyed with other aliment, it does not feem to be an object

---

* It is, no doubt, a fact, that the ANNOTTA belongs to a clafs of plants, many individuals of which are of a poifonous nature. The faftidious, however, have lefs to fear, fince the celebrated THEA (tea) ftands not only in the fame *clafs*, but in the fame *order*, with BIXA *orellana*. See vol. i. p. 290.

ject of enquiry. If fo inconfiderable a portion
were capable of doing any degree of injury,
thoufands muft long ago have been poifoned
by eating cheefe. It might, neverthelefs, be
well, both for the manufacturers and the confumers of cheefe, if fome regulation could be
made, refpecting the material of colouring.

4. RENNET. The prudent manager of the
MABERLEY dairy cures her own " vells":—
under a conviction, refulting from long experience, that more depends on the vell itfelf,
than on any particular method of preparing
rennet from it.

Her method of *preparing the vells* is the
fame as that given in the Rural Econ: of
Norf: m. 108. Being firft made perfectly
clean by wafhing, they are falted, and laid
down, in an earthen veffel, for a few days.
They are then taken out; the firft pickle
drained from them: refalted; and put down
in jars. She feldom ufes them under one
year old: fhe fometimes keeps them two or
three years before fhe ufes them.

Her ordinary *method of preparing her rennet*
is to lay the vells in falt and water, which has
been boiled with a little black pepper in it:
VOL. II.   I   and

and to add a lemon ftuck with cloves; which
(the lemon) fhe thinks, gives the rennet a
" quicknefs;" but fays, that fhe has put
the vell into a little cold water, and made as
good a cheefe from it, as ever fhe did with
prepared rennet. She never ufes the vells a
fecond time.

The rennet made ufe of at FROCESTER was
prepared in this manner: to two gallons of
water, made falt enough to bear an egg, add
one pennyworth of mace,—one pennyworth
of cloves,—a handful of fweet briar and hawthorn buds,—a fmall quantity of alum (about
the bulk of a fmall walnut)--the fame quantity
of fal prunellæ,—a fmall quantity of cochineal
(a fmall " pinch"—the bulk of half a hazle
nut) and, if to be had, two or three bay leaves.
Pound the alum, falt prunel &c. and having
mixed the feveral ingredients with the falt and
water, add five vells; or, if fmall, fix or feven.
In about ten days, the rennet will be fit for
ufe.

Another recipe which I was favored with,
in this vale, is the following: three handfuls
of common falt to three quarts of water: a
quarter of an ounce of falt petre; as much
black,.

black pepper as will lie upon a fhilling; a fmall
quantity of agrimony; a fprig of fweet-fcented
thyme; a handful of fweet briar;—a handful of the " red buds of hawthorn"; four heads
of fage. Add the ingredients, and boil the
water a quarter of an hour. To the liquor,
when cold, put one vell. The rennet may be
ufed the next day.

I mention the different methods of preparing rennet; becaufe they, in reality, form
a part of the practice I am regiftering. They
are *facts* which ought not to be omitted. Neverthelefs, from what I have been able to learn,
from men who have an opportunity of obferving the effects of different rennets, their efficacy reaches no farther than to do away the
faintnefs of the vells; and thereby render the
rennet perfectly *fweet*.

5. RUNNING. It is well underftood that
the quality of curd varies with the degree of
heat of the milk, at the time of coagulation.
Milk immediately from the cow, efpecially
in fummer, is, in this diftrict, confidered as
being much too warm for running; requiring
to be lowered to a defired degree of heat, before the rennet be added. If the fkim milk of

I 2   the

the preceding meal be not adequate to this intention, *cold water* is added, to reduce it to the required heat; and no evil effect is perceived from the practice. In my own experience, cold water had, in this cafe, a probable bad effect. In the upper vale, I found the use of it, for this purpose, cautiously avoided. Nevertheless, in this vale, there are dairy-women of the first character, who will throw a pailful of cold water among their milk, without being apprehensive of any evil effect. It is highly probable that much depends on the specific quality of the water, used for this purpose. The water of the upper vale is not of the best quality. The waters of Cheltenham, or those of Harrowgate, might have a still worse effect.

Maberley, 4 *Oct:* 1783—half past seven, in the morning. Heat of the air in the dairy-room 58°—of the milk when stirred up with the rennet 86°—covered with cheese cloths, came at half past eight—one hour—at 84°. The curd untender.

Note—the small loss of heat in this instance is probably owing to the quantity of milk and the *closeness* of the morning.

Maberley,

Maberley, 4 *Oct:* 1783. Half paſt four in the afternoon. The air 62°. The milk 84°. Came at half paſt five—one hour—at 81½°. The curd delicate.

Frocefter, 9 *Oct:* 1783. Twenty minutes before eight, in the morning. Heat of the air in the room 53°. Of the milk 81°. Covered firſt with cheeſe cloths and afterward with a thick woolen cloth. At a quarter before nine, the coagulation having then begun to take place, the ſurface was broken with a ſkimming diſh, to haſten the coming. A practice not uncommon in this dairy, where the milk is run peculiarly cool. At nine, the coagulation was complete. One hour and twenty minutes. The heat of the whey 76°. The curd extremely ſoft and delicate.

6. THE CURD. *Maberley,* 4 *Oct:* 1783. Morning. The curd *broken* with a double cheeſe knife (ſimilar to that deſcribed in v. i. p. 270. but with only two blades) and *alſo with the hand* ; keeping it in motion with the diſh.

In this dairy, the cheeſe tub is ſcarcely left from the time the curd comes, until it be *gathered* in a maſs. As the curd ſettles, the dairywoman keeps collecting it, with her hands,

to

to one fide of the cowl; carrying the mafs round the tub, from time to time, to collect the fcattered curd the fafter. The whey is laded off, into a large oval tub, to ftand for cream. The curd being laid bare, the fkirts of the mafs are cut off and piled upon the reft; at the fame time gafhing the body of the mafs, to let out the whey, which may have been fhut up in gathering. The remaining whey is ftrained through a fieve, to collect the crumbs of curd; of which the Glocefterfhire dairywomen are fcrupuloufly tenacious.

The curd being thus freed from the principal part of the whey, but not yet from the whole of it; it is put into naked vats; (preffing it well in with the hands; rounding it up in the middle, in the ufual way;—throwing a loofe cloth over,—and tucking it in) and the vats fet in the prefs; in order to free it the more effectually from the remaining whey.

Having ftood ten or fifteen minutes in the prefs, it is turned out of the vats, into the cheefe tub again;—broken fmall with the hands; and cut ftill fmaller with the double knife.

It

It is now *ſcalded*, with *water lowered with whey*; about three parts water to one part whey*. The heat, in the inſtance under notice, 108°. The quantity a pailful;— thrown upon the crumbled curd; and the whole ſtirred briſkly about; mixing the curd and the ſcalding ſtuff, evenly together. The heat of the mixture 84°.

Having ſtood a few minutes for the curd to ſubſide, the liquor is laded off; the curd collected; and *vatted* in this manner: an aſſiſtant takes the curd out of the tub; the manager trimming it into the vatts; both of them preſſing it hard with their hands; freeing it, all they can, from the ſcalding liquor.

The vat about half full, a little *ſalt*, about an ounce, is ſcattered over the ſurface, and worked in among the curd; the vat filled up; and the maſs turned two or three times in the vat; the edges being pared and the middle rounded up, each turning. At length it is turned into a cloth, in the manner which has been de-

I 4   ſcribed

---

* Scalding with *all whey* is in *this* diſtrict reckoned injudicious: there is an idea that " whey may be heated until it be ſour."

ſcribed in the upper vale, and placed in the prefs.

Note. In this inſtance, one of the vats being found too full, and another not ſufficiently, a thin ſlice was ſhaved off the one and laid upon the other, without any breaking or intermixture, to make the parts incorporate.

Maberley, 4 *Oct.* 1783. Evening. The method of *breaking,—collecting,—*and *freeing from the whey,* the ſame as in the morning. The heat of the ſcalding liquor in this inſtance 106°. which was lowered by the curd to 90°. the quantity and quality nearly the ſame as in the morning.

*Note,—*the quantity of curd being in this inſtance conſiderably leſs than it was in the former, the heat of the mixture became of courſe greater than it was in the morning. Here lies a delicacy of management: it is not the heat of the *ſcalding liquid,* but that of the *mixture* which gives the texture of the curd. A circumſtance this excellent dairywoman is fully aware of. She therefore keeps ſome of the hot liquor back; and having ſtirred the mixture, adds, or witholds it, as her judgement directs her: *regulating the heat of the mixture to the*

the ſtate of the curd: thus ſhe ſcalded 84°. with
84°.—81½°. with 90°.

Froceſter, 9 *Oct.* 1783. The curd *broke*
with a double (one-edged) knife, alone, without uſing the hand, immediately, in the operation ; keeping it moving, as in the other
inſtances, with the diſh: the operation taking
up about ten minutes.

Having ſtood about twenty minutes to ſet-
tle, the curd was *collected* with the diſh, hands,
and arms, to one ſide of the cowl ; the whey
laded off; the curd collected nearer together;
preſſed gently in the bottom of the cowl;
and put into vats and the preſs, to free it from
the remaining whey.

Note. Here we have a material difference in
the practices of the two vales: in the upper
vale it is recommended to get the curd " hard
together" with the hands in the bottom of the
cowl; but ſubjecting it to the power of the
preſs is a much higher kind of compreſſion.
There, the curd is, through the ſpecies of
milk, leaner than it is here; where a little
" fat" is not miſſed ; and thus ſqueezing the
curd, while ſoft, may, perhaps, aſſiſt in freeing

ing it from that fuperfluous richnefs which
may promote its heaving.

Having remained full twenty minutes in the
prefs, the curd was returned into the cowl,
cut fmall with the double knife, and *fcalded*
with a pailful of *hot water**, lowered by a
dafh of whey, to 124°. which the curd reduced
to 95°.

Note. The fcalding liquor, in this inftance,
almoft wholly water, became, after it had ftood
fome time upon the curd, as rich to all appearance as whey: a yellow oil fwimming on the
furface !

7. CHEESES.   1. *Management in the prefs* †.
Maberley,—having ftood about an hour in the
prefs, they are turned into finer cloths ; and,
about two hours afterward, *falted* the firft time,
and turned into the fame cloths. In the evening, thofe made in the morning are again
turned

---

* If the water be fuffered to *boil*, all is fpoilt ! How nice,
or how *myfterious*, is this art.

† PRESS. The preffes, which I faw in this vale, were
moftly loaded with gravel, in cubical boxes, raifed by rollers,
and made to fall horizontally on the cheefes. The Maberley prefs is double ; each divifion of it, holding fix or eight
thin cheefes. In very large dairies ; efpecially where much
thick cheefe is made ; three or even four preffes are requifite.

turned, and again falted;—and the fame
repeated next morning: the furface of each
cheefe being falted three times, befides the
little ftrewed among the curd. The enfuing
evening they are bare-vatted; and the next
morning finally taken out: each cheefe ftanding four meals in the prefs.

The *method of falting*, in this dairy, varies
from that which has been defcribed. The
cheefe is falted in the vat. On taking it out
of the prefs the cloth is thrown back and the
upper fide falted: the edges are then raifed up
with the cloth (one part after another) high
enough above the rim of the vat to be conveniently falted:—the cheefe being turned, (in
the fame manner as it would be if the falting
were not done) the other fide is falted; the
cloth fpread over; and the vat returned to
the prefs.

Frocefter;—the cheefes having ftood fome
five or ten minutes in the prefs, they are turned
into dry cloths, of the fame degree of finenefs
as thofe taken off. In thefe, they ftand in the
prefs, until the next meal; when they are
falted the firft time. The fecond meal they
are again turned into the fame cloth, and
falted

falted the fecond, which is the laft, time. The
third meal the cloths are taken off; the cheefes
being then put into the bare vats; in which
they remain fo long as there is room for them
in the prefs; perhaps three or four days.

Spare curd. I obferved a different management of fpare curd, here, to that defcribed in v. i.
p. 306. Here I found it cut into flices, falted,
and left fpread upon an inverted vat, until
the enfuing meal: when it was broken and mixt
promifcuoufly with the frefh curd. But under
this management (though kept only one meal)
it is found injurious to the cheefe; and is
therefore to be avoided with all poffible care.

2. *Management on the fhelves.* Where a
large dairy of cows are kept, the dairyroom
fhelves are not fufficient to contain the young
cheefes; which, in large dairies, are carried,
immediately from the prefs, into an upper
room, fitted up with fhelves for their reception.
Here they are turned, generally once a day;
and remain under this treatment, until they
have acquired a fufficient degree of texture, to
enable them to undergo the operation of
" wafhing": a work which is gone through
every

every three, four, or five weeks, as conveniency, or want of room, may require.

3. *Cleaning.* This is done, here, in a manner similar to that which is described in v. i. p. 310. In some dairies, water is used; not whey; and in autumn, when the weather gets cold, the water is moderately warmed. Hot water is thought to soften the rind too much, and is deemed improper.

Note.—In the operation of washing, the firmness or solidity of the cheeses is seen in their specific gravity; by observing which of them sink and which of them swim in the water. If they sink, they are of a sufficiently close texture: if they swim, they are " hove ",— that is, either porous, or hollow in the middle. This is a very simple, and it seems, a very certain ordeal.

4. *Painting.* Cheeses rich in quality, and well manufactured; more especially, I believe, the produce of some particular soils; acquire, by age, a variegated colour; particularly at and near the surface; which becomes *clouded* with red. This natural effect is not unfrequently observable in Cheshire cheese : which being (until very lately) suffered to appear in

its

its natural colours, the redening parts fhow
themfelves evidently, through the palenefs of
the ground they appear in. I have alfo feen an
inftance of this effect in fome Glocefterfhire
cheefe, of a curioufly fine quality, and great
age.

The exact time when the *imitation* of this
natural effect took place, or by whom it was
firft practifed, I have not been able to learn,
with any degree of certainty; notwithftanding
it is a late *invention*. Like the internal co-
ing, it probably originated in *fraud*. It
was, perhaps, in the firft practifers, an *artful
trick*; an *impofition* on the purchafer. At prefent, however, it is practifed through very different motives. The dairywomen, one and
all, diflike it. The labour and expence of *colouring* they beftow with chearfulnefs; but the
act of *painting*, tho' done with lefs trouble
and lefs expence, is fet about with reluctance,
and fpoken of with difguft; efpecially by experienced dairywomen; who prefer the blue
difk and the yellow edge to any artificial red-
nefs.

At prefent, the painting of cheefes is practifed merely as a *characteriftic*. It is done at
the

the requeſt of the immediate purchaſers ; who cannot diſpoſe of them (without being ſuſpected at leaſt of impoſition) as " Gloceſterſhire cheeſe", unleſs they bear its characteriſtic.

Formerly, Glocesterſhire cheeſe was known by the height of its internal colour. *Colouring* was then its characteriſtic. At length, however, the art of colouring began to travel into other diſtricts ; it is now become in a manner general; and colouring has not, for ſome years paſt, been characteriſtic of Glocesterſhire cheeſe. The cheeſe of this diſtrict, however, has ever been, and probably will continue to be, in high eſteem. Some evident mark, ſome ſpecific character, is therefore required, by the dealer at leaſt, to diſtinguiſh it, at ſight, from that of other diſtricts: and it may be a moot point whether the practice of *painting* originated in fraud ; or whether it was firſt intended to be, what it really has been, a characteriſtic of Glocesterſhire cheeſe. Be this as it may, it ſeems to be almoſt certain that it will not long be able to maintain its character ; if it has not already loſt it. The art of painting has begun to travel; and will,

in

in all probability, foon become the general practice.

Thus it appears, that the Glocefterfhire dairy is fuffering through its own artifice. Had it not firft taught the art of colouring, its cheefes might ftill have been diftinguifhable, in their native colours, by the fuperior bluenefs of their fides, and the golden hue of their edges. It likewife appears evidently, that Glocefterfhire is able to give the fafhion to the colour of cheefe. The Glocefterfhire dairywomen have therefore, now, a fair opportunity of atoning for the fins of their anceftors; and of giving a characteriftic to their cheefes, which cannot be univerfally counterfeited: namely its own natural colour. Could they mufter courage enough to leave it to nature for one feafon only, the characteriftic would be eftablifhed, and the fafhion for uncoloured cheefe would be fet. Other diftricts would in confequence follow the example; and the prefent filthy practices be got rid of, in a way more ready and more effectual, than by any compulfory means that could be made ufe of. If a certain noble Earl would fignify a wifh that the cheefes produced upon his eftate

ſhould

fhould appear in their NATURAL COLOURS ;
his tenants love his Lordſhip too well ; to fuffer them to go to market in any other.

5. *Management on the floor.* The cheeſes
being cleaned, and afterwards difguifed in a
way unworthy of record *,—they are taken to
the cheeſe chamber ; entering what I call the
fecond ſtage. In fome dairies, the floor is prepared with fucculent herbage, in the manner
which has been defcribed ; and in others it is
only rubbed clean with a cloth. Cheeſes be-
dizened in fcarlet require not a blue coat: neverthelefs, the fucculency of the herbage is
thought by fome to keep the rind fupple and
free from cracks, and to kill or prevent mites.
In the cheeſe chamber, they are turned twice
or three times a week, and wiped with a cloth
about once a fortnight: remaining in this
ſtage

---

* Neverthelefs, as an *actual operation* in the prefent practice of Glocefterfhire, it ought to be mentioned. The *materials* Spanifh brown, and Indian red; fometimes mixed;
fometimes ufed feparately. The *method* varies: fome " dab"
on the colouring, wet, with a cloth ; others, while the furface is moiſt, throw it on, dry, in " pinches", irregularly ;
rubbing it in with the hand. The latter is allowed to be the
more miftrefsly manner.

ſtage until they are firm enough to ſet on-edge, or put into piles.

6. *Treatment of marketable cheeſe.*—From the "cheeſe chamber" they are removed into other rooms ; and placed in rows on-edge, or put into piles, of a height proportioned to their degrees of dryneſs. Here they remain until they are ſent to market. If, in a large dairy, they do not go off regularly, at the ac-cuſtomed times, every room in the houſe, every upper room at leaſt, will be full of cheeſes.

8. MARKETS. The produce of this vale, like that of the vale of Gloceſter, is all pur-chaſed by what are called " cheeſe factors" ; though, in reality, CHEESE MERCHANTS. Al-moſt the whole produce of the vale of Berkeley paſſes through the hands of two men: Mr. BIGLAND of FROCESTER, and Mr. HICKS of BERKELEY *. Each purchaſer has his particu-lar dairies: which he takes, year a fter year, at ſuch prices, as their ſeveral ſpecific qualities are entitled to ; and the market price, at the time of delivery, will afford: ſometimes with, but

---

* To whom, alſo, I am indebted for good offices.

but frequently without, any previous bargain being made.

9. PRODUCE. Three fpecies of produce deferve notice.

1. The produce of a given quantity of milk.

2. The year's produce of a cow.

3. The annual produce of the diftrict.

1. *Produce of milk.* By a pretty accurate calculation, in the upper vale, I found that a cheefe weighing fomewhat more than 11 lb. (namely a "ten" to the cwt:) took about 15 gallons of milk (ale meafure) or one gallon and one third to 1 lb. of *twomeal cheefe.* From two inftances, minuted with tolerable accuracy in this diftrict, the proportion appears to be in one inftance fomewhat more, and in the other fomewhat lefs than 1 lb. of curd to one gallon of *new milk.* Thefe proportions, however, are offered merely to convey a general idea of the fubject. The milk was guaged with a common rule, and the curd eftimated by the vats: neverthelefs, the calculations are fufficiently accurate for this intention.

2. *The*

2. *The year's produce of a cow.* A dairy of 40 cows made, in October, about 60 lb. of cheese a day. But the cows were then going off their milk: suppose, that in summer they produced 70 lb. a day; and calculate on seven months, at 65 lb. a day. On this calculation, the forty cows produced 121 hundredweight; or three hundredweight (of 112 lb.) each cow. A dairy of a hundred cows produced, on a par of years, five hundred pounds worth of cheese yearly. Supposing the par price was 33s. 4d. a hundred, the weight, under this supposition, was 300 cwt: or, as before three hundredweight each cow.

3. *The annual produce of the district.* In conversing on this subject, with the man best able to adduce the requisite data, we were led into calculations; which, though they only prove, with respect to the annual produce of cheese in this district, the well ascertained fact that it produces from *a thousand to twelve hundred tons a year*; yet, in other respects, they are interesting; and place the RURAL ECONOMY of the district, as a DAIRY COUNTRY, in a more striking point of view, than

could

could, perhaps, be effected by any other means.

The general mode of calculation, here, is by the rent of the land: reckoning that the cheefe fhould, at 30s. a hundred weight, pay the rent of the land occupied by the cows. The vale has been already eftimated at 50,000 acres. But it contains two or three arable townfhips; the roads &c. are alfo included in this number: fuppofing three-fourths of it to be grafsland in the occupation of dairy-farmers; and fuppofing the rent of grafsland, taken acre with acre, to be 20s. an acre; which is underftood to be at prefent near the truth*; the rental value of the dairy farms of the vale is 37,500l. A thoufand tons at 30l. a ton produce 30,000l. Twelve hundred 36,000l.

To bring the calculation within narrower compafs, and to eftablifh it on better-known data, a particular townfhip was fixt upon. This townfhip contains 2,000 acres; and makes, on a par, fifty tons of cheefe a year. But, being a marginal townfhip, part of the land

---

* Thefe calculations were made in 1783.

land is *arable*, and fome young ftock are reared in it. Deducting one fourth for arable land, rough grounds &c, the remainder is 1500 acres of dairy-farm land. The medium rent of thefe 1500 acres is laid at 20s. an acre, or 1500l. Fifty tons of cheefe at 30l. a ton produce 1500l.

It alfo comes out, by the laft calculation, that if 1500 acres produce 50 tons of cheefe, each acre produces 75 pounds weight.

To eftimate the proportion of cows to acres, a farm of 100 acres, grazed wholly by cows, was chofen. This farm maintains twenty five cows, fummer and winter. Each cow, therefore, occupies four acres. Four acres, at 75 lb. of cheefe an acre, produce 300 lb: which, being the produce of a cow in this calculation, is 36 lb. lefs than the eftimated produce of a cow in the calculation aforegoing, on that fubject.

If, as in the firft calculation, we eftimate the medium produce of the vale at 1100 tons, and the quantity of land occupied by cows at 37, 500 acres, it follows, that each acre produces only 65 lb: confequently, on this calculation,

lation, each cow occupies more than five
acres of land of a middle quality.

It is, however, fufficiently afcertained, by
annual experience, that three hundredweight
of cheefe may be taken as a fair eftimation of
the produce of a cow. From two hundred
and a half to three hundred and a half, according to a variety of circumftances, includes,
perhaps, the produce of every dairy in every
year. It appears to be likewife fufficiently afcertained, by a long courfe of experience,
that the aggregate produce of the diftrict, is,
on a par of years, eleven hundred tons.
Hence it follows, on thefe premifes, that the
number of cows applied to the purpofe of the
dairy is feven thoufand three hundred and odd.
Confequently, if we allow four acres to a cow,
the number of acres appropriated to the dairy,
in this diftrict, is fomewhat lefs than thirty
thoufand.

But the hundred acres, on which the above
calculation was founded, are above par as to
quality; and it is probable that, on a par of
land each cow occupies more than four acres.

On the whole we may venture to fet down,
in numbers fufficiently accurate to convey ge-

neral

neral ideas;—that the vale contains fifty
thoufand acres of furface;—that *two thirds* of
it are occupied by *cows*; that the cows are
in number from feven to eight thoufand;
and that their annual produce of cheefe is
from one thoufand to twelve hundred tons.

IV. WHEY BUTTER. The butter made
from the rich wheys of this diftrict is of a good
quality: if well manufactured, and eaten
while frefh, it is fuperior to the milk butter of
many diftricts. Indeed, it is here equivalent,
in price, to milk butter; not more, I underftand, than a penny or twopence a pound difference. I met with an inftance, in which they
were both of them contracted for, by the year,
by the fame perfon; the milk at 7½d. the
whey at 6½d. a lb. It is not unfrequently fold
at 7d. or 8d. a lb. (of 18 oz.)

The principal *market* is Durfley; where it
is bought up, chiefly, by huckfters for Stroud,
and the manufacturing country which fur-
rounds it. This accounts for the demand and
the price.

The *produce* of whey butter is laid at half a
pound a cow a-week. But I have known an
inftance, in which a pound a week has been
made.

made. And, perhaps, three quarters of a
pound may be taken as the medium produce
of each cow. Confequently, the aggregate
produce of the diftrict is upwards of five
thoufand pounds a week. A quantity, which
could not well be difpofed of, at any price,
were it not for the circumftance of a manufacturing diftrict being fituated in its immediate neighbourhood.

I have been told that it is, or has been, a
cuftom, in fome dairies, to give the whey
butter as a perquifite, or as wages, to the
manager. But this is evidently injudicious;
as it induces her to impoverifh the curd, to
enrich herfelf. Befides, where a large number of cows are kept, the aggregate value of
the whey butter, in the courfe of the feafon,
is confiderable. Suppofe three quarters of a
pound a week at 6d. a pound, and reckoning
the feafon feven months, the grofs produce is
about half a guinea each cow.

V. Swine. *Maberley*, 7 *October* 1783.—
The whey of this dairy is given to the hogs as
faft as it is fkimmed; or paffes through the
hog-tubs, as conveniency fuits. There are
now in the fties five large hogs fatting on beans
and

and whey; and five more very large ſtores
(of the Shropſhire breed) at whey and acorns.
Ten ſwine to forty cows. See v. i. page 317.

Acorns are here in high eſteem as a food
of ſwine. The farmers ſeem to be as anxious
about their acorns as their apples. They
conſider them as the beſt of fatting. They
think the acorns make the bacon firm;
and cauſe it to weigh better than bean-fed
bacon!

How various are opinions, in different diſtricts, on the ſame ſubject. In many parts
of the kingdom acorns are, in a manner neglected as hog-food; and are ſeldom conſidered as an eligible material of fatting. They
are thought to make the bacon *hard:* here
they only make it *firm.* Does the whey take
off the aſtringent quality of the acorns? Or
are the acorns of this diſtrict of a more fattening quality than thoſe of the reſt of the
kingdom?

The price of acorns, here, is 1s. 6d. to 2s.
a buſhel; according to the ſeaſon; and according to the price of beans. But few are
ſold. Every farmer collects his own, or tends
his

his pigs upon them. In one inftance I faw the wafh carried, in a barrel-cart, into the center of the grounds; by the fide of a hay-ftack; under which the pigs refted.

Acorns are this year (1783) unufually plentiful. Several trees have broken down with them. I have feen one bending like an apple or pear tree under its load. Do not thefe circumftances evince a fingular fruitfulnefs of foil; and fhow the peculiarly fattening quality of the products of thefe vales?

NORTH

NORTH

WILTSHIRE.

THE DISTRICT which bears this name is an extensive tract of middleland country; lying, in a vale-like flat, between the hills of Wiltshire and those of Glocestershire; winding from the east toward the southwest; lying, chiefly, within the limits of Wiltshire; but extending, with its northeastern margin, into Glocestershire.

On the east, this district has no NATURAL OUTLINE: the vale of White-Horse being a continuation of it in Berkshire. The southwestern extremity is closed by the hills in the environs of Bath, on the border of Somersetshire.

The EXTENT, lengthway, is about thirty
five miles. The mean width about fifteen:
containing more than five hundred fquare
miles. It may be eftimated at three to four
hundred thoufand acres.

The CLIMATURE of North Witfhire is forward: peas were moftly harvefted; and fome
wheat cut; the 25th July (1788):—more
than a week before the vales of Glocefterfhire.

The SURFACE is uneven; abounding with
fwells and hillocks: fome of them rifing
abruptly, and to a confiderable height above
the general level of the diftrict. Bowwood
rears its head above the reft. But even this
lies much below the downs that overlook it.
The fouthweft quarter, on the contrary, dips
below the general level; forming a valley,
which gives paffage to the Wiltfhire branch
of the Avon.

With refpect to SURFACE WATER;— the
middle being the higheft part of the general
level, the diftrict forms a kind of double
vale; dipping towards each extremity; though
not perceptibly, to the diftant eye. Springs
are abundant. Rivulets numerous and fmall.
Thofe of the eaft end fall gently toward the
Thames.

Thames. Thofe of the fouthweft, more rapidly into the Avon; whofe bed lies low; collecting as well the fprings of the vale, as thofe
of the margins of the hills on either fide. As
it appr aches the neighbourhood of Bath, the
valley grows deeper and narrower: the character of the country changing, from a vale-like
expanfe, to a broken furface; a croud of hills;
a ftyle of country between the beautiful and
the romantic.

The vegetable PRODUCE of this diftrict is
chiefly *grafs*. Perhaps two-thirds of it is in a
ftate of *old grafsland*: one fourth *arable*. The
reft *woodland*.

The APPLICATION of the grafsland is principally to cows;—whofe milk is, in a manner
wholly, converted into CHEESE;—the manufacturing of which was the only object that
led me into the diftrict.

NORTH WILTSHIRE CHEESE is at prefent,
in the firft eftimation among thofe, who in-
dulge their appetites. It has a richnefs, and
at the fame time, a mildnefs, which recommends it to many, in preference to that of
Glocefterfhire; even of the vale of Berkeley;
whofe cheefe, though of the firft quality as to
richnefs,

richnefs, has in general a fharpnefs, a degree of pungency, which is offenfive to fome palates, though coveted by others: the produce of each diftrict may, therefore, be faid to have itsexcellence.

To endeavour to render an account of the DAIRY MANAGEMENT of NORTH WILTSHIRE, as interefting as the fubject will permit, and as intelligible as the nature of it requires, it will be neceffary to examine ftill farther the fite, or fcene of management, and the elements or materials, from which the products arife, as well as the means of production; and for thefe purpofes it will be requifite to examine, feparately, the following fubjects.

I.   Eftates.
II.   Farms.
III.   Soils.
IV.   Water.
V.   Herbage.
VI.   Cows.
VII.   Management.

I. ESTATES.   This fertile diftrict is chiefly the property of men of large eftates; and

and may boaft of fome capital RESIDENCIES.
BADMINTON, the principal refidence of the
DUKE OF BEAUFORT, is feated on its northern
margin: as BOWWOOD, the refidence of the
MARQUIS OF LANSDOWN, is on the fouthern.
LORD BOLINGBROKE and SIR JAMES LONG
have feats near its center. Befides thefe, and
the refidences of feveral GENTLEMEN, the
DUKE OF MARLBOROUGH, LORD CLAREN-
DON, and other Noblemen have off eftates in
different parts of the diftrict.

The yeomanry is inconfiderable. The occupation being almoft wholly in TENANTS.

The RENT of grafsland is from twenty to
thirty fhillings an acre. Twenty five fhillings
may, perhaps, be taken as the prefent medium rent. Grafsland, therefore, lets higher,
here, than in the vale of Berkley : not, however, owing to its fuperior quality, or to its
being more *dearly* rented; but to the circumftance of its having, moftly, a mixture of arable land lying among it; a circumftance,
which that of the vale of Berkley is in want
of.

The TENANCY of the diftrict varies: fome
eftates remain *at will*; while others have been
long

long let under *leafes*; fome of them of twenty-one years.

To the honour of this diftrict, it may, I believe, with truth be faid, that although *requifite alterations* have of late years been made, little of that *oppreffion*, which has manifefted itfelf in many diftricts, has taken place in this. The good opinion and confidence, which ought ever to fubfift between landlords and their tenants, appear to be ftill fufficiently maintained in the diftrict under obfervation.

II. FARMS. There are few diftricts of the ifland, equally habitable, equally well foiled, and principally in a ftate of grafsland, in which farms are fo *large* as in North Wiltfhire. Middleland countries being early inhabited, the lands became much divided; and the diftinct occupations, where they have not been defignedly thrown together, ftill remain fmall. But here, farms of two or three hundred a year, are common. Some of five or fix hundred. And one (at leaft) of feven or eight hundred a year.

The CHARACTERISTIC of farms has been intimated. Some of them are all *grafs*; but,

Vol. II. L in

in general, they have a portion of *arable* land belonging to them : a circumstance favorable to a dairy. One of the largeſt dairymen in the diſtriĉt, who has not this advantage, not unfrequently fetches his ſtraw for litter, ſix or ſeven miles !

From the preſent PLAN of farms in general, we may conclude, that they have long lain in their preſent form, and are not recent aggregations of farm and farm. The houſe is generally near the center, with large cowgrounds reaching up to the yards. The grounds, too, appear to be proportioned to the ſizes of the farms. On the largeſt, grounds of fifty acres, or more, are not unfrequent : though ſmaller grounds, admitting of a change of paſture, would, perhaps, be more eligible.

The YARDS are, in general, mere milking places ; without any ſhelter for cattle in winter ; when the cows (where the land will bear them) are foddered and milked abroad in the grounds. Some farms, however, eſpecially where the ſoil is tender, have ſhedded yards : I ſaw one (the largeſt farm, I believe, in the diſtriĉt) which has a ſpacious yard, nearly incloſed

clofed with fheds; there being fhed-room on
the farm for near a hundred cows.

The yards are not unufually *paved*, with
brick-fhaped ftones, fet edge-way: in one inftance, I found them floored with *afhes* of
clods, cut out of open drains, &c. laid about
a foot thick. Thefe bind, and make an excellent bottom. If they fhovel up, they are
good manure. It might be good management, when materials can be had, to renew
them, as they become faturated with the fer-
tilizing quality of the dung.

III. SOIL AND MANAGEMENT.—
The SPECIES of foil is various. In general,
a rich, deep, productive loam. Some of the
fwells are of a ftiffer more clayey foil; and
fome of them, towards the north fide of the
diftrict, of a " brafhy" nature: appearing as
detached *waves* from the Cotfwold hills.——
While part of the fummit of one (the lovely
fwell on which Swindon ftands) is literally a
blowing fand.

The SUBSOIL, too, is various: in many
places a *calcarious rubble*, or even a kind of
rock, rifes up to the foil, and this in the

L 2   low

low flat parts of the diftrict: an uncommon circumftance. In the valley of Avon, a ftratum of *gravel* intervenes between the foil and a bed of *blue marl*; which, from fome experiments recently made, appears to be very beneficial to grafsland; though, by analyfis, it proves to be weak in calcariofity.

A diftrict which, by natural fituation, is low, and whofe furface is, at the fame time, raifed into inequalities; efpecially where the fubftrata are of different qualities; cold fpringy plots will neceffarily arife; and UNDERDRAINING become requifite. In this diftrict much has been done. Toward the eaft end of it, *ftones* are plentiful. In the valley of Avon, fome *turf-drains* have been made, which thus far ftand very well. I here faw an inftance of fub-draining *rufhy interfurrows* of high wide ridges; and with good fuccefs*. Some yards of each furrow, which, formerly, bore nothing but rufhes, or other paluftrean weeds, now produce herbage equal, or nearly equal, to the reft of the land: a fpecies of improvement, which is wanted in almoft every grafsland diftrict.

* By Mr. BFAMES of Avon.

The

The MANURING of grafsland is, here, pretty common: but the fame bad effect, on the cheefe made from land recently manured, is obferved, here, as in the vales of Glocefter-fhire. Judicious dairymen, therefore, mow, invariably I underftand, the firft year after manuring.——The fecond year they find it may be paftured by cows with a degree of fafety.

On a dairy farm, where cows are foddered upon the land, little manure is raifed. The "hog pounds" are the principal fource; and the produce of thefe, valuable as it might be made, is, I am afraid, fuffered, in general, to run wafte into the common fhores. One judicious manager, however, is preparing a ciftern to receive the liquor of his hog-fties, intending to carry it out in carts, and fcatter it upon his lands in a liquid ftate; while another* fuffers it to run into a wide open refervoir, in which mould and earth of different forts are fhot. When thefe are faturated, they are carried away as manure, and frefh materials thrown in: a practice, which, I am perfuaded, will, in the end, be more beneficial

L 3 (as

* Mr. ISLES of Shaw.

(as the manure will be more durable) than diluting the drainage with water, and carrying it on as liquid manure.

IV. WATER. The numerous fprings and rivulets, with which the diftrict abounds, afford convenient watering places. But with refpect to the *quality* of water, as a beverage for cows, from which cheefe is to be made, I have not, in this diftrict, been able to come at any information. It is a fubject, which does not appear to have been thought of, much lefs agitated, or made the fubject of obfervation or experiment. Intelligent dairymen *think*, that running water *muft* be beft; but their opinion appears to be little better than furmife; without any folid foundation to ground it upon.

V. HERBAGE and MANAGEMENT. From a general view of the diftrict, in the month of *July*, I could perceive no material difference, with refpect to the SPECIES of herbage, between this diftrict and the vales of Glocefterfhire. The RAYGRASS, DOGSTAIL,

and

and WHITE TREFOIL were then the prevailing herbage of the pasture grounds.

Here, as in the vale of Berkeley, the grafs-lands are moftly very old —their AGE, in ge-neral, unknown: forty years is the youngeft I heard of. The entire diftrict appears to have been heretofore under the plow; though few traces of common field are at prefent evident.

This diftrict and the vale of Berkeley, which are feparated by the Stroudwater hills, fome eight or ten miles acrofs, are, in many re-fpects, fimilar, and different from all other diftricts I have hitherto examined.

The MANAGEMENT of grafslands, in this diftrict, is fimilar to that of the vale of Berke-ley.—The cow grounds (which are pretty uni-verfally fkimmed with the fithe once, at leaft, in the fummer) lie near the houfe, and the mowing grounds at a diftance: the chief dif-ference between the two diftricts is, that North Wiltfhire abounds with " WATER MEADS,"— in fituations, which will admit of this ad-mirable improvement.

VI. COWS. The dairies of this diftrict are large. Several, I believe, of a hundred cows

L 4 (I faw

(I faw two of this fize) forty or fifty a common-fized dairy.

The species of cow is, invariably, the *longhorned*; which has here been the eftablifhed fpecies, time immemorial! I did not, at leaft, gain any evidence of its firft introduction; or of any other fpecies being prevalent in the diftrict.

Many of thefe cows are *purchafed*; but numbers are every year *bred*,—and have, time immemorial, been bred in this diftrict; where they appear to be as fully eftablifhed, as they are in Leicefterfhire, and the other midland counties.

The principal *place of purchafe* is High-worth, near the eaftern extremity of the diftrict; to which great numbers are brought, weekly, during fome months in the fpring, from Staffordfhire and the other midland counties. The prices given for cows, *with calves at their feet*, at that feafon, is extraordinary. There is one man, in the neighbourhood of Swindon, who has not given lefs than fifteen or fixteen pounds, or guineas, during the laft ten years! From twelve to fifteen is the ordinary price. None but prime cows are
b rought

brought into the country. Even the Glocefter market is generally picked, by dealers, to take into Wiltfhire.

The cows, which are *bred in the country*, are not inferior to thofe driven into it. Bulls bear a good *price*; but are not let at the extravagant rate which they have of late years arifen to, in the midland counties. Mr. BADON of Dey-houfe, near Swindon, has a fine dairy of three or four fcore cows, moftly of his own rearing. But Mr. BEAMES of Avon, near Chippenham, ftands firft in the diftrict as a breeder. He has forty cows, which, in mould—though not in fize—may vie with any dairy of cows the mid-land country can produce; and has, this fea-fon (1788) a lot of the eveneft and moft beau-tiful yearling heifers I have ever feen in any country. But he has hired bulls from the midland diftrict; the fountain-head, at pre-fent, of this fpecies of cattle. Neverthelefs, it may be faid, without rifque, that, at prefent, no diftrict in the kingdom, of equal extent, can fhow fuch herds of cows, whether for num-ber or value, as are, at this time, in the diftrict under notice.

The

The MANAGEMENT of DAIRY COWS is much the fame, here, as in Glocefterfhire: except that they are, here, more generally kept out, during winter, in the open grounds; which, in general, are better able to carry them, without injury, than are thofe of Glocefter-fhire; where the fubfoil is more retentive.

The hay is all carried onto the land, upon mens' backs (a laborious employment) and fcattered regularly over the ground; foddering on frefh ground every day: by which means the land is equally benefitted, and the hay eaten up clean.

One particular, refpecting the fummer management of cows, deferves to be mentioned. It is ufual for dairymen to keep a few *fheep* among their cows. About one fheep to a cow. But there are men, here, and thofe of the firft character as dairy farmers, who object even to this fmall number: alleging, that a few fheep are nearly the fame trouble as a flock; and that, by nibbling out the choiceft herbage, they are enemies to the cheefe cowl. Neverthelefs, there are others of opinion, that, on very fat land, land too rich for cheefe, fheep are beneficial to the dairy; and they may be

right:

right: there certainly cannot be a more ingenious method of impoverifhing the pafture of
cattle, than that of mixing fheep among them.

VII. MANAGEMENT.   This will require to be fubdivided as in the other diftricts.

1. MANAGERS.   Through the intereft of
AMBROSE GODDARD, ESQUIRE (Member for
the county) who has a confiderable eftate lying round his refidence at SWINDON ; and by
the affiduities of Mr. FARMER, one of the
moft confiderable cheefe factors in the diftrict ; I gained free admiffion to fome of the
firft dairies in the eaftern part of it: and
through the obliging affiftance of Mr. BEAMES
of AVON, my information in the fouthweftern
quarter was rendered equally valuable.

I had an opportunity of feeing the entire
proceffes of fix different dairies, from forty to
a hundred cows each: and faw a fufficiency of
others to gain a general idea of their management.

Mr. ILES of Shaw, in the Swindon quarter,
who may, I believe, be called the firft dairyman in the diftrict, and who is equally able
and

and ready to inform, was particularly obliging in ſhewing me his own and his neighbours management. Mrs. Badon of Deyhouse, near Swindon, a moſt experienced and intelligent manager, and whoſe management is, in many reſpeƈts, ſingular, was equally liberal of information. And Mr. Rich, of Foxham, in the Chippenham quarter, a ſkilful and attentive dairyman, whoſe cheeſe has long been held in the higheſt eſtimation; and which is, in reality (this year at leaſt) the moſt uniform, and the moſt highly flavored dairy of cheeſe I have any where taſted,—was not leſs ſolicitous in giving me, without reſerve, the wiſhed for intelligence *

2. Dairyroom.

---

* One general remark, reſpeƈting the dairywomen of this diſtriƈt, requires to be made. It is cuſtomary, even in the largeſt dairies, for the oſtenſible manager, whether miſtreſs or maid, to perform the *whole* operation of making cheeſe ; except the laſt breaking &c. and the vatting ; in which ſhe has an aſſiſtant. But this, in a dairy of eighty or a hundred cows, is too great labour for any woman : it is painful to ſee it. In one inſtance, in this diſtriƈt, a man was employed in this laborious department : and, in a large dairy, it is certainly man's work. A curd-mill (ſee York: econ: v. ii. p. 291.) would leſſen the labour conſiderably.

2. Dairyroom. The " *dey*houfes" of this diftrict, are fpacious and commodious*. Set round with preffes and whey leads†: no fhelves: the area being left free for the cowls churns, &c. The floors of ftone.

Cleanlinefs is feen in every dairy: a degree of neatnefs is obfervable in fome. Every thing is conducted in a fuperior ftyle. There are men of independency and fpirit, who fet the example. Mr. Iles's dairyroom and " cheefe-lofts" form an exhibition worth going fome miles to fee.

The North Wiltfhire dairyrooms, in general, have OUTER DOORS; frequently opening under a penthoufe or open leanto fhed: a good con-veniency; affording fhade and fhelter; and
giving

One for forty cows, meafured 20 by 16. One for a hundred, 30 by 40; befides a back leanto for whey leads &c.

† WHEY LEADS. They have, here, a peculiarity which is noticeable. Inftead of a pin or plug being made ufe of to ftop the outlet pipe in the bottom of the lead; the pipe is furnifhed with a common turn-cock; and in fome cafes, I was told, the pipes are continued from the leads to the ciftern or general refervoir; thereby faving the la-bour of carrying out the whey in pails. But quere, may not the whey in this cafe corrode the pipes and be injurious to the hogs?

giving a degree of coolnefs to the dairyroom. In one inftance, I obferved two doors: a common clofe-boarded door on the infide; and an open-paled gate-like door on the outfide: giving a free admiffion of air, in clofe warm weather; and, at the fame time, being a guard againft dogs and poultry. A conveniency, which would be an improvement to any dairyroom in the fummer feafon.

3. UTENSILS. Similar to thofe of Glocefterfhire. The weight of the *prefs* is a box filled with fand or gravel. The dimenfions of one, filled with fand, was 18 inches fquare, by two feet two inches long, on the infide (meafuring the depth of fand only). A cubical inch of the fand, when *dry*, weighs 368 grains; confequently, the whole weight of *fand* is not quite four hundred weight.

The " broad" *vats* the fame dimenfion as thofe of Glocefterfhire: namely 15½ diameter. The " loaf" vats 10 to 12 inches diameter, by four to fix inches deep. The vats are moftly without holes in their bottoms; that they may retain the brine the longer.

It is obfervable, that the *pail* of the Avon quarter is the large one-handled pail of Glocefterfhire;

cefterfhire ; while, about Swindon, the common pail of the fouthern counties (iron hooped,
with an iron bow) is univerfally in ufe ; carried on yokes, in the London manner.

The *cowl* is proportioned to the fize of the
dairy.   I meafured one near four feet diameter: yet this is fometimes too fmall to contain the milk of the dairy.   In this cafe, two
cowls are ufed: and, when part of the whey
is laded off, the two parcels of curd are mixt
and broken together.

4. MILKING.   The hours of milking are
very early.   In the morning, the cows are generally in the yards, by four o'clock ;—in the
afternoon, by three.   In fome dairies, and in
the middle of fummer, the cows are in the
yard, and the whole family up, by three
o'clock in the morning !   Thus dividing the
two meals equally.

The number of milkers are proportioned to
the number of cows—ten cows to a milker is
the general allowance.   In large dairies, the
principal part of the milkers are labourers, or
their wives, or daughters.

The cows are milked promifcuoufly ; and
only once over at a meal; not *ftroked* or drawn
a fecond

a fecond time; as they are in many diftricts:
a practice, which I have not obferved either in
Glôcefterfhire, or Wiltfhire.

The OBJECTS of the dairy, which, in this
cafe, will be required to be noticed, are

Calves

Cheefe.

I. CALVES. The calves, which are not
reared, are fatted by *fuckling*, for the London
market. Moftly fent up *dead*;—cut up in
quarters;—and packed in hampers with damp
cloths. The common age of butchering fix,
feven, or eight weeks.

Here, inftead of calf *pens*, or *ftages*, CALF
STALLS are in ufe. Each calf has its feparate
ftall, about two feet wide and four feet long;
juft room enough to lie down; on a platform
of boards or laths; with a range of troughs
before their heads; with which, in this cafe,
they ftand toward the wall; tied up fhort, as
aged cattle: a plan which might well be
adopted by the fuckling farmers about the
metropolis. It has many advantages over
the *pens* there in ufe.

II. CHEESE.

II. CHEESE. The SPECIES of cheefe made here are various. Early in fpring, *foft* thin cheefes are made, and fent up weekly to the London market. Some dairies, it feems, put the whole, or a principal part, of their make in *nets*. But the common make of the diftrict confifts of

> Thin cheefe,
> Broad-thick, and
> Loaf cheefes.

The thin and the broad-thick forts are fimilar to thofe of the vale of Berkeley; and are, I underftand, fold in London as double and fingle GLOCESTER. It is the narrow LOAF CHEESE, which goes under the name of NORTH WILTSHIRE cheefe; and which has of late years become fo high in fafhion as to fetch fifteen or twenty fhillings a hundredweight more, at market, than thin cheefe,—of perhaps a fuperior fpecific quality !

It may reafonably be afked, why is any other fpecies made in the diftrict. The anfwer is, every one makes loaf cheefes who *can*, with any degree of *certainty*. They not only require more *fkill*, and more *labour*, than thin cheefes; but it is generally believed

VOL. II.   M   that

that much depends upon the *ground* from which they are to be made. The fact is, I understand, that more than half the make of the district goes to market, in the form of thin cheese, which, at prefent, is not worth more than 27 to 28s. a cwt. while not one fourth of it is fent in loaves, which, notwithstanding the low price of cheese in general, is worth from 45 to 50s. a cwt. !

Loaf cheeses, however, have their difadvantages ; though not equal to the prefent difproportion of price. They require not only more labour ; but more prefsroom ; and what is ftill more inconvenient, efpecially to the *neceffitous,* they do not come fo quick to market ; requiring a much longer time to ripen in, than thin cheeses: confequently more loftroom is likewife neceffary.

Neverthelefs, thefe inconveniences are inconfiderable, when compared with the advantage they have at market. Every man, therefore, whofe fkill and grounds will permit him, and who is not in neceffitous circumftances, makes loaf, or *thick* cheese; which, in general, bears a price approaching to that of loaves.

The

The MANAGEMENT now requires to be par-
ticularized.

1. SEASON OF MAKING. In large dairies,
cheefmaking is continued *throughout the
year!* Not only cheefe for the *family*; but
factor's cheefe, alfo, is made through the winter feafon. In one dairy, I faw a very confiderable parcel of broad-thick cheefe, which
was literally made in *winter*. Many tons of
factor's cheefe is every year made, in this·
diftrict, entirely from *hay*; which, if good,
is faid to afford not only clofer, but richer
cheefe, than grafs. Winter-made cheefe,
however, is long in ripening, and is liable to
be fcurfy and white-coated. But time over-
comes one of thefe difadvantages, and a coat
of red paint the other.

2. MILK. The *fpecific quality* of the milk
is not here debafed. The milk is run neat,
or nearly neat, from the cow. The Glocefterfhire practice of " keeping a little out", for
milk butter, is not here in ufe. It is not, at
leaft, the common practice of the country,
for the cheefmakers to *fell* milk butter. In
one or two inftances, which I attended to more

M 2   clofely,

cloſely, not a drop was added to the new milk neat from the cow.

3. COLOURING. The colouring of cheeſe has been long a practice, in this diſtrict. The oldeſt dairywoman I converſed with (ſixty or ſeventy years of age) does not recollect to have ſeen cheeſe made with its natural colour. She remembers very well the introduction of the "ſtone colouring"; the preparation of annotta, now in uſe; and has herſelf made uſe of the "powder colouring"; ſaunders; which, ſhe ſays, was uſually boiled among a little milk, previous to its being put into the cowl.

At preſent, the material, and the method of uſing it, is the ſame as in Gloceſterſhire; except that a new ſpecies has lately made its appearance; giving the milk and the curd a beautiful *yellow* hue; very different from the *redneſs* communicated by a ſuperfluity of the common colouring. The baſe appears to be annotta; the difference being in the preparation.

The colour preferred, by the cheeſe factors of this diſtrict, is that of well coloured beeswax. Cheeſe of this colour will fetch more,

by

by some shillings a hundredweight, than pale under-coloured cheese, or that which is too highly reddened.

4. Rennet. I met with nothing new, in this district, respecting rennets; except in one dairy; in which a peculiar mode of preparation is made use of.

The usual method is to make as much, at once, as will last several days; perhaps weeks; or the whole season. But, in this instance, it is *made fresh every day*: that is, fresh brine is added every day; and never more than two vells—here provincially " rades"—are suffered to lie in the jar at once. The older of them is marked with a skewer; and as soon as it grows stale, is taken out, and a fresh one added.

This method of preparing rennet has been now continued through two or three generations. All I can say farther of it is, that the dairy, in which it is used, produces (if any one dairy has a decided preference) the best cheese of the district: but whether from the rennet, the ground, or the management, or from the three jointly, is by no means evident.

M 3   5. Running.

5. RUNNING. The milk is univerſally run as it comes from the cow ; or as it *happens* to be lowered by the little ſkimmed milk, which is put into it. Its degree of heat I never ſaw tried; not even with the hand ! It is *ſaid* that, in very cloſe weather, the firſt milking is ſometimes kept in ſeparate veſſels, or ſpread thin in a whey lead ; but in general, I apprehend, its degree of heat, during the ſummer ſeaſon, is never attended to ! A faꬶ, which I could not have believed, had not my own obſervation, ſtrengthened by the thermometer, convinced me of it. I had conceived, that the ſuperior excellency of the Glocefterſhire management conſiſted very much in running the milk cool ; and expeꬶed to have found it run ſtill cooler in Wiltſhire. But the following memorandums, accurately taken, are a convincing proof of the contrary.

Swindon, Monday evening (21 *July* 1788). Heat of the air in the dairyroom 60°: milk 87½°: uncovered: came in one hour and ten minutes: whey 85°: curd of a middle quality.

Deyhouſe—Tueſday evening. Air 63°: milk 88°: not covered: came in half an hour: " too
much

much rennet": whey 86°: the curd untender ; but far from being of a bad texture.

Weſtleycot—Wedneſday morning. Air 60°:
milk 86°: uncovered: came in three quarters
of an hour: whey 84°; the curd of a good
quality.

Shaw—Wedneſday evening. Air 62°: milk
87°: not covered: came in about an hour:
whey 86°: (quantity very great:) the curd of
a good quality.

Avon—Thurſday evening. Air 60°: milk
88°: cloſely covered with a thick woolen
cloth, to make the top and the bottom come
together: came in about an hour: whey 87°:
the curd very good.

Foxham—Friday evening. Air 60°: milk
91°. ! covered with a thin cloth: came in one
hour: whey 89 ! Nevertheleſs, the curd
delicately tender ! ! !

6. CURD. The management of the curd
depends, in ſome meaſure, on the ſpecies of
cheeſe. Thin cheeſe requires the leaſt care
and labour ; and thick cheeſe leſs than loaves;
which require the beſt ſkill and induſtry of the
manager.

In this department of the cheefe manufac-
tury the North Wiltfhire dairywomen excel. It
appears to be their *forte*. In it they feem to
think the principal art confifts. It will therefore be proper to defcend to its minutiæ.

1. *Breaking.* This is done entirely with
the hand and the difh: no knife in ufe, here,
as in Glocefterfhire. In fome dairies, great
caution is obferved in the firft fracture of the
curd ; which is done, either with the hand,
or the difh, moved gently in the center of the
cowl; dividing the curd into large fragments ;
fo as to let out the whey, leifurely, to prevent
its carrying off with it the " fat" of the curd.
When the curd has funk a little way down in
the whey, it is broken more freely ; and,
having ftood again to fubfide, and the clear
whey on the top being laded off, it is reduced
to a degree of finenefs proportioned to the fpecies of cheefe. For thin cheefe, it is broken
as fine as curd generally is in Glocefterfhire ;
for thick cheefe, ftill finer ; and for loaves, it
is reduced, as it were, to atoms.

In fome dairies, it is violently agitated
among the whey, with the hands, throwing it
up from the bottom of the cowl, making it
boil

boil up at the top, like a ftrong fpring gufhing out from below the furface. This is called " beating" it: a practice which is objected to by judicious dairymen; though I fee moft dairywomen do it, more or lefs, in the laft breaking in the whey.

2. *Gathering*. The ordinary practice is to lade off the whey as it rifes; preffing down the curd with the bottom of the lading difh ; to fink it the fafter, and render it the firmer.

In one inftance, and this in a dairy whofe practice is intitled to the firft degree of attention, the curd, inftead of being preffed with the back of the difh, is, while yet fufpended in the whey, gathered, with the bowl of it, to one fide of the cowl; firft carrying it gently round the cowl to collect the curd more effectually. The whey, by this means, is got off much clearer, " greener"—than it is when the curd is preffed, in a foft pappy ftate; a practice, which, undoubtedly, impoverifhes the cheefe.

Moft of the whey being got off, the cowl is heeled (in the common practice) to get the curd into a mafs on one fide of it. The cowl is then replaced upright ; the fkirts of the

mafs

mafs cut off and piled upon the reft; the mafs
gafhed with a long knife; and the whey laded
off; fopping it up dry with a cloth.

The mafs of curd is now pared down flice
after flice, (about an inch thick) and piled on
the oppofite fide of the cowl; at intervals,
prefling it clofe with the hands, and gafhing
it with the knife, to let out the whey more
effectually. The whole being thus gone over,
the whey, which has been by this means extracted, is laded off and fopped up with a
cloth, as before; and the curd piled a *third*
time; and, in fome dairies, a *fourth* time;
flicing, gafhing, and prefling it with the
hands; making it, by this means, in a manner
perfectly free from whey. A practice, which
was new to me, and which is, perhaps, peculiar to North Wiltfhire.

In one inftance, and that in the practice of
a moft intelligent and experienced dairywoman,
I obferved an improvement of this method of
freeing the curd from the whey. Inftead of
prefling the pile, at intervals, with the hands
(a power which, when the quality of curd is
large, has but little effect) a vat was put upon
it, and loaded with cheefe weights; a cloth
being

being fpread over the bottom of the vat to
prevent their fliding.   As the pile was carried
up or gafhed, the vat was moved from part to
part, fo as to give an even preffure to the
whole.   By this means the whey is, in a manner, wholly extracted.

Some few dairies, it feems, " double prefs"
the cheefes: that is, put the curd in the prefs
before it be fcalded, agreeably to the Berkeley
practice.   But it is confidered as an inferior
method.   It certainly reduces the richnefs of
the cheefe, more than the practice which is
here defcribed; and which, alone, fell under
my obfervation, in Wiltfhire.

3. *Scalding.*   The ordinary method of
fcalding, here, is fimilar to that, which has
been defcribed in the Glocefterfhire practice.
The mafs of curd is broken, to different degrees of finenefs; proportioned not to the
ipecies of cheefe, altogether; but according
to the fkill of the dairywoman.   In a firft-
rate dairy, making loaf cheefes, I faw it broken
very roughly.

The *quality* of the fcalding liquor, too, varies, here, as in Glocefterfhire.   Some fcald
with

with whey: fome with water: others with water lowered with whey.

The *heat* of the fcalding liquor likewife varies, even in the ordinary practice of the diftrict, very confiderably: not, however, as in Glocefterfhire, according to the quality of the given curd; but according to the cuftom of the given dairy! Cuftom, however, which may have been founded on long experience, and may be peculiarly adapted to the *ground*, from which the curd is produced.

In the ordinary practice of the diftrict, the North Wiltfhire dairywomen may be faid to fcald highly. Five, out of the fix dairies, whofe fcalding liquor I tried with the thermometer, heated the *liquor* from 102°. to 140°. The heat of the *mixture*, of the liquor and curd, being from 92°. to 110°. So that, in the ordinary practice of the country, the milk is not only run, but the curd is fcalded, much higher than in the vale of Berkeley. A circumftance, which I did not expect to find in North Wiltfhire; whofe cheefe is characterized by a foft faponaceous texture; diametrically oppofite to that hardnefs,—toughnefs,—which

fcalding

fcalding appears to give to the curd in the firft inftance.

But if a degree of furprize arifes from the ordinary practice of the diftrict, an *excentric* practice, which I was favored with the infpection of, muft be a matter of fome aftonifhment. What renders this inftance of practice the more interefting, is its being ftruck out and purfued, by one of the oldeft, beftexperienced, and moft intelligent dairywomen I have any where converfed with. In this inftance, the curd is literally *fcalded*, with almoft *boiling water!* namely, with boiling water qualified by a dafh of cold water, before it be thrown into the cowl; to prevent its "catching the curd." The actual heat 192°.

It is proper to be underftood, however, that, in this cafe, the curd is not *crumbled*, or broken in the ufual manner, before the fcalding liquor be thrown among it; but is *cut* into checkers, or dies, of about a cubical inch each; with the fame knife, ufed in nearly the fame manner, as in flicing it.

Another peculiarity of this practice is, that the curd is *falted before it be fcalded*—a handfull of falt, to every cheefe, being ftrewed over the

the checkers, fpread regularly on the bottom
of the cowl, and worked in evenly among
them.

This is done in conformity with the general
principle of this practice : namely, " to keep
the fat in the cheefe;" the falt being thought
to harden and clofe the out fides of the cubes ;
thereby preventing the butyraceous particles
from being extracted by the fcalding liquor.
The fact is, the water, inftead of being made
as rich and thick as buttermilk, is left in the
cowl, after the curd is taken from it, thinner
than the cleareft whey; and without a fpeck
of *oil on its furface.*

In one dairy, which I had an opportunity
of obferving, in this diftrict, the fcalding liquor was covered with a *fheet of oil* : which
might have been fkimmed off its furface in
quantity : while in others, whether they were
fcalded higher or lower than this, not a drop of
oil was to be feen; though the MANAGEMENT
in every refpect, was fimilar. The GROUND,
therefore, feems to be the caufe of this difference; which, to me, appears to be a circumftance fingularly interefting.

4. VATTING.

4. VATTING. Nor is fcalding with boiling water; cutting the curd; and falting it before fcalding; the only peculiarities of that fingular dairy. The dies of curd having been ftirred among the fcalding liquor, and lain a minute or two to be thoroughly heated, are taken out of the "fcald" which yet retains a heat of 130°. with difhes, and immediately put into the vats, as hot as the hands can poffibly bear! They prefs into the vats like beeswax, that has been very much foftened by heat, or as cheefe, which is flightly toafted. Two or three vats being filled, they are fet in a fhallow tub, placed on the dairy floor, and a loaded vat put upon them, *to clofe the curd while warm :* in my opinion, an admirable ftroke of practice : it had long ftruck me, in theory, as being likely to be eligible; but was among the laft things I expected to meet with in actual practice.

Thus, not only richnefs, and a clofenefs of texture are probably obtained, by this courfe of treatment; but the farm, on which it is ufed, is confidered as being difficult to make cheefe from; and it is *believed*, that the method of treatment, which is here defcribed, is

the

the means of preventing the cheeses from heaving. The fact is, the cheese (thin cheese) appears to be, with this treatment, above par as to quality.

The methods of *vatting* in the other dairies, which I examined, were various. In some, the scalding liquor was laded off, and the curd rebroke and *salted in the cowl*; while in others, the curd was taken warm out of the liquor, and *salted in the vat*; thin cheese with a small handful in one layer,--thick with two small handfuls in two layers,—loaves with two handfuls in three or four layers;—spreading and rubbing in the salt evenly among the curd.

The dairy, which has been mentioned as being celebrated for cheese of a superior quality, scalds highly (130°.) and vats the curd warm out of the scalding liquor; while it retains 105°. of heat. Nevertheless, in a neighbouring dairy, which makes very good cheese, the curd is put cold into the vats.

What can we infer from the aggregate of these circumstances? There appears to be but one alternative. Either different grounds require very different management: or the art of cheesmaking is less mysterious, than has hitherto

therto been imagined. To make good cheefe *fometimes*, from *fome grounds*, is, I believe, a very eafy matter; but to make good cheefe, at *all times*, and from *all grounds*, on a *cer-tainty*, is what no perfon has yet been able to perform. Neverthelefs, I am more and more clearly of *opinion*, that with leifure and perfe-verance, affifted by a degree of chemical know-ledge, and a proper apparatus, this object, difficult and defirable as it may be, is at-tainable.

7. The CHEESE. 1. *The management of the cheefes in the prefs* is, here, much the fame as in Glocefterfhire. They are generally *falted twice*; (only one inftance of the contrary;) and *remain in the prefs* a time proportioned to the given thichnefs: thin cheefe, three or four meals: thick cheefe, four or five meals: loaves, five or fix meals.

2. *The cheefes on the fhelves.* From the prefs they are carried into rooms, fitted up with fhelves, for their reception; fome of them very commodiously: an entire lining round the walls, and, perhaps, a ftage or two in the middle of the room; with only gangways,

VOL. II.   N   wide

wide enough to pals conveniently, between them.

On thefe the young cheefes remain until they be cleaned, or until the fhelves be full; turning them as often as the weather and their refpective ages require.

3. Them ethod of *cleaning* varies: in fome dairies, the fummer cheefes have nothing done to them; except having their edges wiped. The blue coat rifes foon enough, and fufficiently, to hide their roughnefles. In others, they are only fcraped, dry (by the milking man) and in others wafhed and brufhed with a pail brufh, without being fcraped. I met with no inftance, in which they are foaked by the hour in water, and afterwards fcraped, as in Glocefterfhire. Some object even to *weting* them: all to *foaking* them: not only as making them foft, thereby checking their ripening, and backening their fale; but as being dangerous to the cheefes; which, if they have the fmalleft cracks, abforb the water, and receive irreparable injury.

4. No *painting*; except of winter-made cheefe; which generally throws out a white fcurfy coat, difficult to be got rid of, in any

other

other way. Thefe are covered with a uniform coat of paint: but the general make of
the country are, as yet, permitted to go to
market in their own blue coats.

5. From the fhelf-room they are taken to
other rooms, provincially " lofts," and fpread
over the floor; which is repeatedly cleaned,
by rubbing it with cloths; but not *prepared*
with fucculent vegetables; except for old thick
cheefes, in order to prevent or kill the mites,
which thick cheefe is liable to be infected with,
before it be ripe enough for market. In this
cafe, the leaves of the elder are, I believe,
principally ufed.

In one dairy, (Deyhoufe) I obferved an ad-
mirable arrangement of cheefe rooms. The
fhelf room is immediately over the dairyroom.
And the lofts, over the fhelf room; with
trap-doors in each floor to hand the cheefes
through. A plan which faves much aukward
carriage, and might well be adopted in every
dairy that will admit of it.

8. MARKET. The cheefe of this diftrict,
like that of Glocefterfhire, is bought up principally by FACTORS, who live in and near
the diftrict, and who fend it moftly to the

London market; the younger by land, the older by water carriage. One factor (or co-partnership of factors) is said to send seven or eight hundred tons annually.

The small cheeses are generally drawn, from the larger dairies, once a month; and down perhaps to five or six weeks old. The large cheeses require a much longer time before they be marketable. The winter, and early spring make, go off in autumn: the latter make the ensuing spring.

Besides what the factors purchase, considerable quantities are still sent, annually, to READING FAIR. The distance thirty to forty miles; according to the part of the district, from which they are sent; hired waggons being employed to carry them.

The PRICE, for the last ten years, has been, for thin cheese, from 30 to 35s. a hundred. For thick 40 to 45s. For loaves 45 to 50s. At present, and last year, thin cheese has been very low: 25 to 30s. The present par price 28s. While thick cheese; and especially loaves; keep up, nearly, at their old prices. There is, at present, from 15 to 20s. a hundred difference, between the prices

of

of thin and loaf cheefes! Neverthelefs, it has been faid, and I believe with truth, that more than half the make of the diftrict is thin cheefe. A ftriking evidence, this, of the prefent imperfection of the art under confideration.

9. PRODUCE. The produce of *milk* I had not fufficient opportunity to attend to accurately. To that of *cows by the day* I was moft attentive. This ran in every inftance, except one, from 2 lb. to 2½ lb. a cow. The one exception was fomewhat below 2 lb.—2¾ lb. has, I am told, been produced, from cows, which came well in together, and were in full milk.

The produce of *cows by the year* is, in this diftrict, almoft incredible. Three to four hundredweight a cow, is, I was affured on all hands, the common produce. Four and a half not unfrequent. Four hundred nearly the par produce. There is a well attefted inftance, in which a fmall dairyman *fold* thirty five hundred weight from feven cows; befides what was ufed in his family! But the cows were in their prime, and extraordinary milkers.

There are two reafons, why the produce of cows, in this diftrict, exceed that of cows,

in

in Glocefterfhire. The cows are larger, and
the feafon of making longer: cheefe is here
made the year round. Whereas, in Glocef-
cerfhire, the feafon of making lafts little more
than feven months of the twelve.

The annual *produce of the diftrict*, has not,
perhaps, been calculated: I met with no eftimate of it. Suppofing one third of the diftrict to be appropriated to cows, and allow
that each acre thus occupied yields one hundredweight of cheefe (calculating on four acres
and four cwt: to a cow) the aggregate produce is, at leaft, one hundred thoufand hundredweight; or five thoufand tons a year.

Admitting that there is a market for the
whole produce of the diftrict, in loaf cheefes,
and taking the medium difparity of price between loaf cheefes and thin cheefes, to be ten
fhillings a hundredweight, or ten pounds a
ton; and allowing that, at prefent, half the
produce of the diftrict is fent to market in the
form of thin cheefe,—North Wiltfhire is fuf-
taining, annually, a lofs of twenty five thoufand pounds, through the prefent imperfection
of the art of cheefmaking.

GENERAL

GENERAL OBSERVATIONS

ON THE

DAIRY MANAGEMENT

OF

GLOCESTERSHIRE and WILTSHIRE.

IN THESE OBSERVATIONS, the article CHEESE will be the only object of attention.

The SPECIES OF CHEESE, produced in this ifland, are various. Its markets, however, are principally filled with two fpecies: the one of a dry loofe contexture, and of a rough auftere flavor: the other, milder to the tafte, and of a clofe waxlike texture. The former is fold under the name of CHESHIRE cheefe; and is, I believe, chiefly the produce of that county: the latter, under the name of GLOCESTERSHIRE cheefe; provided its quality entitle it to that diftinction: if not, it takes, I believe, in general, the name of WARWICK-

SHIRE

SHIRE cheefe ; but, in reality, is produced in feveral counties. The products of Somer-fetfhire, Wiltfhire, Berkfhire, Oxfordfhire, Glocefterfhire, Worcefterfhire, Warwick-fhire, Leicefterfhire, Staffordfhire, Derby-fhire, and Yorkfhire, are very fimilar:—all of them as different from the produce of Chefhire, as if they were manufactured from a different material.

It is this milder fpecies, which is a principal article of food, of various claffes of working people ; and which, therefore, claims the firft and the higheft attention.

GLOCESTERSHIRE has long held a decided fuperiority in the production of this article of human food. At prefent, NORTH WILT-SHIRE is a competitor, and bids fair to take the lead. In thefe volumes, the practices of the two counties are, I believe, accurately and, the more difficult paffages, fully regiftered, down to their loweft minutiæ.

Therefore, without any view to blazon my own induftry, or to fet off, unfairly, the work I am executing, I will venture to fug-geft, that whoever fhall examine, with atten-tion, the three feparate practices, which are here regiftered, will know more of the fubject

under

under examination, than any individual of the
two counties knew at the time of regiftering.

The knowledge, even of practitioners, is
in a manner wholly confined to their own individual practice ; or perhaps to that of fome
few confidential neighbours.

The manufacturing of cheefe is not like
the cultivation of lands. This is a *public employment*, open to any one who travels acrofs
the fite of cultivation: that a *private manufac-
tury*—a craft—a myftery—fecluded from the
public eye: and what may appear extraordinary, the minutiæ are feldom familiar, even
to the mafter of the dairy, in which they are
practifed ! The dairyroom is confecrated to
the fex; and it is generally underftood to require fome intereft, and more addrefs, to
gain full admiffion to its rites.

The information I have been favored with,
while it fhews the fuperior fkill of the Glocefterfhire and Wiltfhire dairywomen, and ex-
hibits the beft practice of the kingdom at this
day, proves, in a ftriking manner, the imperfectnefs of the art; even in thefe long-
experienced and enlightened diftricts. Glocefterfhire acknowledges a degree of *decline*;
and

and Wiltſhire, notwithſtanding the ſpirit of improvement has evidently been ſome time on the wing, confeſſes, with equal frankneſs, that it has not yet been able to reach any degree of *certainty*, much leſs *perfeɛtion*.

At preſent, the art is evidently deſtitute of principles. So far from being ſcientific, it is altogether immechanical. It may be ſaid to be, at preſent, a knack involved in myſtery. Therefore, its *fair* profeſſors, tho' they may claim a degree of NATURAL CLEVERNESS, to which *we* have no pretenſion, and which, only, could have raiſed the art, in the extempore way, in which it is at preſent praɛtiſed, to the height it has attained; having tried their ſkill, *alone*, without obtaining the requiſite degree of excellency, can have no good objection, now, to let us try our *joint* endeavours. And I call upon every man of ſcience, who has opportunity and leiſure, to lend them his beſt aſſiſtance. And would wiſh to recommend to intelligent dairy farmers to be more attentive, than they appear to be at preſent, to what ſo nearly concerns their intereſt.

This in apology for the following obſervations.

In

In attending to the minutiæ of different dairies, and feeing the effects of different modes of management, a variety of ideas would, of courfe, rife fpontaneoufly. Some of them fancying improvements, in the particular management I was obferving; and others propofing a transfer of it, to the different diftricts of the ifland. Such of them as appear to be entitled to attention, and are not interfperfed in the foregoing relations, will be given in this retrofpective view of the fubject.

As a groundwork, it will be proper to afcertain the good and evil QUALITIES of cheefe: the EXCELLENCIES to be obtained; and the DEFECTS to be avoided. In defining thefe, however, we muft not pay regard to the palates of individuals. There is a kind of depravity in fome men's taftes, with refpect to the article of food under confideration, which would fruftrate every attempt at definition.— We muft, therefore, have an eye to thofe good and bad qualities of cheefes, which raife them in value, or depreciate them, at market. Qualities of which the different dealers, in this

article,

article, have ideas, fufficiently accurate for our purpofe.

EXCELLENCIES. Cheefe of the firft quality;—that which comes as near perfection, as the nature of it admits of, or as art can probably approach,—is of a clofe even contexture ; of a firm but unctuous confiftency; of a mild flavor, while young; acquiring, by age, an agreeable fragrance. If a cheefe of this quality be *ironed*, it has fomewhat the appearance of firm butter ; or of wax moderately warmed. If the plug be gently rubbed, the fubftance of the cheefe feems to melt under the finger, which wears it down, as it would fine clay duly moiftened. If the end of the plug be pinched, it yields to the preffure without crumbling ; grinding down, between the fingers, to an impalpable matter——— Cheefe of this defcription, like wine of a good vintage, improves, by age, in mellownefs and flavor.

DEFECTS. The defects of cheefe, in this diftrict, are, *poroufnefs, hollownefs, drynefs ;* and *partial rottennefs* : the *fly,*—fo much to be dreaded in Norfolk,—is not *known* here !—
Where

Where maggots are thought to breed *naturally* in good cheefe.

Poroufnefs. The fubftance of cheefes, having this defect, may be fufficiently unctuous and cohefive; but the contexture is broken, by cells of different magnitudes; and the flavor invariably bad; being pungent to the tafte, and offenfive to the fmell.

Hollownefs. This defect appears to be, generally, though not always, produced by the fame caufe, operating in a different manner. In that, the expanding air is diftributed: in this, it is collected: cleaving the cheefe in the middle: making it bulge out; generally in the center; but fometimes partially toward one edge. The effect, too, is the fame: both of them leaving, in moft cafes, a pungency of tafte, and difagreeablenefs of fmell; qualities, which are increafed by age. Poroufnefs feems to be a weaker effort: hollownefs a higher ftage of defect.

Drynefs. The contexture of cheefe, under this defect, is loofe and incohefive. If a plug be drawn, it is hard and dry to the touch; and crumbles under preffure. It wants unctuoufnefs and flavor; being infipid to the

tafte,

tafte, and inodorous to the fmell. This defcription of cheefe is likewife liable to cleave
in the middle.

" *Whey Botches*" appear on the furface;
and are underftood to be caufed by what is
called " flip-curd"—namely curd, from which
the whey has not been duly exprefled. This
theory, however, does not appear to me to
be altogether fatisfactory.

The CAUSES of the other defects are important objects of enquiry.

The drynefs is underftood to be owing to
fome degree of acidnefs in the milk, at the
time of coagulation; and may originate in
other circumftances.

The caufe or caufes of the other defects
may be ftill more involved in uncertainty.—
Since the doctrine of airs has been agitated,
a general idea has been fuggefted, that *fixed
air* is the latent caufe. But I have not met
with any reafon tending to explain how this
fixed air is let loofe; or why it fhould leave,
invariably, a pungency of tafte and ranknefs
of fmell behind it.

That an expanfion of air takes place is evident; but the *efficient* caufe of this expanfion
                                        may

may be difficult to explain. It may, however, be taken for granted, that whatever is
the *primary* caufe of the pungency and ranknefs, which follows, is the *primary* caufe of
the expanfion: which, indeed, is not, in this
place, the object of enquiry. For it is not
the expanfion; but the pungency and rancidnefs, which conftitute the defect.

To endeavour to afcertain the caufe of the
pungency and rancidnefs, I made fome experiments with cheefe, poffeffed of thefe qualities
in a fuperior degree.

The fpecimen fubjected to thefe experiments was of the *porous* kind. The pores or
cells varying from the fize of a muftard feed to
that of a bean: all of them *glazed* within : and,
to the naked eye, apparently *varnifhed* with a
yellow refinous fubftance ; but, in a glafs,
there appeared to be no *coat* of matter. On
being fcraped with the point of a needle, the
infides of the cells rofe in the fame fnowy
flakes, which every other part of the fubftance
afforded: the colour of the loofened particles
purely white ; notwithftanding in their confo-
lidated ftate they were of a dark yellow—a
wax-colour ; the cheefe having to all general
appearance

appearance been *coloured* ; yet not a particle of the colouring material diſcoverable ! One minute bundle of reſin-like matter, I found lodged among the ſubſtance ; but none in the cells.—The ſmell fetid—the taſte bitter.

EXPERIMENT I. *Tenth of July,* 1788. Placed two pieces, about a cubical inch each, in ſeparate glaſſes. Covered one of them with *cold,* the other with *boiling* water.

Eleventh of July. The colour of the ſurfaces of both of them is changed. That ſubjected to the *cold* water is become pale : that to the *hot,* purely white. The water, in both caſes, fetid. The *cold* water the *ſtronger*-flavored, and the higher-coloured ; the *hot, milder,* and paler. On the top of the *hot,* a few ſmall particles of oil ſwim ; on that of the *cold* ſome large ſpecks appear.

The heat of the boiling water has ſoftened the pulp (but not the rind) of the cheeſe, ſo as to disfigure the cube, and fix it to the bottom of the glaſs. On pouring off the water, and raiſing up this piece, the part, which was in contact with the glaſs, is ſtill of a yellow colour, and retains its fetid ſmell ; while the upper ſurface is pale and in a manner *ſcentleſs.*

The

The *fcent* of the other piece is weakened;
but much of it ftill remains. The *tafte* of
both pieces leffened; efpecially that of the
heated piece.

EXPERIMENT II. *Eleventh July.* Covered
a piece of the fame fpecimen,—(an inch fquare
and about a quarter of an inch thick)—with
rectified fpirit of wine. And put another piece,
(a quarter of an inch cubical) into a vial of
the fame fpirit.

Twelfth July. No apparent change of *colour* or *contexture*: except that the piece in the
phial is fomewhat paler than when it was im-
merged. The *glazing* on the infides of the
cells is ftill perfect. Neverthelefs, the *fmell*
is entirely gone; and the *tafte* rendered perfectly mild: the bitternefs loft. But quere are
they diffipated, or only difguifed by the fpirit?

EXPERIMENT. III. *Twelfth July.* Bruifed
fome of the pulp of the fame fpecimen (dry
and hard) with the blade of an ivory knife;
the granules fmall, but not evenly reduced.
The colour after bruifing, nearly white. Put
equal quantities of it into three feparate glaffes:

VOL. II.   O   covering

covering one with *cold water*—one with *boiling water*—and the third with *spirit of wine*.

Fourteenth July. That upon which the *spirit* was poured, underwent no evident alteration; except that it regained part of its colour. This fettled down and laid clofe, but loofe, at the bottom of the glafs. The *fmell* entirely fled, *or* difguifed.

The *cold water* effected no change, even of colour. The fubject would not mix freely with it. Part of it funk; part fwam on the furface. Yefterday, not having been difturbed, it afforded little or no *fmell*; but this morning, on being ftirred up, it proves as fetid as the original cheefe. The crumbs, which now fubfide, have a fomewhat curdlike appearance.

The *hot water* produced, immediately, a milky liquor;—which prefently divided into *curd* and *whey*; exactly refembling fcalded curd, with its fcalding liquor ftanding upon it. The curd as white, almoft, as fnow; the water pale and oily. Yefterday, the water emitted no fmell : today, the curd, which has formed itfelf into a compact mafs at the bottom

tom of the glafs—a *cake of perfect cheese curd!*
—is in a manner *fcentlefs,* and *taftelefs.*

Thus, from the whole, and from every part of this evidence, it appears, that the immediate caufe of the pungency and rancidnefs of cheefe is an ESSENTIAL OIL; which fpirit of wine *diffolves*; and which is rendered *volatile* in boiling water.

The excellencies and defects of cheefe being enumerated, and the probable caufe of the principal defect pointed out,—it will now be proper to view the following heads feparately; examine ftill farther into this caufe; and endeavour to point out fome probable means of avoiding its evil effect: and, at the fame time, to endeavour, by fcattering a few rays of light on the general fubject, to relieve it, in fome fmall degree at leaft, from its prefent obfcurity.

Seafon,
Soil,
Water,
Herbage,
Managemen

SEASON. It is a fact, well eftablifhed, that the feafon has great influence on the quality of

cheefe;

cheefe; efpecially on the defect more immediately under notice. In 1783, a dry hot fummer, fcarcely any dairy could make good
cheefe. In fome dairies more than half the
make was hollow; and even in the beft dairy
I had an opportunity of examining, numbers
were "eyey": while in a common feafon; and
more efpecially in a cool fummer; the fame
dairy has fcarcely a defective cheefe.

This corroborates the idea of an ESSENTIAL
OIL being the caufe of the defect. It is annually
proved in the practice of numbers, that plants,
in general, afford a quantity of effential oil,
proportioned to the warmth of the feafon they
grow in. It is likewife known, in the dairy
counties, that cheefes made from the grafs of
autumn feldom or ever heave. At that feafon the finer blade graffes are chiefly produced.
Few *flowers*, or *aromatic plants*, mix with
them. Befides, the weather being generally
cool, a lefs proportion of oil is probably raifed,
at that feafon of the year.

SOIL. It has been obferved that the beft
cheefe is made from the leaft productive
foils: not, perhaps, fatter than cheefe made
from richer more productive foils; but freer
from

from the defect under notice. This is accounted for in the principle laid down: the
unproductivenefs of the inferior foils has been
faid (without any regard to this theory) to be
owing to their *coolnefs*: another ftriking circumftance in favor of the principles offered.

Another obfervable circumftance, with refpect to foils, is that of their being injured by
manuring:—it being a fact fufficiently afcertained, in each diftrict, that clofe, well flavored cheefe cannot be made, or is with much
uncertainty produced, from land that has
been recently manured. But whether the manure, itfelf, be the immediate caufe; or whether it only change the *herbage*,—appears to be
a moot point.

WATER. This is a fubject to which no one
feems to have paid the fmalleft attention. I
have not been able to gather any information
refpecting it, which is interefting. Neverthelefs, it is probable, that much may depend upon it. It feems *reafonable* that a *plenty*
and *purity* of water fhould be conducive to the
production of good cheefe: it is *probable*
that a *deficiency* of water may increafe the proportion of acrimony in the milk.

O 3 HERBAGE.

HERBAGE. Each fpecies of plants has its
peculiar organization ; which either enables
it to make choice of its food, or gives it a fa-
culty of changing, whatever it imbibes, to its
own fpecific nature ; or, which to me is moft
probable, each plant is poffeffed of thefe two
powers jointly. It is evident, that the qualities of mild, fweet, bitter, acrid, and poifonous are all of them produced by different plants
growing in the fame foil.

By analyfis, their component particles are
found to be extremely different in *proportion*,
at leaft. Thus one plant (the favin) yields
a quantity of fluid effential oil more than equal
to one feventh of its own weight: while another (the rofe) feldom perhaps affords the proportion of one to a thoufand. Hence, on the
theory offered, *much—very much indeed—*
may depend on the SPECIFIC QUALITY OF
THE HERBAGE.

In North Wiltfhire, an experienced and
very intelligent dairywoman obferved, that
when the " crazey" (the crowfoot) is in full
blow, fhe finds her cheefe particularly inclined
to heave: while a dairy farmer of the higheft
clafs, in the fame diftrict, has obferved, that,
when

when the creeping trefoil—white clover—
(trifolium repens) has been in full blow, and
in particular abundance, he has heard the
loudeſt complaints of the licentious diſpoſition of the cheeſe.

It is not probable, that any one ſpecies of
plants is the ſole cauſe of the diſorder. Almoſt every cheeſe has its peculiar flavor, and
its different degree of acrimony. Nothing
is more likely to give that almoſt cauſtic
quality, which ſome cheeſes are poſſeſſed of,
than the common and the bulbous crowfoots :
not only their flowers, but their leaves, are
ſingularly acrid. On the other hand, there
are ſeveral circumſtances which render it probable, that a redundancy of the creeping
trefoil tends to aggravate the diſorder. Dry
ſeaſons, by keeping the graſs ſhort, give it
an opportunity of ſpreading. Manure is well
known to encourage it ; ſometimes in a ſingular manner. Sheep-feeding paſture grounds
produces a ſimilar effect ; partly owing, perhaps, to the blade graſſes being kept ſhort;
and in part to the ſoil being meliorated
by a freſh manure : and it has been obſerved
that a ſuite of cowgrounds, which have been
occaſionally *fed hard with ſheep*, are very dif-

ficult

ficult to make cheese from : while *a few sheep among cows* may, by picking out the clover, be serviceable to the dairy.

Other plants, probably, have a bad effect; and to ascertain them is an object worthy of attention. It is probable, however, that the mischief is effected by some common article or articles of herbage; and not by a few *weeds* which can easily be extirpated : nevertheless, it would be useful to know, not only the herbs, but the parts of them, which cause the evil.

The *age* of herbage may likewise influence its effect. It has been generally understood, that cheese of the first quality cannot be made from *young leys* : nothing but *old turf* being esteemed equal to its production. I have been informed, however, that there is, or was, an instance, in these districts, in which good cheese was made from *fresh land*; from land which was kept alternately in corn and grass. In my own opinion, more depends on the quality of the *subsoil*, and the *species* of herbage, than on its *age* : or, in other words, the effect appears to me to be produced by the species of herbage and the temperature it

feeds

feeds in. I have traced the roots of old turf, in different parts of this diftrict, to two or three feet deep. Here the plants, notwithftanding the fubfoil may be abforbent, probably feed in a *cool* fituation, undifturbed by the immediate influence of the fun, and on foils thus fituated much may depend on the age of the herbage: but it ftrikes me that young grafs, of a proper fpecies, may, upon *cold land*, produce good cheefe, though it fhould feed near the furface. This, however, by the way.

From the aggregate of the foregoing evidence we may infer, that the defects of porofity and hollownefs are principally owing to the SPECIES OF HERBAGE: very much, however, depending on its STATE OF GROWTH; very much on the SEASON; much on the nature of the SUBSOIL; fomething on the AGE OF THE SWARD; and fomething perhaps on the SOIL. I wifh, however, to have it underftood that the inference here drawn is not confidered as *conclufive :* all that appears to me is its *probability*. The theory of an art is feldom brought to light in a ftate of perfection. It generally requires to pafs, progreffively,

greffively, the feveral ftages of infancy, ado-
lefcence, and manhood; rifing by flow fteps
to maturity.

MANAGEMENT. The prefent imperfection
of the art ftands confeffed on all hands; and,
even with the joint affiftance of fcience, it may
never be raifed to perfection. Neverthelefs,
it is evidently capable of improvement, and
of being raifed nearer to perfection than it is
at prefent. Different GROUNDS (a term
which aptly comprehends herbage, foil, and
fubfoil) may require different modes of management: but fo it is in the raifing of corn;
diffimular foils require diffimular treatments:
yet we fee fine crops of wheat growing on
almoft every fpecies of foil. Coagulation appears to be a much lefs fickle procefs of nature than fermentation: neverthelefs we find
the art of brewing (in the larger brewries)
is raifed to a degree of certainty.

The milk,
The coagulum,
The coagulation,
The curd, and
The cheefe
will each require to be feparately examined.

THE

THE MILK.   Three things are here wanted.

A teft of the quality of milk ;

A mode of correcting an evil quality ;

A gauge to afcertain the exact quantity.

That fome milk is fufficiently pure, to require no correction, is evident, from cheefe
of the firft quality being made from it, genuine, as it is drawn from the cow.

In all human probability, however, the
caufe of the defect, more particularly under
notice, is lodged in the MILK ; and a *teft* to
difcover it would be valuable.

In the vale of Berkeley, I was told, there
are dairywomen who will judge, by the *fmell*
of the milk, whether the curd to be produced
from it will, or will not, make a heaving
cheefe.

This circumftance is highly probable. For,
if the heaving be caufed by an ESSENTIAL OIL,
the *fmell* is the eafieft, and, perhaps, the moft
certain teft it can be brought to.   The odour
of plants (in general) lies wholly in their effential oils.   Draw off this, they become fcentlefs ; the whole of their odour being found in
the oil.   The various *effences* of the fhops are
no other than the effential oils of the feveral

plants,

plants, whofe names they refpectively bear.—
And it appears to me more than probable,
that were the effluvia which rife from milk
warm from the cow, to be *concentrated*; that
is, collected into a narrower compafs, thereby
encreafing the flavor;—the quality might be
judged of with fufficient certainty. A fimple
apparatus might be rendered applicable to this
purpofe.

Correcting. A redundancy of odour being
difcovered, the means of doing it *fufficiently*
away would be the great thing defirable. It
is probable, that a *degree* of odour, a *due portion* of flavor, in the milk, may be neceffary
to the production of well flavored cheefe.

If rancidity be the effect to be guarded
againft; and if effential oil be the caufe of
rancidity; an evident, and eafy mode of puri-
fication prefents itfelf.

It is well known, that all effential oils are
of a volatile nature. The heat of boiling water will caufe all of them to quit their native
fubftances. Some will quit and fly off with
a much lower heat. In the loofe ftate, in
which they lie in milk, they might, no doubt,
be eafily diffipated. Ventilation, alone, would
probably

probably go near to effeƈt the defired purpofe.
A fmall addition of heat would, perhaps, render it fully adequate to the intention. By an
increafe of heat, the end might be obtained,
with a degree of certainty.

Two inconveniences would attend this mode
of correƈtion. An increafe of labour ; and a
lofs of time. But *theory* fuggefts another fimple apparatus, adapted to common ufe, and
manageable by the moft ignorant dairy girl,
which would render the extra labour and the
lofs of time inconfiderable, compared with the
advantage to be obtained by the ufe of it.

In this place, it will be proper to mention
an attempt, which has been made, in this
diftriƈt, to correƈt the milk. But not, from
what I can learn, with much fuccefs. Before
I made the foregoing experiments, it ftruck
me, that fome chemical preparation might be
hit upon for this purpofe ;—and that which is,
perhaps, moft likely to effeƈt it has been ufed
in this inftance : namely, the *vitriolic acid* :
or, as it is commonly called, the *fpirit,* or the
oil of vitriol.

A dairywoman, who tried it, put about a
teacupful into feventy or eighty gallons of
milk

milk. But fhe found it interfere with the rennet, fo as to difturb the " coming." That
is, being a ftrong acid, it brought on a premature coagulation. She, therefore, laid afide
the ufe of it. Neverthelefs fhe, and others,
who have given it a fuller trial, are of opinion,
" that it helps to keep down the cheefe."

This circumftance, it is obfervable, ftill
farther corroborates the theory offered; and
in an interefting manner; as it is an evidence,
that the *heaving*--the *immediate effect*--is caufed
by an effential oil; a confiderable portion of
which the ftronger acids have a power of *fixing*
in a refinous ftate. It is, therefore, highly
probable that, by a fufficient quantity of concentrated acid, the caufe might be fufficiently
overcome. But fuppofing this mode of correction to be practicable, the practice could
not be recommended.

Gauge. At prefent, the proportional quantity of curd to a given quantity of milk appears
to be very uncertain. A dairywoman feems
to be under no certainty, until fhe has, as it
were, meafured it in the vats. Running the
milk cool is thought to leffen the quantity of
curd. The proportion is thought to be greater

in

in autumn than in fummer. Some cows are thought to afford more curd than others.— This is an interefting fubjeƈt, and requires to be ftriƈtly enquired into.

To come at this proportion, the firft thing is to afcertain the exaƈt quantity of milk. A rod graduated to the given cowl (by an exaƈt gallon meafure) would give it at fight; without the trouble, or the danger, of calculation being incurred.

THE COAGULUM. Notwithftanding the ftomach of the calf is the eftablifhed coagulum of milk for cheefe;—it may, or may not, be the beft, which nature affords for that purpofe. Coagulation may be produced in a variety of ways, and the beft ought to be fought for. The great objeƈt feems to be to reduce the whey to the moft aqueous ftate poffible.— Not only the quantity, but the richnefs, and even the dietetic quality of the curd is, perhaps, given by the coagulum. The theory of coagulation appears to be, at prefent, imperfeƈtly known, or not in any degree underftood; though, perhaps, a fubjeƈt of fome importance, in medicine, as well as in rural economics.

A *teft*

A *teſt* of the *ſtrength* of the coagulum uſed; and a *meaſure* to aſcertain an exact *quantity*; are much wanted: in order that a given quantity of milk might have a due quantity of *proof* coagulum aſſigned it. This, with a little induſtry, might no doubt be accompliſhed: and being once fixed on mechanical principles, neither time nor labour will be loſt by it.

COAGULATION. The *thermometer* is a certain guide as to the heat of the milk; as well as of the air, in which it is to be coagulated. Thus far we might, therefore, go, on mechanical principles; and regulate the *time of coagulation*, and the *quality of the curd*—with a degree of certainty: provided the *quality of the air*, in which the curd is generated, have no influence, by its action on the proceſs of coagulation, on the quality of the curd.

I have obſerved, in one or two inſtances, that in a *cloſe muggy air*, the curd has appeared to come prematurely, and to be of an inferior quality. But even ſhould this, on due enquiry, be found to be a real circumſtance in the general law of coagulation, its evil effect might, perhaps, by due attention, be guarded againſt. If any particular ſpecies of air ſhould
be

be found to be conducive to good cheefe ;—
either during the coagulation, or while the
manufacture is carried on; how eafily might
the required atmofphere be given; either to
the containing veffel, or to the room in general ?

The method of *regulating the heat of the
milk* may be a thing of fome importance.—
Water may, or may not, be proper for this
purpofe.

The due length of *time in coagulating* requires, likewife, to be enquired into. Perhaps a rapid coagulation, not only renders the
curd tough; but, by giving a greater quantity, injures its richnefs. Hence, on a lean
foil, it may, perhaps, require to be carried
on more deliberately, than on a rich one. It
will, I am perfuaded, be found, on due examination, that the quality of the curd is in
great part given by the PERIOD OF COAGULA-
TION.

The *point of maturation* wants to be afcertained. I know no guide to it, at prefent,
which can be defined with fufficient accuracy,
If the curd be broken prematurely, a portion
of it may be loft: if it remains too long be-

fore it be broken, fome worfe confequence may follow. Hence, it appears to be only common prudence to keep the veffel clofely *covered* during the coagulation, that the whole may reach the proper ftate of maturity at the fame time.

CURD. This may be called the ftage of *manufacture*. The firft ftep toward perfection is to provide a fuitable material; the next, to manufacture it in the moft perfect manner.

Separating the curd from the whey is a point of management, on which the *richnefs* of the cheefe, perhaps, very much depends. The object to be aimed at, in this operation, is to draw off the whey as clear—as *green*—as may be. For this reafon, it ought not to be fuffered to remix with the curd, after it has once been diflodged from its cells: much lefs to have the curd broken fmall among it; thereby faturating it with the richer particles. An apparatus, fufficiently manageable in common ufe, and one which would, probably, fave much labour and much time, might, I believe, be rendered equal to this intention.— Should it be faid, that what is loft to the cheefe is faved in the whey,—the reply is, that the injury

injury does not proceed from the *quantity* loft;
but from the *quality* of the entire cheefe being
lowered, by the lofs of part of its moft valuable particles. If an inferior kind of cheefe
be required, the milk ought to be reduced,
previous to the coagulation. From the rich
foils of thefe diftricts, cheefe of a fuperior quality may be made; though the curd be impo-
verifhed in the operation of making it. But
on leaner foils, not a particle of the natural
richnefs of the milk fhould, in ftrictnefs, be
fuffered to efcape among the whey.

Scalding the curd is an operation, which requires to be examined into. It is peculiar to
this quarter of the kingdom. It may or may
not be neceffary to the production of cheefe of
the firft quality. It unavoidably carries off a
portion of the richer particles of the curd.—
Were it not for this inconveniency, it is probable, that the caufe of heaving might, by
breaking the curd fmall, and fcalding highly,
be diffipated in this operation. Even when
the curd is cut into cubes, we find that high
fcalding has a probable good effect *. *Cutting*
                                          the

* See NORTH WILTSHIRE, page 173.

P 2

the curd, inftead of *breaking* it, certainly pre-
ferves the richnefs, but may prevent the free
efcape of the offenfive matter. Neverthelefs,
in the inftance of practice referred to, it feems
to anfwer the purpofe required by the excellent
dairywoman who ufes it. It has, indeed, more
ingenuity in it than all the other operations I
have met with in the art.

Another circumftance in the operation of
fcalding is noticeable. It feems to be indif-
putable, that the curd fhould be fcalded *evenly*.
But, by the prefent method in ufe, the fame
cowl of curd is fcalded with various degrees of
heat. That which the fcalding liquor immediately falls upon is fubjected, perhaps, to
150°. of heat; while that which is afterwards
ftirred up among the liquor has not, perhaps,
more than 100°. This, and the practice of
leaving the cowl uncovered, during the coagulation, may account for the otherwife, perhaps, inexplicable circumftance of one cheefe
of a good, and another of a bad quality, being
made from the fame cowl of curd: a circumftance, which is mentioned with confidence
in different diftricts. If the curd be fcalded,
it ought, in my idea, to be plunged wholly,
and

and inftantaneoufly, into the fcalding liquor; and not the fcalding liquor poured upon the curd, in the manner in which it is at prefent. Some prudent dairywomen, I have obferved, lower the firft dafh of fcalding liquor thrown in, and ftir the curd up among this, before the reft be added. This leffens the evil very confiderably, but may not altogether prevent it.

Salting the curd is a matter entitled to attention. It ftrikes me, that much, if not the whole, of the fuperior pungency, which is moftly obfervable in the Berkeley cheefe, may be owing to the great *quantity of falt* ufed in that diftrict: while the mildnefs of that of Wiltfhire, and efpecially of the two-meal cheefes of the upper vale, may arife from the comparatively fmall quantity, which is ufed in thefe. The quantity of falt ufed in the lower vale is, in the eftablifhed practices of the two vales, twice, or, perhaps, near three times as much as in the upper: and although, in Wiltfhire, the quantity mixed with the curd be full as much as in the vale of Berkeley, that rubbed on the furface is very confiderably lefs. This is a point of management, which experi-

ment

ment would readily determine. Something, too, may reſt with the *method of ſalting.*——Whether the whole ſhould be rubbed on the *ſurface*; or whether it ſhould be partly or wholly *mixt with the curd*; or communicated in the form of *brine*, is a ſubject worthy of enquiry.

Correcting the curd by ſome chemical preparation, ſo as to prevent the cheeſe from riſing, may be practicable; but it is probable, that although the *riſing* were to be prevented, ſome part at leaſt of the badneſs of *flavor* would remain, after this mode of correction; which, in theory, is much leſs eligible, than that of purifying the milk, previous to the coagulation.

The ſhape of the vat is not unworthy of attention. It is obſervable, that cheeſes ſhrink in width, but not perceptibly in thickneſs :—thus, a cheeſe made in a vat fifteen inches and a half wide, and an inch and a half deep, does not, at three or four months old, meaſure more, perhaps, than fourteen inches in diameter; yet retains a thickneſs equal to the full depth of the vat. This ſeems to be accounted for in the ſpecies of compreſſion, to which

which cheefes are fubjected. Curd being a
fubftance of a tough cohefive texture, does
not, like water, or other liquid " prefs upward, downward, fideway, every way, and
equally in all directions;" but, in a vat of the
ordinary form, is preffed much more downward, than it is fideway;—more flatway, than
it is edgeway: hence, in drying, the cheefes
fhrink principally in width: and hence, *all
cheefes of the common form have a neceffary
propenfity to cleave in the middle.* For the
edge, or outer rim, having a greater quantity
of furface for the atmofphere to act upon,
fhrinks fafter, or attempts to fhrink fafter,
than the central parts of the difk; which, of
courfe, acquire a natural propenfity to bulge
out, to allow for the contraction of the edge:
while the edge acquires a fimilar inclination
to crack, to give the requifite circumference.
If, however, a cheefe be of a clofe cohefive
texture, the powers gained, by this inequality
in drying, may not be fufficient to caufe either
of thefe effects. But, if it happen to be of a
loofe crumbly texture; or, if the texture fhould
be broken or opened by an internal rarefaction;

P 4 it

it is left at liberty to act; and, in the latter cafe, is affifted by the internal expanfion.

The degree of propenfity is in proportion to the diameter of the cheefe. Therefore, in this point of view, broad vats are lefs eligible than narrow ones.

There are, however, fome ftrong reafons in favour of the prefent form of thin cheefes in thefe diftricts. If they were made narrower and of the fame thicknefs, their number, and, of courfe, the labour and the requifite prefs room, would be greater. If their thicknefs were increafed they would be more liable to rife, and would not be fo foon ready for market, as they are at prefent: nor would they, perhaps, if made narrower, be fo convenient to the dealers.

To the confumer, however, the prefent form is extremely aukward, and the caufe of unneceffary wafte. It appears to me that, in regard to the conveniency of the confumer, no cheefe fhould be lefs than three or four inches thick; nor the diameter of cheefes of that thicknefs, more than ten or twelve inches.

In

In North Wiltſhire, we find the form of vats varying very much. The *thin* and the *broadthick* cheeſes are ſtill made in vats exactly of the Gloceſterſhire dimenſions. But almoſt every dairy has vats of various forms and ſizes; ſo that *ſpare curd*, a thing to be ſtudiouſly avoided, is ſeldom heard of there.

Vatting. With reſpect to the perfect "cloſeneſs" ſo much admired in the texture or ſubſtance of cheeſe, ſomething may depend on the vatting; or rather on the heat, at which the curd goes into the preſs. If the common air, which is neceſſarily ſhut up, in greater or leſs quantity, with the curd, be, at the time of ſhutting up, in a ſtate of rarefaction, it will, as it cools, condenſe, and, as it were, aſſiſt the preſs in giving the requiſite compactneſs. Beſides, curd, like wax, is ſoftened by warmth; becomes pliable; and may be preſſed into a cloſer, more uniform ſubſtance, than cold curd is capable of forming. The latter part of this poſition never ſtruck me ſo forcibly, as in ſeeing the actual effect of heating curd very highly, in the inſtance of practice I ſaw in North Wiltſhire. See page 175.

CHEESE.

CHEESE. It is not an extraordinary circumftance for the cheefes to "*heave in the prefs*:"
in which cafe, it feems, no weight is able to
keep them down. They fet men's laws at
defiance. In this cafe, it is the practice of
moft dairywomen, I believe, to take it out;
break it down fmall; and refcald it. This,
I underftand, generally allays the commotion,
fo far as to prevent its rifing in the prefs a
fecond time.

The *weight of the prefs* may be a thing of
fome importance, in the manufacturing of
cheefe. It feems to be a fact, fufficiently eftablifhed, that *net cheefes* never heave; nor
are found to be "eyey;" but are invariably
clofe *. I was affured, by an authority which
I have no reafon to doubt, that in Wiltfhire,
where (as has been already faid) quantities of
net cheefes are made for fale, it is no uncommon circumftance to form, out of the fame
cowl of curd, preffed cheefes which heave, and
net cheefes which are perfectly clofe: it is
farther remarked, in that obfervant diftrict,
that the heavier the prefs is, the greater propenfity

---

* In making NET CHEESES, the curd is fqueezed, by hand,
into the nets as clofe and tight as poffible; but receives no
other compreffion.

penfity the cheefes have to heaving; and that filling the vats too full has a fimilar effect.— Thefe appear to me moft interefting circumftances; and fuggeft a variety of theoretic ideas; which, however, it might be imprudent to rifque on the prefent foundation.

It may be unneceffary to obferve, that an experimental enquiry into the art under confideration would be vague, without fome method of *identifying the fubjects of experiment.* Some permanent mark is requifite. Numbers are, perhaps, the beft reference. In Norfolk, I made ufe of the *numeral characters,* cut out of plate iron. Common *figures,* of the fame or other metal, would be ftill more fimple. Thefe lying upon the cheefling, while in the prefs, fink into the rind, and leave a lafting impreffion.

The aftermanagement of the cheefe. Perhaps the principal improvement to be made in this ftage of the art, is that of ftriking out fome practical method of HASTENING THE MATURATION OF CHEESES. Wine mixed with the curd brings on a rapid advance of ripenefs. In Glocefterfhire, I had an opportunity of obferving the effect of three or four glaffes of

white

white wine thrown partially among the curd, during the operation of vatting. In a few months, the parts which had imbibed the wine, had paffed the point of maturity, and were haftening down the ftage of decay! Therefore, it is evident that, *by compofition*, a fpecies of ripenefs may be rapidly brought on; and the qualities of cheefes thus ripened, might, no doubt, be infinitely diverfified. And, perhaps, by other means, the *curd alone* might be haftened to a more *natural* ftate of ripenefs.

But enough of reflection. It is my prefent intention, fhould leifure and opportunity favor it, to purfue the enquiry, practically, at fome future time. Left, however, my intention fhould not be accomplifhed, I have thought it right, in this place, to throw open, to others, the more effential part of that which I had laid up, for my own future government.

HERE-

HEREFORDSHIRE.

IN EXTENT, Herefordſhire ranks among the ſmaller counties. Its OUTLINE forms nearly a circle. The mean diameter, about forty miles: including ſomewhat more than twelve hundred ſquare miles, or about eight hundred thouſand acres.

The SURFACE is broken in a remarkable manner. No wide open vale, nor any extenſive range of hill, appears in Herefordſhire. In the north-weſtern quarter, ſome ſeparated links of the Welch mountains riſe above the hillocks and minor hills, which are ſcattered over the reſt of the county; but much the greater part of it reſembles the ſweetly broken country in the central parts of Kent; which, as Gloceſterſhire, has its beautiful features; but Herefordſhire may be ſaid, without flattery, to be altogether beautiful.

The

Its RIVER is the WYE; which takes an extenfive fweep through the fouthweftern quarter. From a bend toward the center of the county, the LUG,—a fine brook,—branches northward; collecting, with its various branchlets, the waters of the north and eaftern quarters of the county. Each brook, and almoft each rivulet, has its " bottom" or valley; with meadows in fome places of confiderable width; and with meadow-banks, broken yet fertile; fteep enough to give beauty to the furface and geniality to the foil; yet not too fteep for the purpofes of cultivation.

The SOIL everywhere fertile: no watery bottoms; nor thinfoiled barren hills; except, perhaps, in the northern and weftern outfkirts. Every other part is uniformly productive. The eaftern fide of the county is moftly a ftiff clay, of great ftrength and tenacity; moftly red, but in fome places of the ordinary colour. The weftern fide is lighter; but ftill a productive foil.

From this defcription, which is no way exaggerated, the county of Hereford may well be deemed a delightful land to *live* in: and it
abounds

abounds in RESIDENCES,—*in defiance of bad roads.*

The ROADS of Herefordfhire may well be proverbial, in England: they are fuch as one might expect to meet with, in the marfhes of Holland, or the mountains of Switzerland. Even the entrance into the county,—from the foot of Mayhill to Rofs ;—the principal tho-roughfare from London to Hereford, Here-fordfhire—and *part* of South Wales, would not be deemed a fufficient by-road, in many parts of the kingdom. The narrow foreft lanes and hollow ways ftill remain: in many places it is impoffible for two carriages to pafs each other; while in fome, the bared rock, worn into inequalities, by heavy rains, and by being travelled upon century after century, is the prefent turnpike road ! Such a road in Yorkfhire, though leading only from vil-lage to village, would be indicted: and how thofe who travel, at leaft annually, through this dangerous pafs, can fuffer it to remain in its prefent difgraceful ftate, can be accounted for no other way, than in their being accuftomed to worfe in the neighbourhoods of their refidences. The lands in fome parts of

the

the county would be improved one fourth of
their prefent value by good roads. At prefent,
fix or feven horfes are neceffary to drag a load
of corn to market. Yet materials are fingularly abundant, in almoft every part of the
county. A century ago, other counties lay
under fimilar circumftances.

INCLOSURES. Herefordfhire is an inclofed
county. Some few remnants of common
fields are feen in what is called the upper part
of the county; but in general it appears to
have been inclofed from the foreft ftate;
crooked fences, and winding narrow lanes.—
Thefe circumftances affift in giving badnefs to
the roads and beauty to the country.

The PRODUCE of Herefordfhire is uncommonly various: in a general view, however,
it falls under the idea of a *corn country*. The
bottoms, neverthelefs, furnifh great quantities
of *grafs*, and the fides of the hills luxuriate,
in a fingular manner, in *wood*—chiefly oak.
Herefordfhire, at this time, could fhow more
YOUNG OAKS than, perhaps, any other county
of the kingdom: while the immediate banks
of the vallies, and the fkirts of the higher hills
are ftrewed with orchards: in fome places,
and

and feen in fome directions the bofoms of the fwells appear to be covered with fruit trees; which, at the time I faw them, were covered with fruit of the fineft quality.

The OBJECTS OF HUSBANDRY are principally CATTLE, SHEEP, *fwine, corn, hops* *, and FRUIT LIQUOR. The two firft, and the laft, were the objects, which led me, in October 1788, to an excurfion into this county.

My route was *Rofs, Ledbury, Bromyard, Leominfter, Weobley, Manfel, Hereford, Rofs,* which laft, and its neighbourhood, I likewife vifited in 1783.

---

* HOPS. Confiderable quantities of hops are grown in Herefordfhire; efpecially about Bromyard;—in that part of the county bordering on what may be called the Hop Diftrict of Worcefterfhire. I wifhed to have made myfelf acquainted with the culture of hops in this part of the kingdom; but had not fufficient leifure to pay due attention to it. The plow appears to be more freely ufed here than in Kent.

C A T T L E.

THE HEREFORDSHIRE breed of cattle,—taking it all in all,—may, without rifque I believe, be deemed the firft breed of cattle in this ifland.

This fuperior variety of the middlehorned breed has been noticed; and its oxen minutely dfcribed *. In general appearance, the Herefordfhire cattle refemble very much thofe of Suffex: except in their fuperior fize: and ftill more nearly the prefent breed of the Vale of Pickering †: notwithftanding thefe feveral diftricts are feparated near two hundred miles every way from each other; with other breeds of cattle intervening. Their frame is altogether *athletic*, with the limbs, in moft cafes, fufficiently clean, for the purpofe of travelling.

---

* See vol. i. p. 245.

† See YORK: ECON: vol. ii. p. 185.

ing. The form of many of them, as BEASTS OF DRAUGHT, is nearly complete.

Befides their fuperiority as beafts of draught;—and their being eligible as dairy ftock (being in this refpect fimilar to thofe of Glocefterfhire) ;—the females, at leaft, fat kindly at an early age ; the ftrongeft proof of their excellency as FATTING CATTLE. I have feen three-year-old heifers of this breed—to ufe a familiar phrafe—" as fat as mud": much fatter than any heifers of that age, I have feen, of any other breed;—the fpayed heifers of Norfolk excepted.

Viewing the Herefordfhire breed of cattle in this light; which I believe to be a true one; how unfortunate, for the rural affairs of thefe kingdoms, has been the choice of the fpirited breeders of the midland counties ! The fuperior varieties of the midland breed, befide being beautiful in their form, are indifputably well adapted to the GRAZIER, when kept to a proper age: and other varieties are well enough adapted to the DAIRYMEN: but for the ARABLE FARMER, as beafts of draught, they are far inferior to many other breeds ; which, with a fmall fhare of the attention and

Q 2 expence

expence that have been bestowed on the longhorned breed, might, I am fully persuaded, have been rendered equally, or still more profitable as milking cattle and grazing stock ; and, at the same time, have been fit for the purpose of draught:—a use, for which, not the horns only, but their general frame unfits them. I have seen them no where, in common use, as beasts of draught.

Nevertheless, we see the longhorned cattle, not only in full possession of the more central parts of the island, but overrunning the marginal districts in every direction. A circumstance, which to my mind appears to be of serious importance. The working of cattle is in the way of being, perhaps irretrievably, cut off; and, whenever the spirit of breeding shall flag, and the art fall into neglect, the intire country will be burthened with a breed of cattle, *naturally*, the worst, perhaps, it ever knew. The longhorned cattle, in a state of neglect, might, in figurative language, be called creatures without carcase; all horns and hide. With every assistance which genius and spirit can give them, they are barely, if at all, superior, even as grazing stock, to

other

other breeds, which have remained in a ftate
of comparative neglect.

Thefe obfervations refult not from an anti-
pathy to this breed of cattle: nor from a want
of refpect for its prefent diftinguifhed breeders.
Nor do they, I truft, originate in a want of
knowledge of the breed itfelf.   There is no
other breed of which I have had fo much
experience.   If, however, after fifteen years
acquaintance, I ftill remain a ftranger to its
merits, and have in confequence formed a
wrong judgement, I wifh and afk to be fet
right.

I am the more defirous to form an accurate
judgement of the longhorned breed of cattle,
as I hope to have, very foon, an opportunity
of digefting my ideas refpecting it, and of purfuing its excellencies as far as facts will enable
me.   There are, undoubtedly, fome varieties
of it raifed to an almoft incredible height.
And left, infatuated with the faiinefs of their
form, I may, in their praife, be led beyond
truth, I have, here, compared their GENE-
RAL NATURE, with that of a breed, which I
confider as the firft the ifland affords, that, by

having

having a standard to refer to, I may be the better enabled to regulate my judgement.

In Herefordshire, WORKING OXEN are the principal object of breeding. Great numbers of cattle are here in use, as beasts of draught. Half the plow teams appear to be of oxen; which are, likewise, often used in carriages: The ox cart—provincially " wain" *—is here a common implement. They are still, in general, worked double, in yoke; even in the deep-foiled parts of the district; with, however, some few exceptions.

One circumstance in the management of cattle, in this county, is to me à matter of some surprize. The spaying of female calves is not here a practice. This circumstance is the more remarkable, as the excellency of SPAYED HEIFERS, not only as beasts of draught, but as fatting cattle, is indisputable: and still more extraordinary, as, Herefordshire not being a dairy country, numbers of female
calves

---

* WAINS. So lately as fifty years ago, the WAIN was the only carriage of the district : there being many men, now living, who remember the first introduction of WAG-GONS.

calves muſt every year be fatted for the butcher. How much more eligible management it might be to caſtrate, indiſcriminately, the handſomeſt, and cleaneſt, of ſuch males or females, not wanted for the purpoſe of breeding, as drop in the rearing ſeaſon.

The oxen are bred, chiefly, in the northweſtern quarter of the county; but, more or leſs, in every other; except the Ryeland quarter. They are moderately worked, until they be five or ſix years old; at which age they are ſold moſtly in good condition, but ſome times out of the yoke, to the graziers; principally, I believe, of Buckinghamſhire, Wiltſhire, Warwickſhire, Gloceſterſhire, and the neighbouring counties.

At HEREFORD FAIR the 20 October (1788) there were about a thouſand head of cattle; chiefly of this breed, with a few Welch cattle. A large proportion of them were grown oxen, full of fleſh, and ſold, or worth at the ſelling prices of the day, from twelve to ſeventeen pounds an ox. The moſt *valuable* collection of cattle I have met with out of Smithfield: and by much the *fineſt* ſhow I have anywhere

ſeen.

feen. Had they been arranged in a proper fairftead, inftead of being huddled together, as they were, in the ftreets of the town, they would have formed a ftill finer exhibition *.

---

* The impropriety of continuing to fhew cattle for fale in the ftreets of towns is evident at Hereford ; whofe ftreets having been newly paved in the London manner, the town's people, to fave their windows, and to preferve a paffage to their houfes, very prudently run a rope on the outfide of the foot-pavement ; by which means the cattle are either crouded together in the middle of the ftreet, creating a ftate of confufion I have nowhere elfe obferved ; or, if headed againft the rope, ftand with their fore feet in the kennel ! An *aukwardnefs* which needs not to be defcribed.

S H E E P.

SHEEP.

HEREFORDSHIRE has been celebrated, time immemorial, for a peculiar
breed of fheep—called the RYELAND breed;
from an indeterminate diftrict, in the fouthern
quarter of the county, which goes by the
name of Ryeland; on which this breed of
fheep are principally reared.

The Ryeland fheep are remarkable for the
fweetnefs of their mutton; but ftill more for
the finenefs of their wool; which may be faid
to rival that of the growth of Spain. If the
Spaniards improved their wool, by any breed
of Englifh fheep, it was moft probably by
that of the Ryeland of Herefordfhire; not by
that of the Cotfwolds of Glocefterfhire.

The "Ryelanders" are a fmall, white-faced,
hornlefs breed. Their form (though little
attended

attended to) is often beautiful; and their
flefh of the fineft quality. The ewes run from
nine to twelve or fourteen, the wedders from
twelve to fixteen or eighteen, pounds a quarter.

In the MANAGEMENT of the ftoreflocks of
this breed a ftriking peculiarity is practifed.
Inftead of folding them in the open field,
agreeably to the practice of other diftricts,
they are generally fhut up, during the night,
in a building, which is provincially termed a
" cot",—and the practice termed COTTING.

The cot is generally, I believe, the ground
floor of a large building, which is chambered
at five or fix feet high. The fize is, of courfe,
in proportion to that of the flock. From thofe
which I have meafured, a yard fquare to a
fheep may be taken as the medium allowance
of room. Racks are fixed up againft the
walls; and, in the larger cots, fome of which
will cot two hundred fheep; other racks are
fufpended acrofs the middle of the room, and
hoifted as the dung and litter rife.

Their FOOD in the cot is fometimes *hay*,
and fometimes *barley ftraw*; but moft commonly *peas halm!* A food, which, it feems,
is particularly affected by fheep: a fact, which

the

the reſt of the kingdom does not ſeem to be fully poſſeſſed of. The halm, however, is not, I find, always thraſhed clean; the under-ripe pods being frequently left unbroken for the ſheep. The offal is ſtrewed about as litter; and the cot cleaned out once or twice a year; or as often as neceſſity, or conveniency, requires. The manure is eſteemed of the firſt quality.

The ADVANTAGES of cotting are not ſpoken of with ſufficient clearneſs to recommend it, without trial on a ſmall ſcale, to other diſtricts. The advantage generally held out is, that it fines the wool; but diſcerning men obſerve that, in the ſame proportion as it curbs the growth of the wool, it checks the growth of the ſheep; being in this effect worſe than folding.

The dung is, no doubt, of great value: and I have been told, by an intelligent huſbandman, that " cotted ſheep never rot;"— provided they be kept in the cot in the morning, until the dew be off the graſs. This accords with the theory above offered (ſee vol. 1. page 210.): the warmth of the cot promotes perſpiration: the dry food abſorbs the ſuper-
fluous

fluous moifture of the ftomach; and keeping them from the grafs, until the dews be
gone of it, is a ftill further preventive of fuperfluous moifture. I have, however, heard it
intimated, that if ground "be given to rot,"
cotting will not, with certainty, prevent it:
neverthelefs, I am inclined to believe, that
cotting, *properly*, would prevent it.

Ewes, when full with lamb, are feldom, I
underftand, cotted; but, after lambing, the
cot is found highly beneficial to the young
lambs; preferving them equally from cold
and from vermin.

The PRACTICE OF COTTING has probably
arifen in the tender nature of the Ryeland fheep,
which cannot ftand the fold. Attempts, it
feems, have been made to fold them, but always with great injury to the flock. Houfing
them was, therefore, the only means of collecting their dung; and rendering them moft
ufeful in an arable country: befides preferving
them from the vermin of the woodlands, with
which this diftrict has formerly abounded, and
with which it ftill abounds.

This breed of fheep appears to be an object worthy of national attention. Large fums
are

are annually paid to Spain for wool. The wool of the Ryeland fheep is ufed in the fame intention, as that of Spain. Though not fine enough as an entire fubftitute for Spanifh wool, it fupplies its place, I underftand, in fome degree. In 1783, Ryeland wool was fold for two fhillings a pound, when the ordinary wool of the kingdom was not worth more than fourpence a pound. Spanifh wool was then three fhillings. Ryeland wool *cotted* and *trended** was, this year, (1788) fold for near two fhillings; and Spanifh, I underftand, is worth about three fhillings.

It is, I believe, an inevitable confequence, that fhould the fupply of Ryeland wool be difcontinued, an increafed fupply of Spanifh wool would be neceffary. On the contrary, fhould the internal fupply be augmented, the wants from abroad would be diminifhed, proportionably. Should the longwooled breed of fheep, which is now working its way into all quarters of the kingdom, gain a footing, and acquire

* This wool appears to have been formerly confidered as a national object. It is under the infpection of " fworn trenders;" who free it from dirt and offal, and make it up in trendles, or round bundles, for fale. Wool thus made up bears a price of about half-a-crown a ftone (of 12¼ lb.) more than wool of the fame quality, in its rough ftate.

acquire fafhion, in Herefordfhire, the Ryeland breed may, in a few years, be irretrievably loft.

The farmer's object is the aggregate profit
of his flock: no matter, to him, whether it
arife from wool or carcafe: and, if the carcafe
of the Ryeland fheep had not been of fuperior
value, it is probable the breed would long ago
have been extinct. For although the wool of
this breed is fold at a high price, the quantity
cut, from a given number of fheep, is in the
inverfe proportion. *Cotted* fheep feldom, I
believe, afford more than a pound and a half,
each fheep;—while from fome breeds of the
kingdom, feven or eight pounds of wool are
cut,—worth, at prefent (1788) 8d. or 9d. a
pound; or twice the value of the Ryeland coat.
—The fheep of thofe breeds are, however,
larger; but not in this proportion.

What I mean to intimate in this cafe is, that
the continuation of the fupply of Ryeland wool
is, at prefent, in a ftate of uncertainty; and I
leave it to thofe, whofe province it more nearly
concerns, to devife the proper means of preferving and encreafing the ENGLISH BREED OF
FINEWOOLLED SHEEP.

THE

THE

MANAGEMENT

OF

ORCHARDS AND FRUIT LIQUOR,

IN

Herefordſhire and *Gloceſterſhire.*

THE CULTIVATION of FRUIT TREES, for the ſole purpoſe of LIQUOR, is peculiar to the weſtern provinces. The ſouthern counties, when the London markets are over-ſtocked with fruit, make a ſort of liquor from the ſurplus: but the eaſtern, the northern, and the midland counties may be ſaid to be as much unacquainted with the buſineſs of a liquor orchard, as they are with that of a vine-yard.

yard. Even Staffordſhire, which is divided from the cider country by a narrow ridge of hill only, has not, generally ſpeaking, a barrel of cider made within it.

HEREFORDSHIRE has ever borne the *name* of the firſt cider county :—GLOCESTERSHIRE, however, claims a preference in the two moſt celebrated fruit liquors the diſtrict affords.— WORCESTERSHIRE, and MONMOUTHSHIRE have their claims of excellency. May-hill may be conſidered as the center of this diviſion of the cider country*.

FRUIT LIQUOR is here an object of RURAL ECONOMY; and, though inferior to moſt other of its objects, was a ſecondary inducement to my viſiting the diſtrict. In 1783, however, I was unfortunate : it was not a general fruit year. But this year (1788) has made up for the diſappointment. There are men who will this year make a hundred hogſheads, that, in 1783, did not " wet the preſs."

But

---

* DEVONSHIRE and its ENVIRONING COUNTIES form another diviſion ; which, though upon the whole much inferior to this, produces one ſpecies of liquor (the coccagee cider) which is in high eſtimation.

But the management of orchards and their produce, though it enters into the practice of almoſt every occupier of land, is far from being properly underſtood. The primary obje&ct; of farmers, in general, has been that of ſupplying their own immoderate conſumption.— The markets for *ſale* liquor has hitherto been confined. In a plentiful year it has barely paid for the *ſlavery* of making it. But the late extenſion of canals, and other inland navigations, and moſt eſpecially one which is now extending between the Severn and the Thames, together with the preſent facility of land carriage, have already extended, and will in all probability ſtill farther extend, the market for fruit liquor; and there may be, henceforward, ſome encouragement for the manufacturing of *ſale* liquor; the right management of which is a *myſtery*, which few men are verſed in, and which I have found ſomewhat difficult to fathom.

I have, however, been the more diligent in my application to this ſubje&ct;, as it is an art which has never been duly inveſtigated. The entire ſubje&ct; having never undergone an analytical examination, no man can be ſaid to

have

have had a view of it, fufficiently comprehen-five, to raife every part to the requifite degree of perfection. The "cidermen"—(the buy-ers of fale liquor,) are far advanced in the or-dering of the LIQUOR; but are unacquainted with the management of ORCHARDS: while the occupiers of orchards are, moftly, as un-acquainted with the proper management of the fruit they grow. A general view of the whole art cannot, therefore, fail of having its ufe; even in the cider countries.

In taking this view, it will be convenient to examine the two main branches feparately; under the heads

MANAGEMENT OF ORCHARDS.
MANAGEMENT OF FRUIT LIQUOR.

ORCHARDS.

ORCHARDS.

UNDER THIS DIVISION of the fub-
ject, it will be proper to view, feparately,

The fituation of orchards.

The foil, &c. of orchards.

The method of raifing ftocks.

The method of planting orchards.

The method of grafting fruit trees.

The after-management of orchards.

And, previous to this detail, to examine
the SPECIES OF FRUIT, which give rife to it.

In the orchards of this diftrict, we find the
APPLE, the PEAR, and the CHERRY. The
laft, however, is only found near towns, and
in young orchards: and although it is probable, that a liquor of fome richnefs and flavor
might be made, from a well chofen variety of
this fpecies of fruit, I do not find that any attempt has been made, in this diftrict, to pro-

R 2   duce

duce from it a vinous liquor. Therefore, the
APPLE and the PEAR, only, are here entitled
to examination.

NATURE has furnifhed us with only one fort
of each of thefe fpecies of fruit : namely, the
common CRAB of the woods and hedges; and
the WILD PEAR, which is pretty common in
the hedges of the diftrict.

LINNEUS, *who knew all nature,* takes no
notice of the APPLE. He, as well as other
botanifts, confider it as a production of ART :
the various forts, with which our orchards
abound, being confidered as no other than
CULTIVATED VARIETIES of the *pyrus malus,* or
CRAB : while all the rich and highly flavored
PEARS, of which gardeners fpeak fo learned-
ly, are confidered as no other than ARTIFICIAL
PRODUCTIONS, from the *pyrus communis,* or
common WILD PEAR.

But we require not the affiftance of botanic
knowledge to convince us, that the numerous
forts of fruit, which are cultivated by orchardmen and gardeners, are not NATURAL SPE-
CIES.

Nature propagates and continues ITS OWN
SPECIES, *by feed.* But the feeds of a given
fpecies,

fpecies, or rather *variety**, of apple will not produce apples of the fame kind; but a number of different kinds, moft of them, probably, refembling the wood crab, rather than the apple which produced them,—let its richnefs and flavor be what they may†.

The fact feems to be, FRUIT is not, *naturally*, a permanent fpecific character: even the native wild crab is fubject to infinite variety, in colour, fhape, and flavor. But, *by art*, the qualities of fruit may be identically preferved.

The

---

* VARIETY. This is a term of natural hiftory. It is applied to the individual of a SPECIES, as that of *fpecies* is to the individuals of a GENUS. Thus *apples* and *pears* are *fpecies* of the GENUS, PYRUS. The *golden-pippin* and the *nonpariel*, *varieties* of the SPECIES, APPLE. To fpeak more generally, SPECIES are (in botany) PERMANENT PRODUCTIONS of NATURE,—preferved, in perpetuity, by NATURAL PROPAGATION. *Varieties*, on the contrary, are *temporary productions* arifing from *accident* or *art*; and, without the affiftance of *artificial propagation*, laft only one generation; dying with the accidental individuals; their offspring, by SEED, reverting back to the NATURAL SPECIES. This definition is, at leaft, fufficiently accurate to be applied to the clafs of plants now under confideration (TREES); tho' not altogether applicable to another clafs (HERPS).

† By repeatedly fowing the feeds of the feedlings, in common foil, the common crab would, no doubt, be produced.

The bufinefs, therefore, of the improvers of fruit is to catch at SUPERIOR ACCIDENTAL VARIETIES, and having raifed them by CULTIVATION, to the higheft degree of perfection they are capable of, to preferve them in that ftate by ARTIFICIAL PROPAGATION.

The law of nature, however, though it fuffer man to improve the fruits which are given us, appears to have fet bounds to his art; and to have numbered the years of *his* creations. Artificial propagation cannot preferve the varieties in perpetuity. A time arrives, when they can be no longer propagated with fuccefs. All the old fruits, which raifed the fame of the liquors of this country, are now loft; or are fo far on the decline, as to be deemed irrecoverable.

The REDSTREAK is given up: the celebrated STIRE APPLE is going off; and the SQUASH PEAR, which has probably furnifhed this country with more *champaign* than was ever imported into it, can no longer be got to flourifh: the ftocks canker and are unproductive. In Yorkfhire, fimilar circumftances have taken place: feveral old fruits, which were productive within my own recollection,

are

are loft: the ftocks cankered, and the trees would no longer come to bear.

The DURATION OF VARIETIES may, however, depend much upon management. For although nature wills that the fame wood, or the fame fet of fap-veffels (for the wood which is produced by grafting is, in reality, no more than a protrufion of the graft,—an extenfion of the original ftock) fhall, in time, lofe its fecundity; yet, it is probable, that the fame art which eftablifhes a variety, may fhorten or prolong its duration.   Much may depend upon the STOCK, and much upon the health of the tree, and the age of the wood, from which the GRAFT is taken.   Or, perhaps, the CANKER (which feems to be the natural deftroyer of varieties) may be checked.   But of thefe in their places.

The popular idea among orchardmen is, that the DECLINE OF THE OLD FRUITS is owing to a want of frefh grafts from abroad—from " Normandy"—under a notion, that the higheft-flavored apples grow there, in a ftate of nature, as the crab in this ifland !

That the firft fruits of our anceftors were fetched from the Continent is highly probable.

But

But it is equally probable, that the forts which
were originally imported, have long ago been
loft; and that the numerous varieties, we are
at prefent poffeffed of, were raifed from the
feed, in this country. MILLER, whofe extenfive practice and connexions enabled him
to be an adequate judge of this fubject, fpeaks
of them as fuch. After enumerating fome
French apples, he fays—" the forts, which are
above-mentioned, are what have been introduced from France; but there are not above
two or three of them, which are much efteemed in England, viz. the French Rennette,
the Rennette-grife, and the Violet Apple; the
other being early fruit, which do not keep
long, and their flefh is generally meally, fo
that they do not deferve to be propagated; *as
we have many better fruits in England,* which
I fhall next mention:" and in mentioning the
GOLDEN PIPPIN, one of the firft apples we
know, either for the table or the cider prefs,
he fays " the golden pippin is a fruit *peculiar
to England.* There are few countries abroad
where this fucceeds well*."

The

---

* At Ledbury, I was fhown a " Normandy" apple :—
this tree, with many others of the fame fort, having been
imported

The STIRE APPLE is generally underſtood to be a "kernel fruit:" and the HAGLOE CRAB, whoſe fame as a cider fruit, is little inferior to that of the ſtire, is ſtill traceable to the parent ſtock. The original tree is ſtill in being.

It is probable, however, that many of our preſent fruits have not been produced from our own native crab; but from the apples which were originally imported. Neverthelefs, it is more than probable, that ſome of the higher-flavored, firmer fruits, as the GOLDEN PIPPIN, have been raiſed, by cultivation, from the native ſpecies. The procefs is ſimple and eaſy: and a young man of ingenuity and enterprize, and in a proper ſituation, might be lefs rationally employed, than in improving this ſpecies of his country's produce.

Elect, among the native ſpecies, individuals of the higheſt flavor. Sow the ſeeds in a highly enriched ſeedbed, in the manner which will be deſcribed. Select, from among the ſeedlings, the plants whoſe wood and leaves wear

the

imported immediately from France. On ſeeing and taſting the fruit, I found it to be no other than the *bitter-ſweet*, which I have ſeen growing, as a neglected wilding, in an Engliſh hedge.

the moft *apple-like* appearance. Tranfplant
thefe, into a rich deep foil, in a genial fituation, and at diftances which will be mentioned;
letting them remain in this nurfery until they
begin to bear.

With the feeds of the faireft, richeft, and
beft-flavored fruit, repeat this procefs. And
at the fame time, or in due feafon, engraft the
wood which produced this fruit, on that of
the richeft, fweeteft, beft-flavored apple : re-
peating this operation; and transferring the
fubject, under improvement, from one tree
and fort to another, as richnefs, flavor, or firmnefs may require. Continuing this double
mode of improvement, until the defired fruit
be obtained.

There has, no doubt, been a period, when
the improvement of the apple and the pear
was attended to in this country. And fhould
not the fame fpirit of improvement revive, it
is probable, that the country will, in a courfe
of years, be left deftitute of valuable kinds of
thefe two fpecies of fruit : which, though they
may in fome degree be deemed objects of lux-
ury, long cuftom feems to have ranked among
the necefaries of life.

Having

Having thus endeavoured to convey a general idea of the nature and propagation of varieties,—it will be proper to enumerate some of the moſt celebrated of thoſe which are now in cultivation, in theſe counties :—to deſcribe, or even enumerate, *all* the preſent varieties of orchard fruit would be impoſſible. They are without number. In Herefordſhire, more particularly, a very conſiderable proportion of the fruit which is grown is "kernel fruit;" is produced from trees that have been raiſed from the ſeed; and which have never been grafted. Conſequently each tree is a ſeparate variety; bearing the name, perhaps, of its planter, or of the "ground" it grows in.

There are, nevertheleſs, numbers which are univerſally known; and ſome of them ſufficiently celebrated to be entitled to notice.

Of APPLES,—the STIRE ſtands firſt in eſtimation. The *fruit* of this variety is ſomewhat below the middle ſize. The form rather flat. The colour a pale yellowiſh white, with ſometimes a faint bluſh on one ſide. The fleſh tolerably firm. The flavor, when fully ripe, fine. It is deemed, by moſt people, a tolerably

rably good eating apple *. The *cider*, which is produced from it, in a foil that is adapted to it, is rich, highly flavored, and of a good body:—its price frequently fourfold that of common fale cider. The thin *limeftone foils* on the margin of the Foreft of Dean, are faid to produce the richeft ftire cider.—The *tree* which bears this apple is of a fingular growth :—remarkably " beefom-headed" :—throwing out numerous, ftraight, luxuriant, upward fhoots, from the crown ; taking the form of a willow pollard ; running much to wood ; and, in deep foils, growing to a great fize before it become fruitful.

The HAGLOE CRAB is, at prefent, next in efteem. It has already been mentioned, that this variety is traceable to the original feed-ling. It was produced, about feventy years ago, in a nurfery among other ftocks raifed from the feed, by Mr. BELLAMY of HAGLOE in Glocefterfhire, grandfather of the prefent Mr. BELLAMY,

---

* There is an apple called the *red ftire* ; but it has no peculiar affinity with the true ftire. In Herefordfhire, about Marcle, I met with a " yellow ftire"—and on the Foreft there is the " kernel ftire" :—both of them probably kernel fruits, which, bearing fome likenefs of the true ftire, have had its name improperly given them.

BELLAMY, near Rofs in Herefordfhire; who draws from it (that is from trees grafted with fcions from this parent ftock) a liquor, which, for richnefs, flavor, and *price on the fpot*, exceeds, perhaps, every other fruit liquor, which nature and art have produced. He has been offered fixty guineas for a hogfhead (about 110 gallons) of this liquor. He has likewife been offered bottle for bottle of wine or fpirituous liquors, the beft to be produced; and this without freight, duty, or even a mile of carriage to enhance its original price.

This fruit, while growing, is nearly white; when fully ripe it has a yellowifh caft; fometimes freckled with red on one fide, like the common white crab. The fize about that of the ftire apple; but the form more oblong. The flefh remarkably foft and woolly, but not dry; being furnifhed with a fheer, but, when fully ripe, fweet juice; which, however, is much fmaller in proportion to the quantity of fibrous matter, than that of moft other apples. The flavor, when ripe, refembles that of the cafhew apple of the Weft-Indies; and, what is remarkable, the texture of the flefh is not unfimilar to the pulp of that fruit. The

cider

cider, notwithftanding the fheernefs of the juice, is, when properly manufactured, fingularly rich ; and, notwithftanding the faint fmell of the apple, is highly flavored: and, what is equally remarkable, the liquor is of the higheft colour, notwithftanding the palenefs of the fruit.

The GOLDEN PIPPIN is in high eftimation as a cider apple ; and may rank as the third of this diftrict. It is more generally known than the Hagloe crab, and, at public market, its liquor, I believe, is generally next in price to that of the ftire apple.

The old REDSTREAK is yet in being. A few old trees are ftill remaining. The *fruit* fmall, roundifh, of a pale yellow ground, with numerous faint-red ftreaks. The flefh firm, full of juice, and, when ripe, finely flavored; a palatable eating apple. The *cider*, at prefent, is not, I believe, in particular eftimation: little, if any genuine redftreak cider is now made. It never was, I believe, equal to that of either of the preceding apples. The *tree* of this apple is of a fingularly aukward growth. Crooked—reclining—ragged and unfightly.

The

The WOODCOCK is another favorite old cider fruit. But is now going off: many old trees, however, are still left in the diftrict. The *fruit* is much larger than any of the preceding forts: above the middle fize. The form fomewhat oblong; with a long ftalk, fet on in a peculiar manner; feigned to refemble the woodcock's beak (hence the name). The colour that of the redftreak, with the addition of fome dark blood-red ftreaks on one fide. The flefh remarkably fine; equally fit for culinary purpofes and for cider. The *tree* large, and ftrongly featured; forming large boughs in the pear-tree manner.

Other favorite cider apples, at prefent, are

The MUST:—an old favorite fruit, of which three forts are enumerated.

The PAUSON:—a middlefized, green apple.

The ROYAL WILDING:—a large white apple.

The DYMMOCK RED: middlefized,—red.

The COCCAGEE: above the middle fize: greenifh white, with an orange blufh:—well flefhed, and highly flavored.

RUSSETS, of various kinds, are in good efteem: particularly the LONGNEY RUSSET.

BROMLEY,

BROMLEY, FOXWHELP, RED CRAB, QUEEN-
ING,—all of them large red apples,—are in
good eſtimation for cider.

Of PEARS, the SQUASH is in much the
higheſt eſteem. It is an early fruit ; remarkable for the tenderneſs of its fleſh. If it drop
ripe from the tree, it burſts to pieces with the
fall : (hence moſt probably its name). The liquor made from this fruit is pale, ſweet, yet
remarkably *clean*, and of a ſtrong body : a
moſt elegant liquor ; if duly manufactured,
from a ſoil which ſuits it. *Taynton*, on the
Gloceſterſhire ſide of Mayhill, has long been
famous for the ſuperior excellency of its
" ſquaſh-pear perry". In price, it bears a
ſimilar proportion to common perry, as the
ſtire cider does to the ordinary kinds.

The OLDFIELD is a favorite old pear; remarkable for the elegant flavor of its liquor.

The BARLAND pear is in great repute, as
producing a perry, which is eſteemed ſingularly beneficial in nephritic complaints ; as

The RED PEAR is for affording a liquor of
ſingular ſtrength. *

The

---

* Frequently, it is ſaid, ſtrong enough to " flaſh in the
fire"

The HUFFCAP, and the SACK, are other pears which have been ufually grafted: and befides thefe and a variety of others, great numbers of " kernel fruits" are found among the pear trees, as well as among the apple trees, of this diftrict.

The PRODUCTION of ORCHARD FRUITS, for the purpofe of LIQUOR, now requires to be examined in detail; agreeably to the fubdivifions of the fubject enumerated at the head of this article. But in giving this general view of the proper management of orchards, the practice of this divifion of the cider country (fo far at leaft as it has come to my knowledge) will be found, in many particulars, improper to be held up as a pattern. The method of procedure, in this cafe, muft therefore be, to felect the beft inftances of the practice of thefe diftricts, and make up the deficiency from my own practical knowledge of the fubject of planting: in order to endeavour to render this article, what I wifh it to be, *general* and *practical*.

I. THE SITUATION OF ORCHARDS. Through the kingdom in general, we fee apple trees in no other fituation, than in fmall

S inclofures

inclofures or yards, adjoining to a houfe or garden; having been planted, perhaps, without much regard either to SOIL or ASPECT: LOCALITY, alone, having determined the fite.

But in this diftrict, LOCALITY, with refpect to the HOMESTALL, appears to have had little weight in determining the fituations of orchards; which we frequently fee fcattered about in every part of a townfhip; perhaps half a mile from any habitation.

In fituations where orchard fruits are fcarce; and where a confiderable market for them is within reach; fuch orchards might be hazardous. But in this country, *fruit* is of little value, until it be converted into *liquor*: a change which thieves,—petty thieves, at leaft,—have not an opportunity of effecting with fufficient fecrecy. Cottagers have no mills. The ftolen fruit muft be carried to a neighbour's mill to be ground. The neighbour knows each man's fruit; and the quantity he grows: and the robbery is of courfe detected. In fmall quantities, efpecially near towns, orchard fruits are no doubt ftolen. But the theft is fimilar to that of ftealing a mefs of turneps in Norfolk:
they

they are never miffed; and the real lofs is inconfiderable; except in fome particular fituations.

Aspect is of much more importance, here,
than locality, and appears to have had due
weight in fixing the fites of orchards, in this
diftrict; for though orchards are found on
every fide of hills, the fouth eaft, with a fkreen
to the north, feems to be the favorite afpect.
The " morning fun" is efteemed genial to
fruit: an old idea; and not merely a popular
notion; though in fome degree it may be
deemed fuch.

It is not probable that the *quality* of the morning rays is much fuperior to thofe of the
noon-day or evening fun (the popular idea);
but it appears demonftrably, that a fouth-
eaftern afpect collects a greater *quantity* of
heat; enjoys a longer day; than any other afpect. It is noon before a weftern afpect *reflects* a ray. In the morning, it will frequently
remain dewy and cold, feveral hours after vegetation has been roufed, againft an eaftern inclination. The afternoon fun is, no doubt,
more intenfe, on the weft than on the eaft
fide of a hill; but its duration is fhort. In an

afternoon,

afternoon, the air is everywhere warm; and a regular supply of warmth appears to be more genial to vegetation, than a great and sudden transition from heat to cold. The coolness of the evening comes on, and vegetation is probably checked as soon, or nearly as soon, in all aspects. Hence we may, I think, fairly conclude, that the southeastern aspect enjoys more vegetative hours, and receives a more regular supply of heat, than any other aspect.

Nevertheless, on a fruit-liquor farm, it may be prudent to have " plantations" in different aspects. Blights (whatever they are) appear to be communicated to the trees by the wind. In 1783, orchard-fruit was cut off in every situation, except a northwest aspect; in which I saw several orchards fully fruited.

A northern aspect, however, has its disadvantage; and although it may, in this country, especially where the soil is warm, produce fruits fit for the purpose of liquor; yet, in the more northern provinces, it may be altogether inadequate to that purpose. A hill dipping to the south partakes of the nature of a south wall. The atmosphere, a few feet from the ground, is probably many degrees hotter on

the

the fouth than on the north fide of a regular
hill: and the richnefs and flavor of fruit depends much on the heat of the atmofphere it
matures in.   The fruit of the branch of a vine,
for inftance, which is introduced into a ftove
or greenhoufe, is much richer and higher-flavored, than that of other branches of the
fame vine, which remain in the common atmofphere. Hence every means fhould be ufed
to render the atmofphere of an orchard as
warm as may be—to collect as much heat
within its area as poffible.   Therefore, while it
enjoys the morning fun, it ought to have a
tall woody fkreen to the eaft, to break off the
peircing winds from that quarter.   The winds
travel horizontally, or nearly fo; while the
fun foon gains a fufficient elevation, to lodge
its rays in the atmofphere of a fkreened orchard.

Much has been faid about FRUIT TREES IN
HEDGES, in the cider counties.   But this fhould
feem to be one of thofe *wild ideas*, which
hafty travellers are liable to catch.   Crab trees,
perhaps, are more common in the hedges of
this, than they are in thofe of other diftricts;
and hedge crabs, here, as in other places,
are fometimes grafted with apples; but I have

met

met with very few instances, in which hedgerows have been designedly, and regularly,
filled with apple trees. About Bromyard, I
saw one or two instances, in which apple trees
form close woody hedgerows ; blowzing out,
on either side, over the adjoining inclosures.
But the practice of planting fruit trees in
hedges, I apprehend, has never been common,
and is now, I believe, wholly laid aside.
There are two disadvantages attend it:—the
hedge is inevitably destroyed, and the fruit is
difficult to collect.

II. THE SOIL OF ORCHARDS. It appears
to be sufficiently well ascertained, in this district, that the same species of fruit, when
produced on different soils, affords liquors of
very different qualities. The *stire apple*, on
the LIMESTONE LANDS of the Forest of Dean,
yields a cider, which is marked by richness,
(sweetness), and fulness of flavor: while the
same apple, in the vale of Glocester, a strong
deep rich soil, affords a liquor, whose predominant qualities, without great diligence in
the manufacture of it, are roughness and
strength.—The *Hagloe crab*, too, seems to require a CALCARIOUS ROCK to give full richness
and

and flavor to its liquor.   The orchard, which
yields the nectarious juice, that has been ſpoken of, has for its ſoil a very ſhallow loam,
lying on a ſoft ſandy rock—provincially ·a
" dunſtone"—which, on examination, proves
to be pretty ſtrongly calcarious ; and is of a
contexture ſufficiently porous and looſe to admit the fibrils of vegetables.

On the contrary, the *ſquaſh pear* draws the
fineſt liquor from DEEP STRONG LAND.   A
plug of ſoil, taken beneath a pear tree, in a
celebrated orchard, in the townſhip of Taynton, is a STRONG BROWN CLAY, without a
particle of calcarious earth in its compoſition.
Nor does the ſubſoil, a ſtill ſtronger RED CLAY,
ſhew the leaſt marks of calcarioſity *.

This contrariety may be reconcileable in the
ſpecific qualities of theſe fruits.   The juice of
the

---

* I have obſerved a PEAR-TREE flouriſh on the ſide of a
COLD BLUE-CLAY SWELL (Laſſington hill) where the ſoil
is ſo infertile that ſcarcely any herbage, except the wood
feſcue, will grow upon it ; and where the native crab evidently ſtarves for want of nouriſhment.   There are many
ſimilar ſwells ſcattered over this diſtrict ; and it is probable,
that their value, (at preſent very inconſiderable) might be
advanced manyfold, by planting them with ſome of the ſuperior ſorts of pear trees.

the pear is naturally faccharine; while that of
the apple abounds with acidity; and, if we
may venture to reafon on a fubject fo little underftood as is that of the vegetable economy,
what is more likely to leffen the proportion of
acidity, than the tree which produces it feeding among calcarious earth; its natural deftroyer?

From the whole of the evidence collected
in this diftrict, I am inclined to believe, that
there are many fituations, even in the more
northern provinces—notwithftanding the difadvantage of climature—in which, with due
attention to afpect, a judicious choice of fruit,
and proper management of the liquor—even
CIDER of the firft quality might be made.—
PERRY of a good quality, I am perfuaded,
might be made in almoft any quarter of the
kingdom.

III. RAISING STOCKS. To convey an adequate idea of the BUSINESS OF THE NURSERY,
it will be proper to divide it into

> The choice of the feed.
> The feedbed.
> Tranfplanting.
> Training.

I. The

1. The SEEDS generally ufed, in this intention, are the kernels of cider apples, feparated from the " muft" or refiduum of the prefs. Thefe are either fown in autumn, or are kept dry in fand, or otherwife, until fpring; care being had, in either cafe, to preferve them from mice, during winter.

When the production of frefh varieties is the principal object, or when fruits, which are yet too auftere, require to be further improved by cultivation, feeds thus obtained may be eligible. But for fruits, whofe flavor is already raifed to the defired pitch, and more efpecially for thofe, which have paffed the point of perfection, as fome of the dry fpungy varieties appear to have done, the feeds fhould certainly be thofe of the natural fpecies,—the native crab,—which moft diftricts produce, and whofe juice will generally repay the trouble of collecting.

2. THE SEED BED fhould be adapted to the intention.—If new varieties, or the improvement of old ones, be the object, the feed bed ought to be made as rich as poffible : perhaps even a frame, or the ftove, might be found eligible. On the contrary, if the prefervation

of

of varieties be all that is wanted, an ordinary loamy foil is fufficient. In either cafe, it is proper that it fhould be perfectly clean, from root weeds at leaft, and that it fhould be double dug, from a foot to eighteen inches deep. The furface levelled and raked fine, the feeds ought to be fcattered on, about an inch afunder, and covered, about half an inch deep, with fome of the fineft of the mould, previoufly raked off the bed, for that purpofe. During fummer, the young plants fhould be kept perfectly free from weeds, and the enfuing winter may be taken up for tranfplantation; or, if not crouded in the feed bed, may remain in it, until the fecond winter.

3. TRANSPLANTING. The nurfery ground, like the feed bed, fhould be enriched agreeably to the general intention; and ought, in common good management, to be *double dug*, at leaft fourteen inches deep; eighteen or twenty inches deep is always preferable.

The feedling plants ought to be *forted*, agreeably to the ftrength of their roots, that they may rife evenly together. The top or downward roots fhould be taken off, and, in
this

this operation, the longer fide rootlets fhould be fhortened.

They fhould be planted in rows, three feet apart, and from fifteen to eighteen inches afunder in the rows'; care being had not to cramp the roots, but to bed them evenly and horizontally among the mould.

If the plants be intended merely for ftocks to be grafted, they may remain, as they generally do, in this and other diftricts, in this fituation, until they be large enough to be finally planted out. But, in ftrictnefs of management, they ought, two years previous to their being transferred to the orchard, to be RETRANSPLANTED;—into frefh, but unmanured, double-dug ground, aquincunx; four feet apart every way: in order that the *feeding fibres* may be brought fo near the ftem (yet have fufficient room to form in) that they may be removed with it, into the orchard : inftead of being, as they generally are, left behind in the nurfery. Hence, in this fecond tanfplantration, as in the firft, the branches of the root fhould not be left too long ; but ought to be fhortened, in fuch a manner, as to induce them to form a regular, GLOBULAR ROOT: fufficiently

ciently fmall to be removed with the plant;—
yet fufficiently large to give it firmnefs and vigour in the plantation.

If the raifing or improvement of varieties
be the object in view, the nurfery ground
fhould be naturally deep and well foiled, and
highly manured; and the plants repeatedly
moved—as every fecond, third, or fourth year
—that they may luxuriate, not only in rich,
but in frefh pafturage; thereby doing, perhaps, all that art can do, in this ftage of improvement, towards giving freedom to the fap
veffels, and fize and richnefs to the fruit.

4. TRAINING. The *intervals* may, while
the plants are fmall, be cropped with fuch
kitchen garden produce, as will not croud or
overfhadow the plants; the *rows* being kept
perfectly free from weeds.

In *pruning* the plants, the leader fhould be
particularly attended to. If it fhoot double,
the weaker of the contending branches fhould
be taken off.—If the leader be loft, and not
eafily recoverable, the plant fhould be cut
down to within a hand s breadth of the foil,
and a frefh ftem trained. Next to the leader,
the ftem boughs require attention. The un-
dermoft

dermoft boughs fhould be taken off by degrees; going over the plants every winter;—
always cautioufly preferving fufficient heads to
draw up the fap; thereby giving ftrength to
the ftems, and vigour to the roots and
branches: not trimming them up to naked
twigs, as in the common practice; thereby
drawing them up prematurely tall, and feeble
in the lower part of the ftems.

The *length of ftem*, to which ftocks are
ufually trained, in this diftrict, is fix feet;—
fometimes to near feven feet;—a height which
is much preferable: half a rod high would be
ftill more eligible. A tall-ftemmed tree is out
of the reach of ftock, and is much lefs injurious
to whatever grows under it, than a low-headed
tree; which, while it is the caufe of mifchief,
is itfelf in harm's way.

The *thicknefs of the ftem* ought to be in proportion to its height: a tall ftock, therefore,
requires to remain longer in the nurfery than
a low one. The ufual fize, at which ftocks
of the ordinary height are here planted out,
is four to fix inches girt at three feet high.—
A fize which they will reach, with proper management, in feven or eight years. The price

of

of fuch ftocks, in this diftrict, at prefent, (un-grafted) is eighteen pence each! *

IV. PLANTING ORCHARDS. In conduct-ing this bufinefs, properly, various confidera-tions are requifite, as

    1. The diftance.
    2. The difpofition.
    3. The time of planting.
    4. Taking up the plants.
    5. Pruning the plants.
    6. Putting them in.
    7. Defending them.
    8. Aftermanagement of the ftocks.

    1. DISTANCE. This depends upon the fite, and the general intention. If a mere ORCHARD be the object; namely, a plantation of fruit trees placed in as clofe order as the nature of fruit trees will admit; the diftance may be much fhorter, than in a FRUIT GROUND, which, notwithftanding the plantation, is in-tended to remain an object of hufbandry.

In this diftrict, we fee fruit trees ftanding at all diftances. In clofe ORCHARDS, ten
yards

---

* I met with one inftance of crabftocks being gathered in the woods; and with a good profpect of fuccefs.

yards feems to be a prevailing diftance.   But
the proper diftance in this cafe depends on
the natural growth of the given trees: from
ten to twelve yards (half a chain) may, in this
intention, be an eligible diftance*.

In the GRASS GROUNDS of Glocefterfhire, and
the ARABLE FIELDS of Herefordfhire, twenty
yards is a common diftance: fome I have
obferved with intervals of twenty five yards.
A chain's length (twenty two yards) may be
taken as a good medium diftance.

In *this* cafe each acre fuftains ten trees; in
that forty.

2. DISPOSITION.   In GROUNDS, the trees
fhould be planted in *crofs lines,* for the conveniency of plowing.   In ORCHARDS, they
ought to be fet in the *quincunx* manner, that
they may have equal room to fpread on every
fide.

3. The TIME OF PLANTING fruit trees is
Oftober, and November ;——or February,
March, or April; according to the feafon and
the

* In old orchards I have found them at only eight yards,
in one inftance only fix yards diftance; but the trees have
not head room to acquire nearly their full growth.

the foil. Where the foil is dry and light, autumn is preferable; as, during winter, the
foil has time, affifted by the winter's rains, to
fettle firmly to the roots. On the contrary,
in a cold, wet fituation, where the foil is tenacious, and the fubftratum retentive of moifture, the fpring months are a more eligible
feafon of planting.

4. In TAKING UP THE PLANTS, more attention is requifite, than is ufually paid to this
operation. Their future progrefs refts principally upon it. The roots ought to be as *numerous*, and as *long* as poffible. For the purpofe of affording immediate fuftinence to the
plant, and of giving it firmnefs and ftability
in the foil. Hence the impropriety of croud-
ing the plants in the nurfery: and hence the
utility of tranfplanting them previous to the
final planting.

5. PRUNING THE PLANTS. The ROOTS
ought not, in *this* cafe, to be touched (except
taking off the downward roots in the center)
but the TOP fhould, at this time, receive the
form, which it afterward ought to take. The
leader fhould be fhortened, and the fmaller
fide boughs be taken off; leaving a proper
choice

choice of the larger fide boughs *entire* and *un-touched**; to draw up the fap; and, in due time, to furnifh proper wood for grafting.— Hence thefe boughs fhould have a proper elevation; and fhould ftand in different directions; that the tree, after it be grafted, may take a regular head. This pruning of the head leffens the power of the wind, and, at the fame time, by affifting the roots, enfures, with common care, the fuccefs of the plant.

6. The METHOD OF PLANTING. This requires particular notice. The ordinary method in the Glocefterfhire cow-grounds; is to dig a hole, wide enough to take the roots (if not very long); which being placed within it, the mould is returned upon them in the order in which it came out; carefully replacing the fods on the furface, that no grazing ground may be loft! A mode of planting, which is too common throughout the kingdom.

A method, which is more likely to fucceed is this: the ground being fet out with ftakes,

driven

---

* Except when the root, for want of due tranfplantation, is weak. In this cafe, the top ought to be reduced in proportion.

driven in the centers of the intended holes, defcribe a circle, five or fix feet in diameter,
round each ftake. If the ground be in a ftate
of grafs, remove the fward, in fhallow fpits;
placing the fods on one fide of the hole. The
beft of the loofe mould place, by itfelf, on
another fide; and the dead earth, from the
bottom of the hole, in a third heap.

The depth of the holes fhould be regulated
by the nature of the fubfoil. Where this is
cold and retentive, the holes fhould not be
made much deeper than the cultivated foil.—
To go lower is to form a receptacle for water,
which, by ftanding among the roots, is very
injurious to the plants. On the contrary, in
a dry light foil, the holes fhould be made confiderably deeper; as well to obtain a degree of
coolnefs and moifture, as to be able to eftablifh the plants firmly in the foil. In foils of
a middle quality, the hole fhould be of fuch a
depth, that, when the fods are thrown to the
bottom of it, the plant will ftand at the fame
depth in the orchard, as it did in the nurfery
Each hole, therefore, fhould be of a depth
adapted to the particular root, which is to be
planted in it. The holes, however, ought,
for

for various reafons, to be made previous to
the day of planting.   If the feafon of planting
be fpring, and the ground and the weather be
dry, the HOLES fhould be WATERED, the evening before the day of planting, by throwing
two or three pailfuls of water into each : a *new*,
but an eligible practice.

In planting, the fods fhould be thrown to
the bottom of the hole; chopt with the fpade;
and covered with fome of the fineft of the
mould.   If the hole be fo deep that, with this
advantage, the bottom will not be raifed high
enough for the given plant, fome of the worft
of the mould fhould be returned, before the
fods be thrown down.

The bottom of the hole being raifed to a
proper height; and adjufted; the loweft tire
of roots are to be fpread upon it: drawing
them out horizontally ; and fpreading them,
in different directions, as the bird fpreads its
foot when it ftands on a level furface : drawing
out the rootlets and the fibres, which feverally
belong to them ; fpreading them out as a fea-
ther, or as the frond of the fern;—preffing
them evenly into the foil ; and covering them,
by hand, with fome of the fineft of the mould:

one

one perfon fteadying the plant; another adjuft-
ing and bedding the roots; and a third fup-
plying the mould: which being raifed high
enough to receive another root, or another
tire of roots, they are to be fpread out horizontally upon it, and bedded in a fimilar manner: thus continuing, until every root be bedded, feparately, horizontally (or fomewhat
declining) freely, yet firmly, among the beft
of the foil: great care being had to work the
mould well in, *by hand,* among the roots beneath the crown, that no hollownefs, nor falfe
filling, may be left: to prevent which, the
mould, after the roots are all bedded, and
covered fome depth, fhould be preffed, or
trodden hard (according to the nature of the
foil and the ftate of the feafon) with the foot:
the remainder of the mould being raifed into a
hillock round the ftem; for the triple ufe of
affording coolnefs, moifter, and ftability to
the plant.

In forming thefe hillocks fome little fkill
is requifite. The foil ought not to prefs
againft the ftem much higher, in the orchard,
thanit did in the nurfery: yet it is proper
that there fhould be a defcent for rain water,
from

from the ftem ; not *toward* it. To this end a
dimple or little difh fhould be made on the
top of the hillock ; and, from the rim of this,
the flope fhould be gentle to the circumference
of the hole ; where the broken ground fhould
fink fome few inches below the level of the
orchard.

Much of this will, no doubt, be deemed tedious and unneceffary : by thofe, I mean, who
have been accuftomed to *bury* the roots of
plants, in the gravedigger's manner: but
I can recommend every part of it, to thofe
who wifh to enfure fuccefs, from my own practice; in which this method of bedding the
roots arofe ; and in which only, I believe, it
has been ufed.

7. DEFENDING THE STOCKS. Plants which
have been properly tranfplanted, in the manner recommended aforegoing ; whofe heads
have been judicioufly leffened ; and which
have been planted in the manner here defcribed; feldom require any other ftay than
their own roots. If, however, the ftems
be tall, and the roots few and fhort, they
fhould be *fupported,* in the ufual manner with

T 3   ftakes

ſtakes, or in a manner which will preſently be mentioned.

The methods of *guarding* young trees from *live ſtock,* in this diſtrict, are various: the cheapeſt, and, perhaps, the moſt common way is that of ſticking ſome tall thorns round the plant, at a diſtance from the root; binding the tops of the thorns with a with, and the middle of them with another; forming them into a ſort of cone round the plant.— This, however, is only a ſlender guard; and the thorns are liable to chafe the ſtem of the plant. I have ſeen many plants materially injured by this method of defending them.

Oppoſed to this, the moſt expenſive guard —not unfrequently made uſe of in the cow-grounds of Gloceſterſhire—are four poſts, put down, in a ſquare, about the plant; with five or ſix ſhort rails on either ſide. The expence of this, if done in a ſtrong workmanlike manner, is too great for common practice.

The next is three poſts, ſet in a triangle, with rails in a ſimilar manner.

In Herefordſhire, and on the Herefordſhire ſide of Gloceſterſhire, where young orchards are kept under the plow, two poſts, only, are

in

in ufe; namely one large poft, flit with a faw, and placed flatway, with the faces to the plant; and about two feet apart; with rails on each fide, nailed upon the edges of the pofts. This is beautifully fimple, ftrong, a fufficient guard, if carried high enough, and out of the way of the plow; which has, in this cafe, nearly the fame poffeffion of the ground, as if no trees were planted.

In this cafe, however, the upper rails fhould be compaffing (bowing outward) equally to protect the tops from cattle, and to prevent the ftems from being chafed againft them. If thefe pofts were put down at the time of planting, fetting them within the planting holes, the roots would not be afterwards difturbed; and, by means of hay-ropes, the plants might be fteadied between the lower rails, without the trouble, or the danger of ftaking.

In this and every other cafe, unlefs the lower rails be placed very near to each other, the bottom of the ftem fhould be guarded againft fheep; which in winter, efpecially while fnow is upon the ground, will peel off the bark of the young trees; and, in a few hours. deftroy the whole plantation.

8. The AFTERMANAGEMENT of the STOCKS
confifts in *watering* them (if requifite) the firft
fummer: not, however, in the ordinary manner, by pouring fmall quantities, from time
to time, againft their ftems; but by throwing
as much at once as the hole will imbibe, into
the trench left within the outer ring, round
the fkirts of the hillocks: thus communicating
coolnefs, and a *lafting moifture*, rather than a
temporary wetnefs, to the immediate region of
the feeding fibers. And, fecondly, in *culti-
vating the hillocks*, fo far as to keep the furface
over the roots free from grafs and weeds, and
the fkirts of the hillocks in a loofe pulverous
ftate, to induce the roots to fpread horizontally on every fide.

In a plantation, whofe foil is kept in tillage,
lefs care is requifite than in a grafs-ground
plantation; in which the circles of broken furface, round the plants, fhould be kept hoed
as a garden; and the covering of foil be from
time to time carefully worked over with the
fpade. As the roots extend, *the circles fhould
be enlarged*, by frefh rings of fward being cut
off and inverted; in order to encourage, by
air and pafturage, their farther extenfion,

V. GRAFTING

V. GRAFTING. By old orchards, it appears that *whip-grafting* near the ground (letting the young plants remain in the nurfery until fit to be planted out,) has formerly been the prevailing practice. But, in this cafe, the planter muft take the nurferyman's word as to the forts; whereas he wifhes to be on a certainty. He likes to fee the grafts taken from a tree, whofe fruit he *knows**. Befides it is thought that whip-grafting, upon free ftocks, has injured fome of the more valuable varieties of fruit. Be this as it may, the practice, at prefent, is in difrepute.

The practice, which has lately prevailed, and which is ftill prevalent, is this: the ftocks, having ftood fome two three or four years in the plantation, until they have eftablifhed themfelves firmly in the foil, and have acquired a fulnefs of growth, are *cleft-grafted,* in the following extraordinary manner.

The entire head of the ftock is cut off!—horizontally, with a faw, about fix feet high:—
higher

---

* It is not enough to know the fort of fruit:—the ftate of the tree, from which the grafts are taken, ought likewife to be known. It is proper to fee that it be in *full health:* and of a *middle age.*

higher if the ftock will admit of it, and the
fort to be grafted be inclined to form hanging
boughs: while an upright clofe headed fort
may, it is thought, be grafted upon a ftill
lower ftock. The top of the ftump, being
cleft, the grafts are inferted, in the ufual manner; by men who go about the country, in the
grafting feaſon, for this purpoſe.

The method of *defending* the *grafts* put in,
in this manner, is perhaps peculiar to this
diftrict. They are inclofed within a kind of
openwork wicker baſket, made fomewhat in
the manner of the bottle-makers baſkets
(prickles) with fplit ozier twigs, about the
fize of the finger. When they are put upon
the ftock, they refemble the top of a tunnel;
about two feet high, and about one foot diameter at the top: they are, however, worked
flat; fomewhat in the form of the mount of a
lady's fan; much broader at the top than at
the bottom. The compoft ufed in grafting
having remained a few days to ftiffen, the bottom part of the guard is wrapt tight round the
ftem, immediately below the loam, upon
which it is bound with rope yarn; fixing it

in

in fuch a manner that the upper edge forms the largeft circle its length will allow.

Thefe wicker guards—provincially called "BRAIDS"—are moft ingenioufly adapted to this mode of grafting: they not only guard againft cattle, but prevent rooks and other birds from difturbing the grafts, before they be eftablifhed in the ftock ; and, what is of fingular advantage to fome forts of apple trees, they fet up a dropping head—giving the fhoots (which afterward become boughs) an upward tendency.

But this method of grafting has its difadvantage: in a fine young orchard, which has been grafted in this manner, in the vale of Glocefter, I obferved, that feveral of the trees are faulty in the crowns of the ftems, which are now eight or nine inches diameter. The defeдt is owing to one of the grafts having mifcarried, by which means a lodgement being made for water, a decay of that fide of the ftump of the ftock has taken place ; creating a fore, which the furviving graft has not been able to heal ; there being now holes nearly large enough to admit the hand. almoft to the

center

center of the ſtem: a premature decay of the tree muſt be the inevitable conſequence.

In Herefordſhire, I ſaw another orchard, (which has been planted in the ſame manner, and which has got about the ſame growth), in which the trees *cleave in the crowns* ; both grafts having in this caſe ſucceeded. The wind having ſplit ſome of them, and others being in danger of ſharing the ſame fate, the judicious occupier of this orchard has ſecured them with iron bolts ; put through the crowns ; having a broad head at one end, and a long iron pin or key at the other. The heads are already over grown, and ſome of the keys nearly buried*.

By letting the ſtocks remain until they be large enough *to be grafted in the boughs*; namely until the trained boughs be about an inch in diameter ; thoſe evils are avoided: the grafting becomes more certain ; there being more chances of ſuccefs ; and the trees, by forming their ramifications in the natural way, are much leſs liable to be torn to pieces by the winds. Some time, it is true, may ſeem to be

---

This, I have ſince learnt, is not an unuſual expedient

be loft; the trees certainly will not come fo foon to *bear*; but it is highly probable, that they will begin to bear a *burden* of fruit fooner, and will, it is much more than probable, continue to bear longer, than trees *grafted in the ftock*.

VI. The AFTERMANAGEMENT OF ORCHARDS. This divides into

The management of the ground,

The management of the trees.

1. The GROUND. It has been already mentioned, that, in Herefordfhire, the foil of orchards is generally kept under tillage;—in Glocefterfhire, in grafs. Not, however, I apprehend, fo much in purfuance of different principles in the managing of orchards; as from the circumftances of Herefordfhire being an *arable*, Glocefterfhire a *grafsland* country.

Either practice has its difadvantage. Fruit trees, when fully grown, efpecially if they are of a fpreading growth, and are fuffered to form drooping branches,—are very injurious to *arable* crops: their roots, their drip, and their fhadows are deftructive, not to corn only, but

but to clover and to turneps*: befides being, under thefe circumftances, ftill farther injurious, by preventing a free circulation of air; and in being in the way of the plow teams; which, when the trees are loaded with leaves and fruit, can frequently with difficulty *creep* under them !

It is obfervable, however, that *tillage* is favorable to the trees; efpecially to the growth of young trees. While in *grafs* grounds (under ordinary management) their progrefs is comparatively flow; for want of the earth's being ftirred about their roots; and by being injured by the grazing ftock; efpecially lowheaded, drooping trees.

After the trees begin to bear, ftock are equally inconvenient; in a fruit ground. Cattle not only deftroy all the fruit within their reach; but the fruit is dangerous to the cattle; by being liable to lodge in their throats, in the manner of fmall turneps. In the fruit feafon, efpecially in windy weather, the

---

* I have obferved, in a fruit ground, in which a remarkably fine crop of young clover was rifing, that, under the *drip* of the trees, there was not a plant ! A piece of turneps I have feen *dotted* in nearly the fame manner.

the cows are frequently obliged to be kept out
of their grounds, at a time, perhaps, when
the grafs is wanted.   Prudent men, however,
endeavour to provide againſt this inconveniency, by eating the fruit grounds bare, before
the gathering ſeaſon: and every prudent man
ought to keep the boughs out of their reach;
that no injury may be ſuſtained, previous to
that ſeaſon; as well as to give air and ſun-
beams to his grafs.

From theſe circumſtances we may conclude, that, in ſituations, in which fruit
grounds can with propriety and conveniency
be kept either in tillage or in grafs, they
ought, while the trees are young, to be kept
under the plow; and that, when the trees become particularly injurious to the arable crops,
the ground ought to be converted to a ſtate of
grafs.

In the deep-ſoiled diſtrict about Dymmock
and Marcle, where the whole country may be
ſaid to be a foreſt of fruit trees,—the occupiers
of fruit grounds, experiencing the evil of trees,
in arable lands, are planting in their grafs
grounds.   This, however, appears to be a
wrong principle.   Let them lay their old
orchards

orchards to grafs : and, if they plant, break
up their young orchards to arable ; this will
be changing the courfe of hufbandry, and be
at once beneficial to the land and the trees.

In the Bromyard quarter of Herefordfhire,
where confiderable quantities of hops are
raifed, it is common to plant young fruit trees
in the hop grounds. The trees, while young,
do little injury to the hops ; while the manuring and cultivation of the hop grounds is
highly beneficial to the young trees. Before
they acquire an injurious fize, the grounds
are worn out for hops, and returned to the
common courfe of hufbandry.

2. THE MANAGEMENT OF THE TREES. If
we view the common practice of the diftrict
throughout, we may fafely conclude, that,
after the trees are out of danger of being
thrown down by cattle, no attention whatever
is paid to them, other than that of collecting
the fruit, when they happen to " hit."

Water boughs are feen dangling, as bell
ropes, perhaps to the ground: while the upper
part of their heads are loaded with wood ; as
impervious to the fun and air as the heads of
pollard oaks, or neglected goofeberry bufhes ;
with,

with, perhaps, an additional burden of mifletoe and mofs to bear.

Indolence and falfe economy are, no doubt, the *principles*, on which this flovenly conduct is purfued. The improvident occupiers of thofe neglected orchards, unmindful of the damage they annually fuftain by the encumbrance of the trees, refufe to beftow a little leifure time, or lay out a few fhillings, to render them productive !

This fhameful management, however, is not univerfal. There are orchards, in every quarter of the diftrict, which appear to have fome little attention paid them ; and fome few, which are in a degree of keeping, equal to the Kentifh orchards.

By taking a view of the NATURAL ENEMIES of fruit trees, we fhall be the better able to judge of the art requifite to their prefervation.

The enemies of the fruit trees under notice are

   A redundancy of wood
   The mifsletoe
   Mofs
   Spring frofts
   Blights

Infects

An excefs of fruit

Old age.

Some of them are beyond human reach; but moft of them are within the controul of art.

A REDUNDANCY OF WOOD is the caufe of numerous evils. The roots, or rather the paf- turage, which fupports them, is exhaufted un- profitably; the bearing wood robbed of part of its fuftinence; and the natural life of the tree unneceffarily fhortened: while the fuperfluous wood, which is the caufe of this mifchief, places the tree in perpetual danger, by giving the winds additional power over it; and is in- jurious to the bearing wood, by retaining the damps, and preventing a due circulation of air.

The underhanging boughs weigh down, efpecially when loaded with leaves, the fruit- bearing branches they are preying upon; giv- ing them a drooping habit; or at leaft prevent- ing their taking, as they ought and otherwife would, an afcending direction; while thofe, which grow within the head, are equally in- jurious

jurious in croſſing and chafing the profitable branches.

The outer ſurface, only, is able to mature fruit properly. Every inward and every un-derling branch ought therefore to be removed: and, in ſome caſes, part of thoſe, which reach the ſurface, might, with propriety, be taken out; to give due health and vigour to thoſe which were left. It is no uncommon ſight to ſee trees, in this diſtrict, with two or three tires of boughs preſſing down hard one upon another; with their twigs ſo intimately inter-woven, that, even when the leaves are off, a ſmallbird can ſcarcely creep in among them. Trees, thus neglected, acquire, through a want of due ventilation and *exerciſe*, a runty, ſtinted habit; and the fruit they bear becomes of a crude inferior quality.

The great object of the fruit farmer is to produce a CROP EVERY YEAR: and nothing is more likely to obtain it than keeping his trees in perfect health, and endeavouring to prevent their bearing beyond their ſtrength, in a ge-neral fruit year.

The MISLETOE is, in this country, a fatal enemy to the apple tree. The native crab
tree

tree is frequently killed by it; and apple-trees too often injured; and this, notwithftanding it is eafily overcome, and is applicable to a profitable purpofe; fheep affecting it as they do ivy: yet fuch is the power of indolence, and fuch the plentifulnefs of hay in this country, that a confiderable portion of the produce, of many orchards, is cut off by this fingular plant.

The ordinary method of clearing trees from it is to pull it out with hooks, in frofty weather, when being brittle, it readily breaks off from the branches.

Moss is chiefly, perhaps, owing to the nature of the foil, and cannot be altogether prevented; but it may in moft cafes be checked, and its evil effect in a great meafure avoided. In Kent, there are men who make a bufinefs of cleaning orchard trees; being paid fo much a tree, or fo much for the orchard, according to the ftate of foulnefs.

In Herefordfhire, I faw feveral orchards, in which the trees were almoft entirely fubdued by this vegetable vermin. Some of the trees, perhaps, with only one bough left alive, and others entirely killed; yet fuffered

to

to remain an encumbrance to the ground, and a difgrace to the country !

What avails the number of trees, if they are not productive ? It is healthy bearing trees, which fill the " drink houfe" and fend a furplus to market. Their encumbrance on the foil is nearly the fame, whether they are barren or fruitful; and it may be a moot point, whether, even many of thofe which are productive, much more than pay for their encumbrance: how ridiculous, then, to fpare any reafonable expence in preferving them in a ftate of health and productivenefs ; or to fuffer thofe to encumber the foil, which are paft recovery.

Spring frosts are an enemy againft which, perhaps, it is moft difficult to guard orchard trees. *Dry frofts* are obferved to have no other effects than keeping the bloffoms back ; confequently, are frequently ferviceable to fruit trees. But " *wet frofts*",—namely frofts after rain or a foggy air, and before the trees have had time to dry,—are very injurious, even to the buds. An inftance is mentioned in which a flying hazy fhower, in the evening, was fucceeded by a fmart froft: that fide of the

U 3   trees,

trees, againſt which the haze drove, was entirely cut off; while the oppoſite ſide, which
had eſcaped the moiſture, likewiſe eſcaped the
effect of the froſt.

Much, however, may depend on the
ſtrength of the bloſſoms. The ſpring of this
year (1788) had its froſts; and all hope of fruit
was more than once given up; yet for quantity
and quality, taken jointly, there has ſeldom,
perhaps, been ſo favorable a fruit year. But
this year, the buds formed and the bloſſoms
broke forth with unuſual vigour; and were
enabled, in their own ſtrength, to ſet common enemies at defiance. On the contrary,
the preceding ſpring, many of the bloſſoms
ſickened in the bud; and thoſe which opened
were weak and languid:—the conſequence
was, in the inſtances I obſerved, ſcarcely an
apple ſucceeded.

The aſſiſtance, therefore, required from
art, in this caſe, is, by keeping the trees in a
healthful vigorous ſtate, to enable them to
throw out a ſtrength of bud and bloſſom;
and, by keeping them thin of wood, to give
them an opportunity of drying quickly, before
the froſt ſet in.

The

The term BLIGHT is as common and as
vague, in this as in other diftricts.   " Black
blighting winds" are talked of everywhere;
but no definite idea is anywhere affixed to the
expreffion.   That corn and fruit become unproductive without any vifible caufe; and
that fruit trees are liable to be infected with
infects, are certainly facts.   But whether the
infects be the caufe or the effects of blights
does not feem to be yet fettled.

This year, if the alarm from fpring frofts
was great, that from black blighting winds
was terrible.   Yet the confequence is an excefs of fruit.   The caufe appears to me evident in the acquired ftrength of the trees: they
had not borne fruit during four years.   The
" great hit", in 1784, had exhaufted them.
They were unable to withftand the attack of
common enemies.   But having, by three years
reft, fully recovered their ftrength and vigour,
they, this year, fet the fame black blighting
winds at defiance, which, next year, may
render them altogether unfruitful.

Two bearing years feldom come together.
Next year, however, will have more than a
fair chance to fet this rule afide, as the inter-

val of reft has been unufually long. A full
fruitage every fecond or third year is all that
is expected.

Are we to fuppofe, from thefe circumftances, that becaufe infects are abundant one
year, they become few in number the year
enfuing ? Or, on the contrary, that becaufe
they were few in number this year, they fhall
be numerous the next ? It would be much
more reafonable to infer, that, the trees having been exhaufted the preceding year, by an
exceffive burden of fruit, are not, without
fome extraordinary circumftances, able to
throw out the fucceeding feafon a fufficient
ftrength of bloffom, to withftand the natural
enemies, with which they are every year af-
failed: or if, through extraordinary circumftances, they fhould throw out fufficient
blow, that the fruit, for want of a due fupply of fuftinence, drops abortively from the
boughs.

Hence, *perhaps*, with refpect to blights,
all the affiftance which art can render is, to
keep the trees in a ftate of healthfulnefs ; and
prevent, as much as poffible, an excefs of
fruit.

INSECTS

INSECTS are not only hurtful to the bloſſoms and the leaves, but the larger ſpecies, are de-ſtructive of the fruit;—eſpecially of pears. In 1783, a ſcarce year of fruit, the *waſps*, which were that year particularly abundant, deſtroyed a great ſhare of the pears, that were produced. In a fruit-liquor country, it might be prudent to ſet a price on the female waſps in the ſpring; by which means the number of neſts might be conſiderably leſ-ſened.

AN EXCESS OF FRUIT has ſeveral injurious effects :—it ſtints the growth of young trees ; and renders trees in general barren for two or three years afterward ; while the weight of the fruit is frequently fatal. I have this year ſeen numberleſs inſtances, in which the main branches of trees have been ſplit off, ſolely by the weight of fruit; and very many, in which the entire tree had ſunk under the weight of its burden.

The ordinary guards, againſt the miſchiev-ous effect of an exceſs of fruit, are props—forked poles—ſet under the boughs.—Twenty

of

of thefe props are fometimes employed in fupporting the branches of one tree *.

It would be difficult to defcribe the burden, which many trees, this year, had to bear. Notwithftanding the trees were as full of wood as neglect could fill them, every twig, within and without, was loaded with fruit. Of trees of luxuriant growth, the moft upright fhoots, even to the fummit, were rendered pendant with the weight of their produce, hanging down on every fide as ftrings of onions; the fruit appearing, to the diftant eye, to cover the entire furface of the tree. I have no-whereelfe feen fruit trees bear fuch extraordinary burdens.

The means of preventing, as much as may be, the evil confequences of an inordinate quantity of fruit, in any one year, is to GRAFT IN THE BOUGHS †; and, when the trees are fully

---

* Thefe, however, are chiefly ufed in clofe orchards; where the lower boughs, being lefs broken by cattle, are longer and more luxuriant than they are in cowgrounds, where props cannot conveniently be ufed.

† In moft of the inftances of fracture, I obferved, that the tops fuffer by halves. One half being fplit off this year, or this hit, the fractured part decays, and the next year,

fully grown, to THIN THE BEARING BRANCHES; thereby endeavouring, like the gardener, to grow fruit every year *.

OLD AGE cannot be prevented; but the natural life of fruit trees may, no doubt, be protracted, by proper management. Stocks of the native crab, grafted in the boughs, is, in this intention, the moft eligible bafis. As taking off the underling and croffing boughs while growing, keeping the head within due bounds, and leffening the quantity of bearing wood when the heads are fully grown, are the moft likely means to give a lafting fuperftructure.

The ftage of decline will neverthelefs arrive, and a deficiency in fruitfulnefs will long precede the general decay.

During

---

or the next hit, the remaining half breaks off. This is evidently the effect of *grafting in the ftock*. The head is formed jointly by the two grafts, which have no other natural bond or connexion, than the ordinary grain of the ftem to hold them in union.

* Young trees, which have been *whipgrafted*, planted out while weak in the ftem, and had afterward fhot freely, I have feen bowing with their heads to the ground, with the weight of fruit, which had been injudicioufly fuffered to mature upon them.

During the decline of fruitfulnefs, there is
a ftage, in which the the fruit no longer re-
pays the encumbrance, which the ground is
fubjected to by the tree. Neverthelefs, we
fee trees ftanding, a burden to the foil, in
every ftage of decay. But how injudicious,
in fuch a cafe, is the conduct of their occupiers. If it be a difputable point, whether
trees in full fruit be beneficial to a farmer, he
may fafely conclude, that, after their fruitfulnefs has in great part declined, they become
injurious to him ; and if the occupier, through
friendfhip from long acquaintance, or grati-
tude arifing from the many comfortable
draughts they have afforded him, cannot mufter up refolution to remove them,—thofe who
have the management of the eftate fhould fee
them taken down, while the wood remains
in a valuable ftate. And not fuffer them,
while the wood is wafting, to remain an encumbrance to the eftate.

In the vale of Glocefter, I faw an inftance
of fome healthy, bearing *apple trees*, which
now wear the fecond tops to the fame ftems.
The firft tops, being worn out, were cut off,
and the ftumps faw-grafted. In orchards,

about

about a houſe, this expedient may frequently be eligible.

It is here obſervable that the ſame judicious manager, in whoſe practice I ſaw this inſtance of renewing the heads of trees, could never raiſe young trees with any ſucceſs, in an old orchard ground. If, in a cloſe orchard, convenient to an habitation in a country where fruit is ſcarce, ſuch an attempt ſhould be made, the ſpecies of fruit ought certainly to be changed; as from apples to pears; or pears to apples.

It is likewiſe obſervable, in this place, that pear trees, eſpecially in a ſtrong deep ſoil, are of much longer duration than apple trees; outliving, it is ſaid, two or three generations; conſequently the two ſpecies ought never to be mixed together in the ſame fruit ground.

GENERAL OBSERVATION. Suppoſing the ground to have been in graſs ſince the trees firſt acquired their growth, it will, on their removal, be ready for a change of management. The larger roots being removed, ſuffer the ground to remain in graſs, until the ſmaller roots be decayed; and then break it up for a courſe of arable crops; in order to

aſſimulate

aſſimilate the roots with the ſoil, and do away the *ſourneſs* of ſward which low-ſpreading trees, as thoſe of fruit, will always produce.

Thus, conſidering FRUIT TREES as a CROP IN HUSBANDRY, the GENERAL MANAGEMENT appears to be this. Plant upon a recently broken-up, worn-out ſward. Keep the ſoil under a ſtate of arable management, until the trees be well grown: then, lay it down to graſs; and let it remain, in ſward, until the trees be removed, and their roots be decayed; when it will again require a courſe of arable management.

FRUIT

FRUIT LIQUOR.

THE SPECIES of FRUIT LIQUOR made in this diftrict are

Cider—the produce of apples alone.

Perry—that of pears alone.

" Cider"—produced from apples and pears jointly; and

" Cider"—made from the common wild crab, and the richer fweeter kinds of early pears.

The two laft fpecies, and much of the two firft, are ufed, inftead of malt liquor, as " family drink": the quantity of *fale* liquor, except on the larger plantations, being fmall, in proportion to that which is confumed in the country.

Thus, farmers, in general, confidering fruit liquor as the beverage of their fervants and workpeople, have no ftimulus toward excellency in the art. If it is but " zeyder"

and

and has body enough to keep ; no matter for
the richnefs and flavor. The rougher it is,
the further it will go ; and the more accept-
able cuftom has rendered it, not to the workmen only, but to their mafters : the cider
which is drank, in this, and all the cider countries, with fo much avidity and in fuch quantity,
is a very different liquor to that which is
drank in the reft of the kingdom. A palate
accuftomed to " fweet cider", would judge
the " rough cider" of the farm houfes, to be a
mixture of vinegar and water, with a little diffolved allum to give it a roughnefs.

Men in general, however, whofe palates are
fet to rough cider, confider the common fweet
fort as an effeminate beverage ; and rough
cider, properly manufactured, is probably
the more generous liquor ; being deemed
more wholefome, to habits in general, than
fweet cider :—even when genuine. That
which is drank, in the kingdom at large, is
too frequently adulterated. The " ciderman"
cannot afford to lofe a hogfhead : if it will not
do, it muft be " *doctored*" : or if found, it may
not be fweet enough for the palate of his cuftomers ; nor high enough coloured to pleafe
the

the eye; but the requifite colour and fweet-nefs, he finds, are eafily communicated.

The great art, however, in manufacturing fruit liquors, whether cider or perry, is that of gratifying the palate and the eye with the juices of the fruit alone. And although farmers in general, more particularly the lower clafs, are very deficient in the management of their liquors,—there are men, efpecially among the more fubftantial yeomanry, and the principal farmers who ferment their own liquors for fale, that are far advanced on the line of right management.

Unfortunately, however, thefe men, priding themfelves, refpectively, on the fuperiority of their liquor (more perhaps than on any other produce of their eftates) become jealous of their art; and are not fufficiently communicative with each other. Hence the difference in their feveral practices; and hence the prefent imperfection of the art. For although each man may produce good liquor, in his turn, no one, I believe, pretends to *uniform fuccefs*;—to produce liquor of the firft quality, *with certainty*.

From this clafs of men, chiefly, I have endeavoured to obtain information. I have feen
the practice, in whole or in part, of many individuals ; and have had the fentiments of
many more on the fubject: which, at the fame
time I went over the diftrict (October 1788)
was the prevailing topic of converfation ; and,
it is not probable, that any material circumftance, relating to it, fhould have efcaped
me.

The following detail, however, muft not
be confidered, merely, as the produce of an
EXCURSION. For, although the year 1783 was
not a general fruit year, there was a fufficiency
of liquor made, to enable me to form a gene-
neral idea of its manufacture. And although
the knowledge, then acquired, was not fufficient to fill my regifter completely in every
part, it was enough to enable me to make a
complete ANALYSIS of the fubject : and, during the fummer of 1788, I ftill kept adding
to my collection.

Therefore, *previous* to the excurfion in
HEREFORDSHIRE, my regifter was nearly full,
and *the deficiencies afcertained.* Confequently,
by feeing, there, the practice repeated on a
large

large fcale, and by converfing freely with profeffional men on the fubject, the deficiencies
were filled up, the facts, previoufly acquired,
proved, and the errors, of courfe, corrected.
Befide, fince my return, and after I had digefted the information acquired, I have had
an opportunity of feeing the different ftages
of the art, as practifed by a *profeffional* man,
whofe liquors are in the very firft eftimation.

To adapt a regifter of this art to the public
eye, and to render it as clear, yet full, as the
nature of it requires, it will be neceffary to
defcribe, diftinctly and minutely, its feveral
ftages. And, previous to this detail of the
art itfelf, it will be proper to take a view of
its requifite APPARATUS.

A MILL HOUSE, on an orchard farm, is as
neceffary as a barn. It is generally one end
of an out building : or, perhaps, an open fhed,
under which ftraw or fmall implements are
occafionally laid up.

The fmalleft dimenfions, to render it any
way convenient, are twenty four feet by twenty ; with a floor thrown over it, at feven feet
high ; with a door in the middle of the front,
and a window oppofite; with the mill on one

fide, the prefs on the other fide, of the window; as much room being left in front, towards the door, for fruit and utenfils—
as the nature of the mill and the prefs will
allow.

The MILL confifts of a ftone wheel—provincially a "runner"—fomewhat in the fhape
of a corn millftone—running on its edge in a
circular ftone trough—- provincially—- the
"chace."

The fize of the runner varies from two and
a half to four and a half feet diameter, and
from nine to twelve inches in thicknefs; which,
in general, is even like that of a grindftone:
not varying like that of a millftone: the weight
one or two tons.

The bottom of the chace is fomewhat wider
than the runner, that this may run freely.—
The inner fide rifes perpendicularly, but the
outer fide fpreads, fo as to make the top of
the trough fome fix or eight inches wider than
the bottom;—to give freedom to the runner,
and room to fcatter in the fruit, ftir it up while
grinding, and take out the ground matter.
The depthnine or ten inches.

The

The outer rim of the trough is three or four inches wide, and the diameter of the inner circle, which the trough circumfcribes, from four and a half to five feet; according to the fize of the mill *.

The entire bed of a middle-fized mill is about nine feet—fome ten—fome few twelve feet diameter : the whole being compofed of two, three, or four ftones, cramped together as one; and worked, or at leaft finifhed, after they are cramped together.

The beft ftones are raifed in the Foreft of Dean. They are moftly a dark reddifh gritftone—(noncalcarious)—working with fufficient freedom, yet fufficiently hard, for this intention. The bed of the mill is formed, and the trough partly hollowed, at the quarry; leaving a few inches at the edge of each ftone, uncut out, as a bond to prevent its breaking

in

* This is fometimes raifed by a table of thick plank fixed upon the ftone; with a curb of wood, leffening to an angle, fixed upon the circumference of the trough; making the whole depth of the trough about equal to its width at the bottom. This leffens the quantity of the ftone; and the plank upon the center anfwers a purpofe hereafter to be noticed.

in carriage. Much depends on the quality of
the ftone. It ought not to be calcarious—in
whole or in part—as the acid of the liquor
would corrode it. Some of the Herefordſhire
ftones have calcarious pebbles in them, which
being of courfe diffolved, leave holes in the
ftone. Nor ſhould it be fuch as will communicate a difagreeable tinge to the liquor. A
clean-grained grindftone girt is the fitteft for
this purpofe.

The runner is moved by means of an axle
paffing through the center ; with a long arm,
reaching without the bed of the mill, for a
horfe to draw by*; and with a fhort one paffing to an upright fwivel, turning upon a pivot, in the center of the ftone ; and fteadied
at the top, by entering a bearing of the floor,
above. An iron bolt, with a large head, paffes through an eye, in the lower part of the
fwivel, into the end of the inner arm of the
axis

---

* The horfe moftly draws by traces ; I faw no inſtance of
the contrary : this, however, is an error : the acting point
of draught; the horfe's fhoulder; ought for various reafons to be applied immediately at the end of the arm of the
axis ; not two or three yards before it : perhaps, of a fmall
mill, near one fourth its circumference !

axis. Thus the requifite double motion is obtained, and the ftone kept perfectly upright (which it ought to be) with great fimplicity, and without ftrefs to any part of the machine *.

On the inner arm of the axis, about a foot from the runner, is fixed (or ought to be, though it is frequently wanting) a cogged wheel working in a circle of cogs—fixed upon the bed of the mill†. The ufe of thefe wheels is to prevent the runner from fliding; to which it is liable, when the mill is full; the matter, when nearly ground, rifing up in a body before the ftone. Befides, by affifting the rotatory motion of the ftone, it renders the work more eafy to the horfe. Thefe wheels require to be made with great exactnefs; and in a country, where carpenters are unaccuftomed

---

* This is the ordinary method of hanging the runner. There is a more complex way of doing it; but I fee no advantage arifing from it. There are fome few mills, it feems, with two runners, one oppofite the other.

† The diameter of the wheel is determined by the height of the axis above the bed of the mill. The diameter of the ring of cogs, by the diftance of the wheel from the center of motion.

tomed to them, a mill wright fhould be employed in fixing them.

The fituation of the mill is fuch as to leave
a horfe path, about three feet wide, between
the bed and the walls; fo that a moderate-
fized mill, with its horfe path, takes up a
fpace of fourteen or fifteen feet every way.

THE PRESS is fituated, as near the horfe
path, as conveniency will allow, for the more
eafy conveyance of the ground materials, from
the mill to the prefs.

The principle of the prefs is that of the
packing prefs and the common napkin prefs;
a fkrew working within a fquare frame.

The fizes of preffes are various. The bed,
or bottom, is about five feet fquare, of ftrong
plank, or of ftone, placed on fleepers, about
a foot from the ground floor; or raifed on
mafon's work, to two or three feet high. On
each fide rifes a ftrong upright cheek, provincially a " fifter;" and acrofs the top (the
upper furface level with the chamber floor)
lies a nut, of dimenfions fuitable to the fize of
the fkrew, which is ufually about ten inches
in diameter. The foot of the fkrew is fquare,
with crofs holes for inferting a lever; or has a
wheel

wheel fixed round it for that purpofe. A finker—provincially the "bridge"—is hung beneath it, and fteadied by the cheeks, in the ufual manner.

The bed or floor of the prefs, which is now compofed entirely of wood, or of ftone*, has a channel cut a few inches within its outer edges, to catch the liquor as it is expreffed, and convey it to a lip, formed by a projection on that fide of the bed oppofite to the mill; under which lip a ftone trough, or wooden veffel, is funk within the ground, (when the bed is fixed low), to receive it.

The prefs is worked with levers of different lengths; firft, a fhort one; next, one of a moderate fize, by hand; and laftly, with a ftrong bar, eight or nine feet long, by means of a fpecies of capftone, provincially a "wind-lafs," an upright poft, about fix inches in diameter,

---

* Formerly it was ufually covered with lead; which, by being diffolved by the acid of the liquor, has probably been the caufe of much mifchief: neverthelefs, lead is ftill fuffered to remain about ciderpreffes. There is a public mill, at Newnham, whofe bed is entirely covered with lead; and I have feen others, whofe lips or fpouts, and, perhaps, a rim round the outer edge, are of that dangerous material.

diameter, with a pike or pivot at either end ; one of them being inferted in the ground floor, the other in a bearing of the chamber. From the upper part of this poft paffes a very ftrong rope, with an eye at the end to receive the end of the bar ; which has a crofs pin, or a fhoulder, a few inches from the end, to prevent the rope from flipping. In the lower part of the poft, about three feet from the ground, is one or more holes, for a lever or levers. By thefe means an exceffive purchafe is obtained.

The UTENSILS belonging to a millhoufe are few : the fruit is brought in carts or bafkets, and the liquor carried out in pails. The *haircloths*, which will be mentioned, are the principal addition to the mill and prefs.

The EXPENCE of fitting up a cidermill houfe depends on the fize and quality of the mill and prefs. One of a moderate fize, for a farm, may be furnifhed, completely, for twenty to twenty five pounds. One, on a fmall fcale, might be furnifhed for ten to fifteen pounds : much depending on the diftance of carriage of the ftone.

This

This expence is ufually borne by the land-lord.

A millhoufe fubftantially fitted up, will laft many years.   I have obferved a mill and prefs which, by the date upon them, have been fet up more than twenty years; yet they appear almoft as frefh as new.   Many of the old mills and preffes, which are feen, may, compared with thefe, feem to be a century old; or, the mills, more particularly, a greater age; and are probably the *original* mills of the farms they are upon.

The GENERAL SUBJECT naturally feparates into the following principal parts.

1. The fruit and its management.
2. Grinding, and the management of the ground fruit.
3. Preffing, and the management of the refidue.
4. Fermenting.
5. Correcting.
6. Laying up.
7. Bottling.
8. Markets.
9. Produce.

I. FRUIT

I. FRUIT. The particulars to be attended to in this firſt ſtage of the art are

    1. The time of gathering.
    2. The method of gathering.
    3. Maturing the fruit.
    4. Preparing it for the mill.
    5. Mixing different ſorts for liquor.

    1. TIME OF GATHERING. This is varied by the ſeaſon and the ſort of fruit. The *early pears* are fit for the mill, in September. This year (the ſeaſon early) there was not, in the middle of October, a ſquaſh pear left in the country for a ſpecimen.

But there are few *apples* ready for gathering, provincially " picking"—before Michaelmas; though the winds ſometimes throw them down, in quantity, before that time. And this year, the drink houſes having long been dry, apples were gathered by the time they were fully grown. Many trees were ſtripped, and their produce made into cider and drank, before Michaelmas.

For ſale cider, however, and for " keeping drink", they are ſuffered to hang upon the trees, until they be fully ripe. This year, (a forward ſeaſon), Herefordſhire was in the height

height of fruit picking, the latter end of October. In the vale of Glocester, the stire apple, a somewhat early fruit, was much of it shook down, by the high winds of September; and many orchards were cleared of them before Michaelmas. But the middle of October, in a common season, is esteemed the time of gathering the stire apple.

The *criterion of a due degree of ripeness*, is that of the fruit's falling spontaneously from the tree. Nature is the best judge of this crisis. No art has yet been discovered to mature unripe fruit, in any way equal to nature's process. Fruit, in all human probability, does not quit the tree (in an undisturbed state) until it has received its full complement of nourishment. But having obtained this (or presently afterward) it is probable, that the fruits, under consideration, are suffered to disengage themselves by their own specific gravity: consequently, to force them away, before that period, is defrauding them, in all human probability, of their most valuable particles.

The harvesting of fruit is widely different, in this respect, from the harvesting of grain; which has the entire plant to feed it, after its

separation

feparation from the foil; while fruit, after it is fevered from the tree, is cut off from all poffibility of a further fupply of nourifhment; and although it may have reached its wonted fize, fome of its more *effential* particles are, it is abundantly evident, left behind in the tree.

Some of the later-ripe fruits, however, will hang on, until they be in danger of being caught in the frofts; which, if fevere and lafting, injure it materially for the purpofe of liquor. In the great fruitage of 1784—a very confiderable part of the beft fruits were in a manner loft by the frofts. The buyers of fale liquors fixt their price, for cider, fo very low—that the farmers, obftinately, fuffered the apples to be frozen on the trees, or in heaps if collected, rather than accept of the price they were offered. The confequence proved difadvantageous to the buyers, as well as the farmers; they being afterwards obliged to nearly double the price, to thofe who had worked their fruit, or had faved it from the froft *.

2. METHOD

---

* With refpect to injury by FROST, however, fome thing may depend on the nature of the fruit. Weak *watery fruit*

2. METHOD OF GATHERING. The ordinary method which I have feen ufed, and which is, I believe, the prevailing practice of the country,—is to fend men with long flender poles or rods,—provincially " polting lugs", to beat the trees; and women, with bafkets, to pick up the fruit. I have feen two men and eight women, thus employed, as a fet; with an ox wain, and a boy to drive it, to receive the apples as they were collected; *clearing the trees as they went.*

But this is contrary to the foregoing principles. The apples of the fame tree differ, perhaps many days, perhaps fome weeks, in their times of ripening; owing to afpect, expofure, and perhaps other caufes which we are unacquainted with. Confequently, fome part of the natural richnefs and flavor of the fruit is cut off fo effectually, that no art can retrieve it: brown fugar and brandy are but mean fubftitutes.

Nor

fruit, probably, receives the moft injury. There is an inftance related of liquor, of the very firft quality, being made from GOLDEN PIPPINS, after they had been frozen as hard as ice.

Nor may the lofs of the richnefs, ftrength, flavor and colour, which are left behind in the tree, be the only evil of the ordinary method of gathering fruit for cider. Every thing depends on the vinous fermentation, which the liquor has to pafs through. If this be interrupted, or rendered complex, by a mixture of ripe and unripe fruits, and the liquor be not, in the firft inftance, fufficiently purged from its feculencies, it may be difficult, afterward, to effect the purgation, without injury to the liquor. Brimftone and bullock's blood may alleviate, but cannot altogether remedy the evil.

Some few men, on thefe principles, or in purfuance of the dictates of their own experience, go over their fruit trees twice: once, when the fpontaneous fall begins to take place, *with a hook*, leaving fuch of the fruit to mature, as will not quit the boughs, with a gentle agitation. And a fecond time, when thofe are fufficiently ripened, or winter is likely to fet in, *with the polting lugs*; finally clearing the trees.

If art may, with propriety, be ufed, in this ftage of the bufinefs, thefe appear to be the moft rational means of applying it.

3. Maturing

3. MATURING GATHERED FRUIT. By way of correcting the crudity of the unripe fruit, which in the common practice has been forced from the trees, in the way that has been mentioned,—the whole is laid together in large heaps, in the open air, *expofed to the weather*, until the ripeſt,—that is to ſay the richeſt and fineſt of the fruit,—is beginning to rot. Thus deſtroying, by an injudicious application of art, the natural perfection of the whole.*

Such, at leaſt, is the ordinary management of fruit; under which management three-fourths, or perhaps a much greater proportion, of the cider produced in the diſtrict, is made.

There are men, however, aware of the impropriety of the practice; but they differ in their ideas on the means of rectifying it. One is of opinion, that the ripe fruit, having dropped
                                    ſpontaneouſly

* In paſſing through the country, in the wane of the gathering ſeaſon, the farm houſes are ſeen ſurrounded with heaps of fruit; expoſed not only to the weather; but, of courſe, to night-robbers! A ſtriking ſight;—to thoſe who are ſtrangers to it.

fpontaneoufly, or having been fhook down by
a gentle agitation of the boughs, fhould lie ten
days under the trees, as it falls ; and then be
gathered, and carried immediately to the mill;
without any further maturation. And, in purfuance of this idea, fome few orchards, and
even cultivated grounds, are feen with fruit
lying under the trees, fo thick, that the foot
could not well be fet down among it.

Others object to this practice ; as expofing
the fruit; not only to pigs and other live
ftock*; but to the weather: alleging that
rain and dews are injurious to fruit after it has
quitted the trees.

Their opinion is, that it ought to drop ripe
from the tree ;—to be picked up while dry ;
and to be kept dry, under cover, fome time
afterward to mature ; and, fome will have it,
to take a degree of *heat*: while others object
violently againft its heating ; confequently
againft lofts ; thinking, that it cannot be kept
too

---

* In a ground of this kind I have obferved a fow fo much
fatiated with highly flavored fruit, as to fmell, perhaps, at
ten mellow apples, before fhe found one to her tooth !
Sheep, 1 have obferved, eat fruit with avidity. Deer are
ftill more partial to it.

too cool, in the open air; and that rain water is not injurious to it.

Reafon and common fenfe, however, object to this. All vegetable fubftances, after they are fevered from the foil, lofe their flavor, at leaft, in being expofed to the weather. With regard to this, apples, as hay and corn, ought, no doubt, to be harvefted dry.

Upon the whole, we may conclude, that, in ftrictnefs of management, fruit ought to drop fpontaneoufly from the tree; to be collected while perfectly dry; and to be laid up, under cover, fpread abroad of fuch a thicknefs as to prevent any injurious degree of heat. It is the opinion of thofe, who are beft able to judge of this matter, and whofe practice accord with their opinion, that, in a room, fruit ought not to lie more than ten inches thick; and that in a fruit-loft a thorough air fhould be preferved.

FRUIT LOFTS. Every mill houfe fhould have a fruit chamber over it; with a trap door to lower the fruit down into the mill houfe.

Since this idea ftruck me, I have feen an inftance, in which it is executed, in a moft

Y 2   convenient

convenient manner. The valve is over the
bed of the mill, and is furnished with a cloth
spout or tunnel, reaching down to the chace;
in which the fruit may, of course, be scattered
at pleasure.

No straw is used in the lofts. Sometimes
the fruit is *turned*. But this, I believe, is not
a common practice.

The *due degree of maturation of fruit* for liquor is, however, a subject, about which
men, even in this district, differ much in
their ideas. The prevailing practice (as has
been intimated) is to let it lie, in heaps, until
the ripest begin to rot, or are actually rotten.
But this is wasting the best of the fruit; and
is by no means an accurate criterion. Some
shake the fruit and judge by the rattling of the
kernels: others cut it through the middle and
judge by their blackness. But none of these
appear to be a proper test. It is not the state
of the *kernels*, but of the *flesh*; not of a few
individuals, but of the major part of the prime
fruit; which renders the collective body fit or
unfit to be sent to mill. It is true, a few individuals, or the kernels of the middle-ripe fruit
may be some guide to the state of the flesh of
the

the majority; but why confult a criterion
when the fubject itfelf is prefent ?   The moft
rational teft of the ripenefs of fruit, which I
have met with, is that of the flefh having acquired fuch a degree of *mellownefs*,—its texture fuch a degree of tendernefs,—as to yield
to moderate preffure.   Thus when the knuc-
kle, or the end of the thumb can, with moderate exertion, be forced into the pulp of the
fruit, it is deemed in a fit ftate for grinding.
Or, in lefs practical terms, the proper ftate of
maturation is when the flefh has acquired its
higheft degree of richnefs, and the kernels
their higheft degree of flavor; and while the
rind yet retains its brightnefs and pungency.

4. PREPARING FRUIT FOR THE MILL.
But although the right management of the
fruit may appear to be pretty accurately underftood; and not difficult to be executed;
yet, in practice, ripe and unripe fruit are
not to be kept feparate fo eafily as theory
may fuggeft.   It is tedious to wait the ripening of every apple, and to collect every apple
as it drops.   Befides, high winds do not always make the requifite diftinction: the unripe and thofe which are fufficiently matured

for

for gathering, are frequently thrown down together: and if the hook be ufed the effect is
in fome degree fimilar.

In practice, therefore, there is only one
method of avoiding a mixture of fruit:—that
of SEPARATING IT BY HAND ; either when it is
laid up ; or at the time of fending it to the
mill. And it is more than probable, that
this is one of the grand fecrets of cidermak-
ing ; by which thofe who excel in the art are
monopolizing the credit of it. It is matter
of aftonifhment, however, feeing the obviouf-
nefs of its utility, that it fhould not long ago
have been adopted in common practice.

Some extra trouble and expence is, no
doubt, incurred by this practice. But there
is no department of *manufacture,* which is not
attended with trouble and expence. If the
ware pay tenfold for it, the expence vanifhes,
and the trouble becomes a pleafurable employment. In the infancy of the woolen manufacture, for inftance, it is probable the entire fleece was carded, fpun, and woven together. But now the forting of wool is become an employment of no fmall importance.
And were the forting of apples for cider, once

to

to become the eftablifhed practice,—farmers would as foon think of fowing wheat and vetches together,—as of grinding unripe, ripe, and rotten fruit together in the cider mill. Yet all the *preparation*, which the apples receive in common practice, at prefent, is that of picking out the " black rotten"—which is generally known to give the liquor a difagreeable flavor: and, even this work, I underftand, is frequently done in a very imperfect manner.

There are, however, fome few individuals, who pay attention to this department of the art. In the practice of one man; a dealer, who manufactures his own liquor; more efpecially ftire cider; and whofe liquors are a proof of the excellency of his practice; I found the *brown* as well as the *black* rotten carefully picked out: even if part of an apple be tainted, the faulty part is cut out; the found part only being fuffered to go into the mill*. And in that of another fuperior manager, whofe practice may be faid to be nearly perfect†, not only the rotten, but the " crabbed"—that is, the

Y 4   fmall

---

* Mr. JONES, CIDERMERCHANT, in GLOCESTER, is the fuperior manager, whofe practice is here fpoken of.

† See page 253.

fmall crude underripe fruit—are picked out,
and thrown afide for family drink;--thus felect-
ing the prime fruit, in a proper ftate of maturation, to be ground, alone, for liquor of the
firft quality.

5. MIXING FRUITS FOR LIQUOR. In the ordinary practice, no ftudied compofition or fe-
lection of forts is made. The different kinds
are mixed, indifcriminately, or without any
other diftinction than that of keeping the early
and the late fruits feparate, and the " old
fruits" diftinct. A judicious affortment of
fruits is, however, fpoken of as highly beneficial to liquor; but I have met with nothing,
in practice, that eftablifhes the pofition: and
it is a well eftablifhed fact, that the finer liquors are made from felect fruits. Neverthelefs, it is more than probable, that the
liquor of ordinary fruits may be improved by
a judicious mixture; and, to thofe who have
much ordinary fruit in their plantations, a
proper mixture of it may be an object of attention. A perfon, in Herefordfhire, is mentioned as an adept in the art of commixing:
not fruit, however, but liquors which have
been feparately drawn, and while they are under

der the procefs of fermentation: while others
are faid to mix the liquors, *according to their
flavors*, after they are manufactured. But
thefe by way of HINTS.

II. Grinding, and the management of the
ground fruit.

1. In the bufinefs of GRINDING, the cider-
ifts of this diftrict are far fuperior to thofe
of the fouthern counties; where, as has been
faid, a kind of cider is fometimes made;
but where the mill not unfrequently confifts of
a wooden roller, ftuck with hobnails, working
againft an upright flab, befet in a fimilar
manner. With this petty machine, the apples are broken, or torn, into fragments, that
the prefs may have fuller power over the
juice, than it would have, if the fruit were
placed in it whole. For there, and everywhere, I believe, except in what are called the
cider countries, it is generally confidered,
that the *cellular juice of the pulp*, only, is the
requifite ingredient of good cider.

In this country, however, it feems to be
generally underftood, that cider made from
the juice of the pulp alone, is far from being
perfect; as wanting, in a great meafure, one
of

of its moſt valuable properties—*flavor*—and
ſome will ſay *colour:* it being likewiſe, I believe, pretty generally underſtood, that the
finer ciders owe their ſuperior flavor to the
kernels, and their colour to the *rind**.

Hence, in grinding, it becomes requiſite to
common good management, that the rind and
the kernels, as well as the pulp, ſhould be
cruſhed or broken in ſuch a manner, as to
enable them to impart their qualities, with
greater freedom to the liquor†.

In

---

* The Hagloe crab, however, is an *evidence* againſt
this idea. It is one of the paleſt-rinded apples, which
grow ; yet produces the higheſt-coloured cider, which is
made. The ſtire apple is likewiſe pale-rinded ; yet affords
a high-coloured liquor. Some are of opinion, that the
rind gives the *ſtrength!* Others, that it communicates
flavor to the liquor. From a ſlight examination of the rinds
of fruit, they appear to be warm and aromatic ; qualities
belonging to eſſential oil ; and, it is probable, the pungency may paſs at ſtrength ; while the aroma may communicate additional flavor.

† The effect of the *ſtalks* of fruit has not, perhaps, been
attended to. Attentive managers pick the largeſt off, in
ſorting the fruit ; but not, perhaps, with ſufficient ſcrupu-
louſneſs. The ſtalks of raiſins are known, I believe, to
have a bad effect on the wine made from that fruit, and
thoſe of apples *may* have a ſimilar effect on cider.

In this intention, the ftone runner and chace are much preferable to the petty contrivance mentioned above; but they are not, in their prefent form, and under ordinary management, by any means equal to the entire reduction of the fruit. I have never feen any ground fruit go to the prefs (except in one inftance) without having a large proportion of unreduced fragments of fruit among it: whereas, on the principles, which are here adopted, the whole ought to be reduced to a ftate of mucilage or pap. Nor have I yet feen any refiduum come from the prefs, without a very large proportion of the kernels unbroken: whereas, on the principles received, every kernel fhould be crufhed.

Having obferved the fimplicity, and high degree of perfectnefs, with which the fugar-mills grind the canes, or rather prefs out their juice, between two plain iron rollers, the imperfections of the cider mill may appear the more ftriking.

But the fugar-cane is a long fibrous body, and readily paffes through between the rollers: whereas fruit, being globular, and of a cellular fubftance, is not eafily laid hold of, or if
caught,

caught, has no lengthened fibres to induce it to pafs, like the cane, between *plain rollers*.

It has, however, been found, that between *fluted rollers* it may be made to pafs; and, in confequence, thefe rollers are in ufe, though not common. They are of caft iron, hollow, about nine inches diameter, with flutes or teeth, about an inch wide, and nearly as much deep. They are fold, I underftand, by the ironmongers of the diftrict. In general, they are worked by hand, two men working againft each other. I have feen a pair adapted to a corn mill, turned by water. Between thefe the fruit paffes twice: the rollers being firft fet wide, to break it into fragments; and afterward clofer, to reduce the fragments. But even this is not a perfect engine: in the refiduum from the prefs, many kernels are found. Befides the acid of the fruit is liable to corrode the iron; and this, in return, to tinge the liquor; though neither of thefe inconveniences are *acknowledged*. In a country, however, where ftone is not eafily to be had, this may, perhaps, be found the moft eligible cider mill.

But

But in this diſtrict, where ſtone is ſufficiently plentiful, the ſtone runner and trough ſeem to be the moſt eligible mill, at preſent known; though it appears to me highly probable, that, with attention and perſeverance, a more per-fect machine might be invented.

Be this as it may, however, the preſent mill appears to be capable of IMPROVEMENT.

It is, at preſent, an *unfiniſhed* machine: I mean when it is firſt turned out of the work-man's hands; time and conſtant wear, does that, in part at leaſt, which the workman leaves undone.

The acting parts of the machine; thoſe which are to bruiſe the rind, and cruſh the kernels; are the face of the roller and the bottom of the trough. But inſtead of their being adapted to each other, in ſuch a man-ner as to effect theſe purpoſes with a degree of certainty, they are left in ſuch a rough un-finiſhed ſtate, as in a great meaſure prevents them, during the firſt fifty years at leaſt, from performing that, which is their principal in-tention. Inſtead of being worked over, and fitted nicely to each other, with the ſquare and chiſſel, they are hewn over with the ſtone
maſon's

mafon's peck only; leaving holes and pro-
tuberances, which would fave even horfe beans
from the preffure; much more the kernels of
fruit. A runner which has been worn two and
twenty years, has holes left in it, which would
lodge half a dozen kernels with fafety.*

To account for this abfurdity feems impoffible. Perhaps the roughnefs was intended to
prevent the runner from fliding; but the ufe
of the cogged wheels has fuperceded this intention. Perhaps it was left to gather up the
fruits with greater effect; but, furely, deep
chifel marks, left in the form of flutes acrofs
the face, would have anfwered this purpofe
better; and would, perhaps, have laid hold
of, and fixed the kernels, fo as to fecure their
being effectually broken, preferable to any
other expedient equally fimple. Or, perhaps,
the *cuftom* was eftablifhed, when the ufes of
the rind and kernel were not known; and time
has not yet corrected the error†.

Be

---

* The argument is, " if it mifs them this time it will hit
them the next." But why throw away time and the work
of a horfe fo idly? Why not hit them, with moral certainty, whenever they fall under the runner?

† Since writing this article, I have been told that the
roughnefs is left to " cut the fruit the fafter" on its being
firft

Be the origin of folly what it may, it is painful to obſerve its effeᴄt. In this caſe, however, the folly, and, of courſe, its effeᴄt, may be eaſily removed. Having made the face of the roller as true as the ſquare and the chiſel can render it, work the bottom of the trough to it; until not a muſtard ſeed can eſcape them. The kernels of fruit are hard, ſlippery, and ſingularly difficult to fix: eſcaping preſſure in a peculiar manner, and with ſingular alertneſs.

Another improvement of the common cidermill appears to be much wanted: namely, a method of preventing the materials, in the laſt ſtage of grinding, from riſing before the runner. And, another, a more mechanical way of ſtirring up, and adjuſting them in the chace.

Until theſe improvements be made, cidermills muſt remain, what moſt of them evidently are, at preſent, *imperfeᴄt machines.*

The

firſt put into the trough! and that on this ingenious principle, ſome will peck their runners over, ſo often as they wear ſmooth! To ſuch cidermakers I would recommend the hobnail mill, which would come much cheaper, rid work ſtill faſter, and ſave the expence of pecking!

The *method of grinding* is to scatter in the whole quantity to be ground together, at once: or, to ease the horse, at twice; observing to put in the whole before any of it be stirred.— A woman, or more frequently a girl, drives the horse, and stirs up the fruit as it is ground, and beats down what lodges on the sides of the trough, with a large wooden spatula, somewhat in the form of a cricket bat: continuing until the whole be deemed sufficiently ground.

The *quantity* ground at each *mill-full* varies very much; even in mills of the same size. A bag—about four corn bushels—is, I believe, the most usual quantity, for a middle sized mill: but much more than that quantity is sometimes ground at once; and, in one instance, I observed only half that quantity was ground together, in a mill of the middle size. From the observations I have made respecting this operation, it appears a great error to grind too much at once. In the instance, in which half a bag, only, was ground, the work seemed to go off quicker, and to be more effectually done, than when the trough is choaked with a greater quantity.

The

The *quantities* ground in a *day*, by mills of the fame fize, varies ftill more.—A man, who has two or three hundred hogfheads of liquor to make, is too anxious to get his work forward, to pay due attention to grinding his fruit; there has been inftances of five or fix hogfheads of perry being made in one day (working early and late:) but three hogfheads of perry, or two of cider, is, I believe, the medium day's work. While fome few men, who know the value of grinding effectually; never fuffer more to be made than one hogfhead of cider a day : reducing, as nearly as the prefent mill is capable of reducing, the entire fubftance of the fruit to a uniform pap or mucilage.

2. MANAGEMENT OF THE GROUND FRUIT. From what goes before it appears, that men, in general, have pretty accurate ideas of the manner, in which fruit *ought to be ground:* though, through a want of leifure, or a want of induftry, and, through the prefent imperfectnefs of the mill, few men approach them in practice : but with refpect to the management of the reduced materials—provincially

the " MUST,*"—they are, in general, fo far
from the line of rectitude, that one would
imagine their faint efforts, at reducing the
rind and kernel, were made in compliance
with cuftom, rather than on the principle of
giving their cider flavor, colour, or any other
valuable quality: for, in common practice,
the pomage is preffed immediately as it is
ground (even though four or five hogfheads
a day are made) No fooner is it out of the mill
than it is into the prefs.

By this conduct, the rind and kernel, let
their powers be what they may, have no time
to communicate their qualities to the liquor.
They

---

* MUST. This term is, here, fomewhat unfortunately
applied. *Muft*, in its accepted fenfe in the Englifh language, fignifies *new liquor unfermented*, whether from the
wineprefs, the ciderprefs, or the mafh vat; but, here, it
feems to ftand for every thing elfe belonging to cider-
making. The ground fruit, before it go to the prefs, is
called *muft*; though from fome expreffions, in ufe, it fhould
feem to mean only the fibres or indiffoluble parts, which are
mixed among the liquor; and the refiduum, after preffing,
is alfo termed *muft*. The term, on its firft introduction,
has evidently been mifapplied. I fhall, therefore, to avoid
confufion, lay it entirely afide. In Surrey the *reduced*
fruit, if I recollect right, is called POMAGE, an apt term
for it: POM-MASH would be ftill more-applicable.

They are not, like the flesh of the apple,
tender cellular pulp; but fibrous and vascular
substances; imparting their qualities less freely
than the pulp; requiring the formal process
of *extraction* before they part with them wholly. It would be equally reasonable to expect
that the whole virtue of hops might be extracted by pouring the wort through them in
a sieve, as to expect that the whole of the virtues of the rind and kernels of fruit can be extracted in a few minutes.

This appears so evidently in theory, that it
is no wonder men of reflection, and who wish
to excel in the art, should let their liquor
"lie upon the must" twenty four hours, or a
longer time; or that others, more fully im-
pressed with this idea, should, after the pomage has lain, in open casks, twenty four
hours or a longer time, *regrind it.*

By this means (supposing the mill to be
perfect) the kernels, which were broken in
the former grinding, being now no longer rigid untractable substances, are reduced to particles of the smallest size; and are, of course,
no longer able to withold their virtue from
the liquor. Consequently, by these means,

the

the entire apple is given to the cider; and (fuppofing the mill to be perfect) every thing done, which art, perhaps, can do, with re- fpect to the grinding and management of the reduced fruit,—previous to the prefling.

III. Prefling and management of the re- fidue.

1. PRESSING. Formerly the pomage was packed up, in a pile, on the bed of the prefs, in *ſtraw*, layer between layer. But at prefent *hair cloths* are commonly ufed in form- ing the pile—provincially the " cheefe"—to be preffed.

Thefe cloths are made of common hair- cloth; fuch as is ufed, or was formerly ufed, in covering maltkilns. The texture loofe, frequently, perhaps, too loofe to be perfect in their intention. The ufual fize about four feet fquare*.

The method of forming the pile varies.— In Glocefterfhire, a wooden rim, frame, mould, or gauge,—about three feet fquare, and four or five inches deep,—is generally ufed in ma- king the " cheefe."—(a term fomewhat auk- wardly

* The price of thefe cloths four to five fhillings each.

wardly borrowed from the dairy)— In this cafe, the gauge is fet, with great exactnefs, every way in the center of the prefs ; a cloth fpread evenly over it; and the pomage laded into it, with a large wooden difh or other utenfil. A fufficient quantity being thrown in to form a layer, from two to three inches thick*, it is fpread evenly with the hands, and worked truly againft the fides and into the corners of the mould; the fkirts of the cloth laid over fmooth, and folded neatly at the corners; a frefh cloth fpread on ; and filled in a fimilar manner; firft raifing the guage a few inches, fo that its upper edge may be level with the cloth when filled. Thus continuing to raife the mould and fill the cloths, until ten or twelve cloths are filled, and the pile is, of courfe, raifed from two to three feet high.

The height of the pile when finifhed, however, depends much on the ftate of the pommage: for, as the pile rifes, the fuperftructure

---

* It is deemed, by judicious managers, a great error to fill the " hairs" too full; as the thinner the layers, the drier will the fubject be preffed.

ture acts as a prefs to the fubftrata; fo that a confiderable proportion of the juice of pears, or of apples which afford much, efcapes during the operation.

The pile being raifed to the defired height, and the top made fmooth and *perfectly level*,— a broad, fquare leaf, of ftrong boards, framed firmly together,— fomewhat larger than the top of the pile,—is placed upon it; and upon this, logs, or blocks— two-and-two acrofs, are piled, until they reach the bridge; the bafe of the fkrew being previoufly wound up to the nut; for a purpofe which will be mentioned.

In Herefordfhire, I obferved, in feveral inftances, a different mode of forming the pile. In this method, no guage is ufed; the whole being done by the eye; nor is the pile carried up either plumb, or fquare.—The corners are cut off; forming four long, and four fhort fides; (for the greater conveniency, I fuppofe, of fecuring the corners of the cloths) and the dimenfion of every layer is leffened, as the pile rifes; fo that when finifhed, inftead of being a cube, or nearly fo, as in the firft mentioned practice, it forms the lower fruftum of a pyramid;

a pyramid; being fomewhat confiderably wider at the bottom than the top.

This, however, appears to my mind an improper form. All fluids endeavour to efcape preffure. If it be applied in the perpendicular direction, they endeavour to fly out horizontally. Thus the pomage (a fubfluid) is forced toward the outer edges of the cloths; which, in this form of the pile, *have no immediate preffure*:—an indirect horizontal preffure, arifing from the natural law of fluids, being all the compreffion which the outer fides of the pile receive.

The method of applying the power of the prefs has been defcribed. It is generally worked by one man; who, with the girl that attends the mill, and a man to fetch in the fruit, and carry away the liquor as the refervoir under the lip of the prefs fills, make a fet, for the mill-houfe.

The preffing is done leifurely: that the liquor may draw off the clearer; and to give the affiftant time to keep the refervoir free.— The firft runnings come off foul and muddy; but the laft, efpecially of perry, will be as clear,

and

and as fine, as if filtered through paper :—a
fweet palatable beverage.

In giving the laſt pinch of the preſs, with
the purchaſe-roller, the man, or men, if more
than one be employed, ſtoop under the rope :
hence the uſe of raiſing the foot of the ſkrew
as high as may be, before the operation commences ; and hence the uſe of raiſing the bed
of the preſs; by which means fewer blocks
are wanted; and a more convenient receptacle
for the juice obtained.

By encreaſing the number of hands to three
or four, the reſiduum may be reduced to almoſt any degree of dryneſs.   Hence the cider
PRESS might be ſtyled A MOST PERFECT EN-
GINE.

2. The RESIDUE. In the common practice
of the country, the firſt reſidue, is either
thrown aſide as offal* (though, perhaps, very imperfectly preſſed) or is returned (deſign-
edly underpreſſed) to the mill, to be "waſhed:"
that

---

* The OFFAL or "dry muſt" is conſidered of little value as manure (but I know not why.)   I have obſerved
poor people carrying it away as fuel.   Pigs will eat ſome
part of it; eſpecially when it has been underground and
underpreſſed.

that is, to be reground, with water, for "family drink*." Thus throwing away, or applying to a mean purpofe, what might, in familiar language, be termed the ESSENCE OF FRUIT LIQUOR! The juices of the rind and kernels; which,—common fenfe would tell us, were we not told it by men of experience and obfervation—come off moft plentifully with the laft runnings†

Hence, men, who excell in the art, continue to prefs fo long as a drop can be drawn; and, unfatisfied with this, return the FIRST RE-SIDUE to the mill, to be REGROUND; not with water, but with fome of the firft runnings of the liquor; moiftening the materials to be ground as occafion requires.

It

---

* SMALL CIDER. When the plantations are large in proportion to the farm, a fufficient quantity of family liquor is obtained, in a plentiful year of fruit, from the wafhings of the refidue, to laft the year round, or a longer time :— where the plantations are proportionally fmall; and in a fcarce year; water is thrown into the mill, while the fruit is grinding; thus lowering the quality, and encreafing the quantity of the liquor. In harveft, it is cuftomary to allow fome malt liquor, or cider " of the beft making."

† It is allowed, however, by experienced managers, that the *richeft* of the liquor comes off with the firft runnings.

It is found, that even breaking the cakes of refuse with the hands, only, gives the prefs frefh power over it: for though it has been preffed to the laft drop, a gallon or more of additional liquor may be got from a prefs full by this fimple means. Regrinding them has a ftill greater effect.

In this ftate of the materials, the mill gains a degree of power over the more rigid parts of the fruit, which, in the firft grinding, it could not reach. If the face of the runner and the bottom of the trough were dreffed with a broad chifel, and made true to each other in the manner which has been propofed; and a moderate quantity of refidue were ground at once; fcarcely a kernel could efcape unbroken; or a drop of liquor remain undrawn.

GENERAL OBSERVATIONS ON GRINDING AND PRESSING. From the foregoing obfervations it appears, *firft*, that the fruit fhould be entirely reduced, before the whole of its virtues can be communicated to the liquor. There is, however, one inconveniency in grinding the fruit very fine: the fubftance, as well as the liquor, efcapes the hair cloth, and fills the fermenting veffel unneceffarily: befides,

perhaps,

perhaps, being injurious during the procefs of fermentation. But this effect may be remedied: I have feen an inftance, in which the firft runnings were poured through a hair fieve to catch part of their foulnefs: a piece of hair cloth thrown over the "tun difh"—would, perhaps, be ftill more effectual. The malt-liquor mafh-tub is furnifhed with a hofe, which ftops a great part of the feculencies. The liquor, in that cafe, comes off almoft clear ; and, *perhaps*, fruit liquor ought to be rendered equally clear, before it be committed to fermentation. This degree of purity is obtainable, by fuffering the foulnefs to fubfide, in the firft cafk, and drawing off the clear liquor, into a frefh veffel, previous to the commencement of the fermentation. By this means, the fermenting veffel, as well as the procefs of fermentation, may be freed at leaft from the groffer foulnefs. In fome cafes, by catching the critical time, and by filtering the lees in the manner which will be defcribed, the *muft* may be rendered almoft perfectly clear.

Secondly,—that the reduced fruit ought to remain fome time, between the grinding and the preffing, that the liquor may have an opportunity

portunity of forming an extract with the
rind and kernels. It is obfervable, however,
that the beft cider, which the art, perhaps,
has yet been able to produce, was made under
different management. But it ought likewife
to be obferved, that the judicious manager of
this cider, grinds only one prefsful (affording
perhaps not quite an hogfhead of liquor) a
day; confequently the firft-ground fruit, has
moft of the day to make the required extract;
and every fucceeding mill-full has a proportionate time: and although the liquor, under
this management, proved excellent, yet had
more of the bitter and fragrance of the kernels
been communicated to it, it *poffibly* might
have been better *.

Thirdly,—that the prefent imperfections of
the mill are fuch as render it almoft impoffible
to reduce the fruit, fufficiently, by a fingle
grinding: but the juice, or a principal part of
it, having been drawn off by the prefs, the refidue is capable of receiving the requifite degree of reduction.

Hence,

---

* An objection to this practice is, that it hurts the *colour*
of *cider*; and the moft experienced managers object to its
lying more than twelve hours on the muft.

Hence, upon the whole, the moſt eligible management, in this ſtage of the art, for thoſe I mean who have leiſure to purſue it, appears to be this:—grind one preſsful a day: preſs ; and regrind the reſiduum in the evening. Infuſe the reduced matter, all night, among part of the firſt runnings ; and, in the morning, repreſs, while the next preſsful is grinding.

IV. FERMENTING. In this department of the art, the niceſt judgement is requiſite, The former are mere manual operations. The right principle being adopted, and a ſuitable apparatus being prepared, the execution requires no great ſhare either of genius or experience. But in conducting the fermentation properly, much ſkill, and a cloſe attention are requiſite.

In the prevailing practice of the diſtrict, the liquor is " TUNNED";—that is, put into hogſheads or other caſks ;—immediately from the preſs. The caſks, in the ordinary practice, being *filled* to the bung hole. Some judicious managers, however, object to the filling up of the caſks; eſteeming it more eligible management to leave them about a

" *pailful*

"*pailful ullage*". While others, ftill more deeply verfed, perhaps, in this myftery, leave an *ullage in proportion to the ripenefs of the fruit:* thus, with liquor from underripe fruit the cafk is filled; but with that from fruit which is more mature, an ullage is left, in proportion to the ftate of ripenefs.

With refpect to the TEMPERATURE of the AIR, in which fruit liquor ought to be fermented, nothing *accurate*, I believe, is to be learnt in this diftrict. Even the profeffional dealers, I underftand, are ftrangers to the ufe of the thermometer! It is, however, generally underftood, that fermenting liquors fhould not be expofed to froft*. But, in the commencement of the feafon, it is thought they cannot be kept too cool. In the middle of October, the air then about 60°. the cafks were placed in fheds, or in airy buildings of the fame, or nearly the fame, temperature as the common atmofphere; and frequently in
the

* Neverthelefs it has been remarked, that froft, previous to the commencement of the fermentation, though it formed a fheet of ice on the furface, had no obfervable bad effect.

the open air*. Later in the feafon, the cafks
are placed in clofe buildings ; with windows,
however, to admit occafionally a thorough
air ; which is generally thought to be falutary
to fermenting liquors. I have, neverthelefs,
feen liquor of the moft delicate kind fermenting in a clofe hovel, without a thorough air †.

No FERMENT whatever is made ufe of. I
have not, at leaft, on repeated enquiry, met
with one inftance of any being ufed : even the
moft intelligent feem furprized at the enquiry.
Let the fpecies of fruit, the degree of ripenefs,
and the weather be what they may, the liquor
is left to fight its way with its own weapons.

Hence

***

* In this cafe the cafks have a fmall piece of file or flat
ftone fet over the bung hole, proped by a wooden pin in a
leaning pofture to fhoot off rain water &c.

† FERMENTING ROOM. In a complete manufactory of
fruit liquor, the fermenting room fhould be under the fame
roof with the mill houfe ; a continuation of the prefs room ;
or at leaft opening into it : with windows or doors on every
fide ; to give a free admiffion of air ; and with fuitable ba-
racadoes to guard againft fevere froft ; with fruit lofts over
it ; and, beneath it, a vault for laying up the liquors, after
fermentation ; with fmall holes in the crown of the arch, to
admit a leathern pipe ; for the purpofe of conveying the
liquors, occafionally, from one fituation to the other. The
dealer's warehoufes are fitted up in a manner fomewhat fa-
milar to this.

Hence the COMMENCEMENT of the fermentation is entirely uncertain. Perhaps, the firft; perhaps the fecond, perhaps not until the third day, or perhaps in cold weather not until a week, or a month; after the liquor be tunned. It is obfervable, however, that liquor, which has been agitated in a carriage; though taken immediately from the prefs, will fometimes, on being laid down, pafs, almoft immediately, into the ftate of fermentation.

The CONTINUANCE of the vinous fermentation (or more accurately fpeaking the firft ftage of it) is not lefs uncertain than its commencement. Liquor, under the laft-mentioned circumftances, will pafs through it, perhaps, the fame day. But lefs agitated liquors, I believe, feldom go through it in lefs than two or three days; will fometimes continue under it five or fix days.

With regard to any CRITERION whereby to judge of the fermentation, as to its being *perfect*, *imperfect*, or *inordinate*, I have not been able to collect a fingle idea worth regiftering. It is a fubject, to which moft cidermakers appear to have paid little or no attention: notwithftanding

notwithftanding they are fully aware of the
change, which takes place during this natural procefs; learning, from their own experience, that the liquor owes its intoxicating
quality entirely to fermentàtion. It is true,
the manufacturers of " fweet cider" pay fome
attention to the fermentation: but their whole
art appears to confift; not in *regulating* it to
any *certain degree*; but in checking it with
every means in their power; preventing,—*as
much as they are able*,—any degree whatever of
the vinous fermentation from taking place!

It is obfervable, that fermentation operates
fomewhat differently on differenc liquors.
Thus, ciders made from fruits properly matured, generally throw up a grofs fpume, refembling that of malt liquor; forming, on the
top, a brown cruft, of a thicknefs proportioned to the fpecies and ripenefs of the fruit;
the riper the fruit the more " brown muft"
is thrown up. Perries, on the contrary, throw
up little fpume, and feldom cover it with a
brown cruft; neverthelefs, I have feen barland
perry with a head refembling that of cider;
which, it is obfervable, is fometimes, like per-

VOL II.   A a   ries,

ries, unable to form ahead; or is intentional-
ly prevented from doing it, by management.

Having remained some days in the first ves-
fel, the liquor is drawn off the lees, and put
into fresh casks: an operation termed
RACKING.

It appears to be fully and universally understood, that there is a CRITICAL TIME OF
RACKING, on which the future quality of the
liquor very much depends. Hence, in the
dealer's warehouses, persons are employed to
sit up all night, to catch the critical minute.
But what is rather extraordinary, men differ
in their ideas with respect to the proper juncture. The prevailing idea seems to be, that
the proper time to rack is at the close of the
first fermentation, *while the liquor is clear:*
embracing the critical time between the sub-
siding of the foulness caused by the motion,—
and the falling of the spume; a circumstance
which frequently takes place a short time after the fermentation ceases; whereby the liquor is not only fouled, but is probably furnished with the seeds of a fresh fermentation.

But rational as this theory may seem, there
are men, whose characters class high as managers

gers of fruit liquors, yet who think it right to rack before the fermentation ceafes ; while the liquor is yet foul !

In common practice, however, the liquor itfelf is feldom examined in judging of this nice point ! Secondary CRITERIONS are applied to. Thus cider, in the practice of fome men, is racked when the brown cruft becomes firm enough, and dry enough, not to ftick to the finger on being touched ; while others ftay until the cruft crack, and the white fcum which has formed under it begin to rife through the cracks. The ordinary criterion of the time for racking perry is " before it has done hiffing". In the particular practice abovementioned the guide is " when it begins to twinge the nofe": that is when the gas flies off in quantity ; which it does when the liquor is at the top of fermentation. While the makers of *fweet* liquors will not even hear them hifs, if they can poffibly prevent the difagreeable found !

The METHOD OF RACKING is to draw off the clearer liquor, at a tap fixed above the lees, and to put it immediately into a frefh cafk, duly feafoned. When it begins to run

foul, the tap is ſtopt, and the remainder is filtered through flannel or canvas bags*; or
for want of theſe, through a hair cloth; the
four corners being hung upon a hook; thus
forming a kind of bag adequate to this purpoſe. The intention being merely that of ſe-
parating the liquor from the lees and ſcum.
The filtered liquor, which ought to drop fine
from the bag, is added to the reſt; from which
it differs in three notable qualities: it is
higher-coloured than that which has not
mixed with the lees: it is no longer prone to
fermentation; on the contrary it is found to
check that of the liquor racked off; and, another, if it afterward loſe its brightneſs it is difficult to be recovered.

The degree of FULLNESS OF THE FRESH
CASK ſeems to be pretty generally the ſame:
the caſk is not filled up; but left with about a
pailful

---

* FILTERING BAGS are made in the form of jelly bags—
the mouth wide enough to receive a wooden hoop, a foot
or fourteen inches in diameter: the depth eighteen inches
or more, tapering to a point at the bottom. Where much
racking is done, theſe bags are hung in a frame, about three
feet high, holding perhaps a dozen bags, with tubs placed
underneath to catch the filtered liquor.

pailful ullage; fo that the furface of the liquor can juft be touched with the finger ;—*the bung being ftill left out.*

The NUMBER OF RACKINGS depend on the ftate of the liquor, and the judgement of the manager. If the frefh fermentation, which moftly commences, in fome degree, after racking, become violent, it is generally un-derftood, that the liquor ought to be racked again, to check it. Hence, in the practice of fome men, the fame liquor will be racked five or fix times. On the contrary, if a fmall degree of fermentation, only, take place; which is, in this cafe, termed "*fretting*"; it is, in ordinary management, fuffered to remain in the fame cafk: but the degree of fretting, which requires the operation of racking, is by no means fettled: one man would rack the fame cafk of liquor, which another would leave for time to quiet. In the common practice of farmers, cider is feldom or ever racked more than once; and perry is fome-times fuffered to remain, until time render it *quiet* and *fine*, in the firft cafk, into which it was tunned.—The general idea feems to be, that frequent rackings *weaken* the liquor, and that much fermentation *roughens* it.　The farmers, therefore, rather choofe to be at the rifque of lofing the richnefs than to lower the ftrength and beftow upon it the labour of racking.

But thofe who manufacture the finer liquors for fale; efpecially, perhaps, thofe who have checked the firft fermentation; think it prudent to repeat the rackings, until the liquor will lie quiet, or nearly fo.　If it cannot be brought into this ftate. by ordinary racking, the frefh cafks are fumigated with fulphur; whofe fumes are found to have a power of filencing, or greatly checking, the fretting. This expedient is termed " ftumming the cafks."

The METHOD OF STUMMING them is this: matches, made of thick linnen cloth, about ten inches long, and an inch broad, thickly coated with brimftone about eight inches of their length,—being prepared; and the cafk properly feafoned; every vent is tightly ftopt, except the bung-hole; a match kindled; lowered down into the cafk; and held, by the end undipped, until it be well lighted, and the bung be driven in; thus fufpending the lighted
match

match within the caſk. Having burnt ſo long
as the contained air will ſupply the fire, the
match dies ; the bung is raiſed ; the remnant
of the match drawn out; and the caſk ſuffered to remain, before the liquor be put into
it, ſome two or three hours, more or leſs according to the degree of force required. For
a few days the liquor retains a ſulphurous flavor, which, however, in a ſhort time va-
niſhes, and no evil effect, I underſtand, is found
to follow the operation.

Thus far the method of FERMENTING IN
CASKS : a mode of fermentation, which ninety
nine hogſheads of a hundred, made in the
country, are ſubjected to. Nevertheleſs there
are ſome few men, in different parts of the
diſtrict, who ferment in VATS or other OPEN
VESSELS.

One inſtance of this practice I met with in
the vale of Gloceſter. In this inſtance the liquor is ſet in cowls or other open tubs, or in
caſks with one of the heads out. In theſe veſſels it ſtands until the firſt fermentation be
pretty well over ; when *the ſpume is carefully
ſkimmed off*; under the idea that it is the ſcum
mixing with the clear liquor, which cauſes it

to

to fret after racking. The fermentation having ceafed, and the lees fubfided, the liquor
is racked off into a frefh cafk, and the lees
filtered in the manner which has been defcribed. In this practice, the liquor is never
racked a fecond time.

Another inftance of fermenting in open
veffels occurs in a practice which has been
repeatedly mentioned; and which is entitled to
the higheft attention*. It is generally fpoken
of as being, what I apprehend it really is, the
firft practice in the country. In this inftance,
the liquor is fermented in BROAD SHALLOW
VATS; not lefs than five feet diameter, nor
much more than two feet deep; each vat containing about two hogfheads. In thefe vats
the liquor remains until it has done " rifing;"
that is, until the fermentation has ceafed, or
nearly fo; when it is racked off, *without fkimming*; the critical juncture being caught before the fpume begin to fall; the whole finking
gradually down together, as the liquor is
drawn off. In this practice, likewife, the li
quor, notwithftanding its fuperior quality, is
feldom racked a fecond time.

GENERAL

* See page 253.

GENERAL OBSERVATIONS ON FERMENTING.

Chemifts enumerate three fpecies of fermentation. The *vinous*, the *acetous*, and the *putrefactive*.

The juices of fome vegetable productions; as thofe of fruits which are inclined to fweetnefs; will, while recent and in their natural ftate, with a due degree of heat, and a free communication of air, pafs fpontaneoufly into the firft or VINOUS FERMENTATION : will acquire heat and motion; become turbid; and, at length, difentangle themfelves from their impurities : throwing down part to the bottom of the containing veffel, part up to the furface; leaving, in the middle, a VINOUS LIQUOR,—furnifhed with a greater or fmaller quantity of INFLAMABLE SPIRIT. Thus *wine*, *perry*, *cider*, and the different kinds of *ale* are vinous liquors; their various degrees of *ftrength* being given by the quantity of inflamable fpirit they refpectively contain.

The veffel ftill remaining in a moderate degree of heat, and being ftill kept open, fo as to allow a free admiffion of air, the vinous liquor will pafs on to the fecond ftage of diffolution—- the ACETOUS FERMENTATION: by
which

which the inflamable fpirit will be thrown off,
and another precipitation of grofs matter will
take place; and the vinous liquor will now be
changed into a dilute vegetable acid, or vinegar; of a *ftrength* proportioned to the
quantity of fpirit thrown off.

The fubject being ftill expofed, the third
or laft ftage, at length commences. The vinegar becomes PUTRID; its acid is deftroyed;
and the remaining contents of the veffel are
found to be, fimply, common EARTH and
WATER.

This being the nature of the expreffed juices
of fruit,—the firft object of the ciderift is to
bring on a due degree of vinous fermentation;
and his fecond, to prevent the vinous liquor
from paffing on to the acetous fermentation.

But, notwithftanding this general THEORY
OF DISSOLUTION, fcience remains deftitute of
a fatisfactory THEORY OF THE VINOUS FERMEN-
TATION. I have not, at leaft, after fome
fearch, been able to find any other than ar-
rangements of well founding words, pleafing
enough to the ear, but affording the under-
ftanding no gratification.——Even the firft
mover, the innate ftimulus, the NATURAL

PRINCIPLE

PRINCIPLE of this fpecies of fermentation does not evidently appear.

In collecting and regiftering the foregoing particulars, refpecting the fermentation of fruit liquor, many theoretic, as well as practical ideas were fuggefted by reflection. But though the former may contain a principal part of the theory required, they are, at prefent, in a ftate altogether unfit for publication.

Therefore, all I fhall attempt, in this place, is to explain more fully the GENERAL EFFECT of the vinous fermentation, on the fruit liquors under notice, and endeavour to draw fome practical inferences.

The moft ftriking effect is that of its giving STRENGTH to the liquor which, before its operation, was not poffeffed of that quality: effecting almoft a total change of its original nature: not only by furnifhing it with an intoxicating quality, which it was entirely free from; but in reverfing, in a remarkable manner, its medical, and, of courfe, its dietetic properties.

Another notable effect is that of its deftroying, or leffening, the SWEETNESS of the liquor The lofs appearing, from the information I

am

am in poffeffion of, to be in proportion to the
ftrength acquired.*

Hence the difference between *rough* and
fweet liquors: the fermentation of the former
has continued until the whole or a principal part
of its fweetnefs was deftroyed: that of the latter has ceafed, or been checked, while a principal part of its fweetnefs remained.

It does not follow, however, that roughnefs is a proof of ftrength, or, fweetnefs of a
want of body. Much depends on the nature
of the fruit; and much, probably, on its ftate
of ripenefs. Rich well ripened fruits afford
fweetnefs enough to furnifh a fufficiency of
ftrength, and enough more to retain a fufficiency of richnefs in the liquor. On the contrary, liquor drawn from harfh and underripe
fruit is exhaufted of its fweetnefs, before it
has acquired a redundancy of ftrength. Or,
if the fermentation be checked to preferve its
fweetnefs,

---

* This, as a general pofition, will, perhaps, be objected
to. Good cider is faid to be made from ill tafted fruit.—
The hagloe crab is mentioned as an inftance. But the harfh-
nefs of this apple proceeds, I apprehend, from its flefh,
its fibres, not from its juice; which, when fully matured,
accords fufficiently with the idea here offered.

fweetnefs, it is rendered, of courfe, deficient in ftrength.

Hence the crude flatulent quality of the common fweet liquors; which are either weak thro' a want of fermentation; or, having been fufficiently fermented, have afterward been fweetened by art. A kind of liquor which is palatable enough to *tafte*, but which, on being *drank*, foon becomes nauceous to the palate.

And hence the preference to be given to liquors of a MIDDLE RICHNESS: ftrong without roughnefs, and rich without fweetnefs. A generous liquor, this, which, to ufe the good fellow's phrafe, may be *fat by*. A liquor, which is feldom met with out of this diftrict, and not frequently in it. A liquor, neverthelefs, which, I am fully perfuaded, men, in general, would prefer to moft foreign fruit liquors that are, at prefent, imported—in difgraceful abundance.

In thefe obfervations, the methods of producing the different fpecies of fruit liquor: namely, the rough,—the fweet—and the generous, pretty evidently appear.

To PRODUCE ROUGH LIQUOR,—chufe auftere fruits: grind them in a crude, under-ripe

ripe ftate; and fubject the liquor to a full fermentation.

To PRODUCE SWEET LIQUOR,—make choice of the fweeter fruits: mature them fully; and check the fermentation of the liquor.

The ordinary *methods of checking the fermentation* have been mentioned to be thofe of racking the liquor, and fumigating the frefh cafk.

But *the ufe of racking* is differently underftood. The prevailing idea feems to be, that the frefh fermentation, or the fretting, is caufed by the fpume or dregs of the preceding; and that by racking the liquor off clear, into a clean veffel, the foulnefs is got rid of.

But the manufacturers of fweet liquors rack under different motives. Their idea is, that racking *cools the liquor*; and, by that means, checks the fermentation. They obferve that the fmaller the ftream, in racking, the more the fermentation is reftrained. And, in purfuance of the fame idea, they frequently fpread the liquor, thin, in open veffels; and fometimes agitate, or rather ventilate it, in this fituation; and obtain the defired end by thefe expedients.

It

It appears to me, however, that the end is gained, not altogether by giving coolnefs to the liquor (though in fome degree it may) but by giving the *principle of fermentation an opportunity of flying off.* Filtering the liquor, drop by drop, is found not to check, but to deftroy the fermentation. Filtered liquor is found even to lower the fermentation of others: not, certainly, by its actual coolnefs; becaufe in this it can differ very little from liquor which has been racked; the atmofphere, in both cafes, prefently reducing them to the fame temperature; but, probably, by the fermentative principle having efcaped, wholly, from the one, its proportion is, confequently, leffened, in the other.

Hence (by the way) it is probable, that by filtering the frefh liquor from the prefs, a valuable antifcorbutic might be obtained: and, under the fame idea, it appears probable, that fweet liquors, duly manufactured, may have their medical virtues.

But leaving this idea to thofe whom it more concerns; and fuch liquors to thofe who may require them; we will proceed to the production of one of a more generous nature. A liquor,

which thofe who drink for fafhion or amufement, or to heighten their friendfhips, or
lighten their cares, fhould encourage ; and
which the manufacturers of fale liquors will
then, of courfe, endeavour to produce. At
prefent, their whole fkill is exhaufted on the
art of rendering their liquors unfit for ordinary
drinking. They are not, at prefent, faleable,
unlefs they are fweet !

TO PRODUCE LIQUORS OF A MIDDLE RICH-
NESS. Much depends on the nature of the
fruit, and much on the *feafon* it is matured in.
The fruits to be made choice of are fuch as
yield juices capable of affording a fufficiency
both of richnefs and ftrength. Such are the
ftire apple, the hagloe crab, the longney ruffet,
the Woodcock apple, the fquafh pear, and,
probably, numberlefs other forts, were their
refpective natures individually examined.——
Neverthelefs, it is probable, there are others
which are altogether unfit for this purpofe;
confequently, altogether unfit to encumber
the ground they grow on.

Much, however, depends on proper *management*. From what has gone before, it appears, that to produce a free fermentation,

air

air and heat—*atmofphere* and *warmth* are requifite.   Warmth to fet in action the fermentative principle.   Atmofphere to receive the
loofened particles to be thrown off.   But it
alfo appears, that the ordinary heat of the atmofphere is, generally, more than fufficient to
give the required degree of motion; and that,
in the manufacturing of the fruit liquors under
notice, *coolnefs*, rather than warmth, is requifite.

Hence the preference to be given to *open
vats*; which at once preferve the required
coolnefs; thereby preventing too furious a
fermentation from taking place; and, at the
fame time, admit a fufficiency of furface, to
render that which does take place, free and
uninterrupted.———Two hogfheads of liquor,
fpread in the vats which have been defcribed,
expofe fome yards of naked furface: while the
fame quantity of liquor in cafks, filled to the
bungs, have only a few inches.   The difproportion of furface more than a hundred to one.

Hence it appears to me evident, that if liquors be fermented in *cafks*; which, only,
perhaps, can be conveniently ufed on a large
fcale; they ought not to be filled; nor ought

VOL II.   B b   they,

they, in my opinion, to lie on the bulge, in the ufual manner; but to be fet on-end, with the heads out; and to be filled to fuch a height, only, as will produce the requifite degree of fermentation.

In whatever fituation the liquor is fermen ted, I am clearly of opinion, the firft effort of fermentation ought not, under ordinary cir-cumftances at leaft, to be fruftrated. But, on the contrary, the liquor ought to be allowed one full free fermentation ; the degree being regulated, not by compulfory means, but by the depth of the liquor; and this by the heat of the air in the fermenting room, and the quality of the liquor.

But having paffed through the firft ftage ; having been racked in the proper juncture ; and being found to have acquired a fufficient body, it may be right to prevent, as much as poffible, a frefh fermentation. Rack, fpread thin, or even filter, to keep it in the defired ftate.

V. CORRECTING. This is, provincially, and aptly enough, termed "Doctoring:" for the want of it implies difeafe. My enquiries, however, have been directed to the art of pro-

ducing

ducing found liquor, rather than to that of healing the unfound. Neverthelefs, on digefting the general mafs of information collected on the fubject, I find a few ideas have, as it were fpontaneoufly, offered themfelves, on this department of it.

The imperfections which art undertakes to fupply are,

The want of ftrength;

The want of richnefs,

The want of flavor,

The want of colour; and

The want of brightnefs; confequently, with the addition of the other two qualities of fruit liquor, acidity and aquofity, or in plainer terms vinegar and water, we have in our power; the whole art of making cider, without the trouble of planting orchards.

The want of *ftrength* is fupplied with brandy or other fpirits, in fufficient quantity, to prevent liquor which has been made from underripe fruit, and has been imperfectly fermented, from being carried off by the acetous fermentation:*   The

* I am informed, that the dealers draw a fpirit, for this purpofe, from the refiduum of the prefs, macerated in water; and diftilled in the ufual manner.

The want of *richnefs* is fupplied by what are generally termed *fweets*,—prepared in a manner which I have not enquired after ; nor has it fallen incidentally under my notice.

To fupply the want of *flavor*, an infufion of hops is fometimes added. This is faid to communicate an agreeable bitter, and at the fame time a fragrance ; confequently becomes a fubftitute for the juices of the rind and kernels, thrown away to the pigs and poultry, through infufficient grinding ; or given to the fervants, through a want of proper preffing.

The want of *colour* is fometimes fupplied by elder-berries, ground among the fruit.— Thefe are faid to give a fine colour, and a kind of flavor, which is not difagreeable.— But they are made ufe of, I underftand, by individuals, chiefly or folely, in making liquor for their own drinking. The univerfal colouring of the *profeffion* is burnt fugar, which gives the defired colour, and a degree of bitter, that is highly commended. There are two ways of preparing this colouring: one of them, by melting the fugar on a falamander, and fuffering it to drop, as it melts, into water ;—the other, to boil the fugar (in this cafe

brown

brown fugar) over the fire, until it acquire an
agreeable bitter; then pour in boiling water,
in the proportion of a gallon to two pounds of
fugar, and ftir until the liquor become uniform.   A pint of this preparation will colour
a hogfhead of cider.

Brightnefs is obtained through different
means.   In ftubborn cafes, when the foulnefs
is great, and the liquor will neither " fine nor
fret"—being what is technically termed " ful-
key"—yet is under circumftances which require that it fhould prefently put on a cheer-
ful countenance—it is drenched with " bullocks blood:" namely the blood of cattle or
fheep: the blood of fwine is rejected with ju-
daical fcrupuloufnefs.

The method of preparing and adminiftring
the blood is this.   The only preparation of it
is that of ftirring it well, as it is drawn from the
animal; to prevent its parts from feparating.
Stirring it one way is not deemed fufficient; it
ought to be ftirred both ways, for about a
quarter of an hour.   The next thing is to en-
quire whether the liquor be in the mood for
" taking the blood;" which it is not, it feems,
equally at all times.   This is done by repeat-

B b 3   ing

ing experiments with it in a phial: if it will take the blood in a vial, it will take it in the cafk. A quart, or lefs quantity, is fufficient for a hogfhead. After the blood is poured in, the liquor fhould be violently agitated, to mix the whole intimately together. This is done by a ftick, flit into four quarters, inferted at the bung-hole, and worked about brifkly, every way among the liquor, until the whole be evenly blended. In about twenty four hours, the blood will be gone down, and the liquor ought to be racked; for by "lying upon the blood," even two or three days, the liquor is liable to receive a *taint*, which is not eafily got rid of. A moft extraordinary effect of this procefs is, that the blood carries down, not only the feculency, but the colour, of the liquor: rendering it, though ever fo highly coloured, limpid almoft as water! This, however, is a lofs which is the lefs regretted; as the means of reftoring it are fo eafy and fo effectual.

The other "forces" made ufe of in giving brightnefs to cider, are the common ones of eggs, and ifinglafs; (or a combination of the two;) ufed as in the practice of WINE merchants;

chants; who, as well as the dealers in CIDER,
have of late years, it feems, made a free ufe
of " THE BLOOD."

VI. LAYING UP. This is one of the moft
difficult fteps to be taken in the management
of fruit liquor; yet appears to be the leaft attended to or underftood.

The common practice is to bung up the
cafks in fome particular month, or at fome
certain time; without any guide to difcrimi-
nate the critical juncture, when each individual requires to be fhut up. Thus the early
made liquor lies open until January or February; that made at Chriftmas is fometimes
left open until March or April.

The intention of fecuring the liquor from
the outward air is, evidently, that of preventing th vinous liquor from purfuing its natural
propenfity; that of entering the *acetous fermentation:* which, according to the general
law of nature, all vinous liquors become liable to; as has been already obferved; on their
being expofed to the outward air, and a moderate degree of heat. Hence, liquors which
have paffed the vinous fermentation, and are
kept open until the warm air of fpring begins

to exert its influence, neceſſarily become vinegar ; or enter into a ſtage of diſſolution,
which, if not timely interrupted, terminates
in vinegar. Hence the number of caſks of
liquor, which are every year loſt, or materially
injured, through a want of due attention to the
time of laying up.

The only CRITERION I have met with for
judging the critical time of laying up is, when
a fine white cream-like matter firſt begins to
form upon the ſurface. But this may be too
late; it is probably a ſymptom, at leaſt, of the
acetous fermentation, which if it take place
in any degree muſt be injurious. Yet, if the
caſks be bunged tight, ſome criterion is neceſſary ; otherwiſe, if the vinous fermentation
have not yet finally ceaſed, or ſhould recom-
mence, the caſks will be endangered, and the
liquor injured. Hence, in the practice of the
moſt cautious manager, whoſe practice I
have had an opportunity of obſerving, the
bungs are firſt driven lightly, when the liquor
is fine and the vinous fermentation is judged to
be over ; and, ſome time afterward, when all
danger is paſſed, to fill up the caſks, and
drive the bungs in ſecurely, with a rag, and
rofin

rofin them over the top. Some open the
cafks again at fix weeks, to refil them; others
think this unneceffary.

It is an idea, pretty generally received I believe among the farmers at leaft, that liquor,
after it has done fermenting; that is to fay, prefently after the laft racking; fhould have
" SOMETHING TO FEED ON":—hence fome
feed it with parched beans; others with egg
fhells; others with mutton fuit, to the quantity of half a pound cut into pieces as big as
the finger, to each hogfhead; and a variety of
other things are put in " to make it keep."
There are men, however, who confider this
as a vulgar error:—being of opinion, that liquor cannot be laid up too clean. Neverthelefs, it appears to me more than probable
that, when there is danger to be apprehended
from the acetous fermentation, *fomething* may
be ufeful. Ifinglafs is thought, by a moft
intelligent manager, to be ferviceable in this
intention; which is, in my idea, that of fixing the principle of the acetous fermentation;
or at leaft clogging it fo far as to leffen its
activity.

The

The dealers lay up much of their liquor in *large cafks* containing from four or five to eight or ten hogfheads (of 110 gallons) each. In thefe cafks, good cider will lie many years. In *hogfheads*, it is fometimes kept three or four years. But it is, obfervable, that if cider be kept too long in cafk, it lofes much of its richnefs and flavor—growing what is provincially called " ftummy"—lofes its mellownefs and becomes heady: This, *perhaps*, is owing to a *decay* of the richnefs, which, before, fheathed part of the fpirit, but being now loft, the fpirit obtains full power of action.

The ufual *place* of laying up liquor is a cellar or a vault; or for want of this, a room fo fituated as not to be liable to fudden change of heat and cold.

VII. BOTTLING. The proper *age*, at which to bottle, depends on the quality of the particular liquor to be bottled. Good cider is feldom fit for bottling, before it be a year old. It is fometimes unfit for this operation until it be two years old; fomething depending on the fize of the cafk, as well as on the quality of the liquor; the larger the cafks the

longer

longer the liquor may be fuffered to lie in
them.

In bottling, as in almoft every other ftep
to be taken in the art under notice, there is a
critical time, which ought to be obferved,
and which, in this cafe, is not difficult to be afcertained. Whatever degree of richnefs and
flavor the liquor has at the time of bottling,
the fame, or nearly the fame, qualities it will
preferve in bottles, for many years. Hence
the critical time of bottling is, when the liquor has acquired, in cafk, its higheft degree
of perfection; whether that juncture happen
in one or two years, or in a longer or fhorter
time.

A perfon, who has paid efpecial attention to
this fubject; and whofe liquor is become in
a manner proverbial throughout the diftrict;
has obferved, that liquor which has been bottled in the fulnefs of its richnefs and flavor,
has been friendly to the habit, paffing off
chiefly by infenfible perfpiration; while the
fame liquor, fuffered to remain in cafk, until
it had paffed this juncture, became armed
at all points; diftracting to the head, in the

firft

firſt inſtance, and injurious to the whole frame.

It is needleſs to ſay, that the liquor ought to be *fine* at the time of bottling. If not ſo at the critical time, the common force of eggs or iſinglaſs is made uſe of.

It ought likewiſe to be bottled in cool weather ; otherwiſe the bottles are more liable to fly.

Good cider ſhould be kept as wine* ; and, as this, may be kept to almoſt any age ; the ſeveral *ſpecies* of FRUIT LIQUOR being very ſimilar in their nature †.

VIII. MARKETS. The principal market for fruit liquor, is LONDON ; from whence, as well as from BRISTOL, it is ſent to the EAST and WEST INDIES, and other FOREIGN MARKETS, in bottles ‡. But

---

Cider, which has been ſweetened, with Liſbon ſugar, by the London dealers, to ſuit the palates of their cuſtomers, is apt to fly. The bottles, therefore, in *this* caſe, ſhould be kept upright. Alſo, when the liquor, tho' genuine, is bottled at an early age, the bottles, in the firſt inſtance at leaſt, ought not to be laid down.

† A Gentleman, near Ledbury, is ſaid to have cider of every fruitage, for more than 20 years paſt.

‡ For FOREIGN MARKETS, fruit liquors ſhould not be bottled, until they have acquired ſome conſiderable age ;

as

But the quantity of liquor fent abroad is in confiderable, compared with that expended in the HOME-CONSUMPTION: not only London and Briftol, but every town of this ifland (as well IRELAND) is fupplied from this quarter of it; in which, only, *fale* liquor is at prefent produced, in quantity.

The immediate PURCHASERS are chiefly *dealers*, who live in different parts of the diftrict, and who fupply the inland markets. UPTON and LEDBURY are the principal places of refidence of what are provincially termed " cidermen"; but HEREFORD, GLOCESTER, and WORCESTER have their buyers. Briftol, too, fends buyers into the country; and, of late years, the London dealers have found their way into it; and, in a plentiful year, buy up great quantities.

The STATE, in which orchardmen difpofe of the produce of their grounds and orchards, is various:

Sometimes

as, otherwife, they are liable to burft the bottles; much lofs having been frequently fuftained by injudicious management, in this cafe. The length of time, they ought to lie in cafk, previous to fhipping, depends on the length of the voyage, and the climate it is intended for.

Sometimes the fruit is fold.

Sometimes the liquor immediately from the prefs.

Sometimes the liquor after the firft racking.

Sometimes the liquor fit for market, in cafks.

Sometimes (but not often) the liquor in bottles.

The growers, in general, object to felling the FRUIT :—the quantity of carriage is increafed ;—they lofe the wafhing of the " muft" for family liquor ;—and the dealers fay they have other reafons ;—they cannot change the fruit, nor, in a fcarce year, dilute or adulterate the liquor. Neverthelefs, confiderable quantities of fruit (efpecially of the fuperior forts of apples) are fold: the dealers, who have conveniency and fkill, like to manufacture their own liquor, from the beginning: or, if this cannot be accomplifhed, to fend a perfon to fee it properly made.

The principal part of the LIQUOR is bought immediately from the prefs; the country dealers, in general, choofing to have the working, at leaft, if they cannot have the making, of their own liquors.—And, in a general light, this is, *at prefent,* eligible: for,

having

having proper conveniency, as well as ſkill,
or proper perſons, to give the buſineſs of fermenting due attendance, the riſque of manu-
faƈture is leſſened: beſides their having, by
this means, an opportunity of ſuiting the taſte
(be it true or falſe) of their cuſtomers.   The
London and Briſtol dealers, have places
in the country, where they work their own
liquors: the former chiefly at Upton; the
latter at Hereford.

The PRICES of orchard produce are very
fluƈtuating; varying with the quantity produced, and the quantity of ſtock in hand.
The prices of hops are not more uncertain
than thoſe of fruit liquors.   One night's froſt,
in the ſpring, has been known to raiſe the ſpe-
culating price three-fold of what it was the
preceding day.

The price of fruit.   In the " great hit" of
1784, common apples were ſold at 18d. to
2s. a ſack (of four corn buſhels)*.   Stire apples

* FRUIT MEASURE. This is as vague, here, as it is
in other places. The dealers generally buy by the "feam"
a kind of indeterminate meaſure ; or by the " buſhel";
containing two " buſhel-baſkets", holding more than a
corn

ples 5s. to 12s. a fack; according to the foil,
and fituation produced in. In 1786, a very
fcarce year, common apples were moftly fold
to the fruit boats, for the Briftol market.
Stire 10s to 18s. a bag. This year; another
hit of unufually fine fruit; common apples
18d. to 2s. Stire 6s. to 14s. 'a bag. The
former the price in the vale; the latter in the
foreft!

Price of liquor from the prefs. That of *common cider* is generally fixt by a meeting of the
dealers, at Hereford fair, the 20 October.
In 1784, they injudicioufly (as has been intimated) fixt it too low; namely 14s. the hogfhead (of 110 gallons)*: the confequence
was

corn bufhel each. But by a *bufhel*, in common language,
is generally meant *two corn bufhels* (of 9½ or 10 gallons)
level: the *fack*—provincially " bag"—being reckoned *two*
" *bufhels.*"

† FRUIT LIQUOR HOGSHEAD. By a hogfhead is underftood 110 gallons. But hogfheads in general do not run
exactly to that meafure; varying from 105 to 115 gallons, wine meafure.

They are made very fubftantially, with oak ftaves and
heads, with very ftrong afhen hoops, and generally with
four, or a greater number of iron hoops.

The price of fuch a cafk varies with the demand. The
ordinary price is a guinea. This year, the coopers taking
the

was, farmers would not fell, and of courfe could not make (not having cafks to hold the whole of their liquor). Some fharp frofts fet in, the principal part of the beft fruit was entirely fpoilt, or materially injured; and the dealers, before the making feafon was over, were glad to give 25s. a hogfhead. In 1786, the dealer's price was five guineas a hogfhead: a rare price. This year they have again fixt it unreafonably low: namely 16s. a hogfhead. The ordinary price of common cider, on *a par of years*, is 25s. to two guineas a hogfhead.

Stire cider is feldom fold from the prefs; either the dealers buy the fruit, or the growers work their own liquor. Its *value* at the prefs is 5l. to 15l. a hogfhead: a price, which the fineft wines are not worth, I believe, in any country, immediately from the prefs.

Common perry has, it is faid, this year, been fold at a guinea a load of three hogfheads!—

Not

the advantage of the feafon, have raifed them to a guinea and a half: fo that the cafk is worth nearly twice as much as the liquor it can contain.

When liquor is fent in to the dealers, they draw it off, and return the cafks, by the team which brought them.

Not a penny a gallon.* Half a guinea to 12s. is the ordinary price. Fifteen shillings is esteemed a high price for common perry.

Nevertheless "*squash-pear perry*" is seldom sold so low as two guineas. It has been sold at 12l. 10s. from the press! The ordinary price is 5l. 10s. a hogshead. This year the price at the beginning of the season was five guineas: considerable quantities—probably some hundred hogsheads—were bought at four guineas. But, before the close of the season, the current price was two guineas. A price, which has seldom been known before. A farmer had four guineas bade for his whole make (from thirty to forty hogsheads); but he refused to sell under a shilling a gallon. The same dealer has since bought a considerable part of it, at two guineas a hogshead †.

The

* In this case, however, it is to be supposed, that the carriage is very short; or the liquor is delivered at the press.

† The EXPENCE of picking, carriage of fruits, hoarding, grinding and pressing, is from three to five shillings a hogshead; according to the labour bestowed, and of course the quantity made in a day. It cannot be made properly under 5s. a hogshead. The price of making at one public mill

The price of liquor once racked is about one fourth more than the price from the prefs; Liquor in this ſtate is bought, chiefly, by houſekeepers, in towns, (and perhaps innkeepers) who have neither conveniency nor ſkill to rack. The one racking being generally the whole that it receives *.

The price of fermented liquor varies much; according to the ſpecies of fruit it is made from. *Common cider and perry* (provided the general market prices remain nearly the the ſame) are worth about one half more than their prices at the prefs; more or leſs, however, according to their prefs prices †.

The

mill (at Rofs) is a ſhilling a hogſhead for the mill only, the employer finding the horſe. At another, (in Newnham) the price of the mill and a horſe is three ſhillings a day, The expence of carriage depends on the diſtance. Four hogſheads are a full load. The carriage may be laid at two to five ſhillings a hogſhead. With the wear and tear of caſks and other utenſils, the medial expence on liquor, ſent in from the prefs, may be eſtimated at ſeven ſhillings a hogſhead.

* In this caſe, the farmer ſometimes lends his caſk to the buyer, charging about five ſhillings for the loan.

† When liquor is ſold in this ſtate, the ſeller's caſks remain with the purchaſer, free of coſt, until they be emptied ; though the liquor ſhauld remain in them two or three years.

The rifque, in ordinary hands, is fomething confiderable. The more delicate liquors, as *ftire cider* and *fquafh perry*, which require great judgement in fermenting, and which (the laft more particularly) frequently turn out contrary to expectation, notwithftanding extraordinary care and fkill may have been beftowed upon them, are fometimes fold at a very advanced price, prefently after laying up. In this recent ftate, each fpecies has been fold fo high as 20 guineas a hogfhead. Their par price in that ftate is 10 to 12 guineas.

The price in bottles. When we confider the very low price, at which fruit liquors are fold, in their recent ftate, and ftill more, when we reflect on the many hundred hogf-heads, which are frequently wafted for want of cafks to put it in *, we become afto-nifhed at the extravagant rate, at which they are fold, in their matured ftate; even in the very center of the diftrict, in which they are produced; efpecially in bottles. The common price at the inns is a fhilling a bottle

---

* In 1784 cifterns were formed in the ground to receive it ; but they did not anfwer expectation ; the liquor was fpoilt. In Perfhore the juice is faid to have run from the pear-hoards, in currents, into the common fhores.

bottle*! While the ordinary price of draught
cider (of perhaps a better quality) is four
pence a quart—feldom more than fix pence
(the London prices!)   But the liquor which
is put into bottles is *fuppofed*, at leaft, to be of
the higher finer kinds; as ftire, and golden
pippin cider, and fquafh perry. Squafh perry,
if any way curious, is fold commonly at 18d.
a bottle.   It has (as well as cider) been fold
at 2s. a bottle.

IX. PRODUCE.   This may be viewed in a
five-fold light.

> The produce of fruit
> The produce of trees
> The produce of ground
> The produce of individuals
> The produce of the diftrict.

THE PRODUCE OF FRUIT depends much on
the *fpecies* of fruit, as well as the *feafon* it is matured

---

* The excife on cider, which paffes through the dealer's,
or the publican's hands, is about eighteen fhillings and fix
pence the wine hogfhead; or about three pence halfpenny
the wine gallon.

The dealer's price, for common liquors, is eight to ten
fhillings a dozen; for finer liquors, ten to eighteen fhillings; with bottles included.

tured in. Pears, in general, yield much more
juice than apples. And some species of apples much more than others. The general
estimation is eight bags of apples, or six bags
of pears, to a hogshead of liquor. Of the
latter, supposing each bag to contain thirty
six gallons, and the hogshead one hundred and
eight gallons, two hogsheads of fruit yield
one hogshead of liquor. Hence some sorts of
apples, as the Hagloe crab and the stire, in
some dry seasons, will require near three hogsheads, or any other measure, of fruit to one
of liquor.

THE PRODUCE OF TREES is extraordinary;
evincing, in a striking manner, the fertility of
the soil of this country. I was shewn a *pear*
tree, off which *two* hogsheads were made this
year; and in the same suite of grounds was an
apple tree, from which the same quantity was
expected to be drawn. But this, supposing the
expectation to be fulfilled, is a rare instance,
I believe. *One* hogshead of *cider*, I understand, is reckoned a great produce: three
barrels a very great yield for one tree. But
three hogsheads of *perry* were, *it is said*, this
year produced by one pear tree!

But

But fruit, this year, is not only large and thickly hung upon the trees, but yields an unufual proportion of juice; which is neverthelfs efteemed to be of a good quality.

THE PRODUCE OF GROUND. I have been informed, and by an authority which I have no reafon to doubt, that twenty hogfheads have been made from an acre of ground;— a clofe orchard. This is not improbable; for it appears, above, that forty trees may ftand tolerably well on an acre of ground: fo that the produce, in this cafe, is only half a hogfhead each tree.

THE PRODUCE OF INDIVIDUALS, in a plentiful year, runs very high. This year, there are feveral men, who will make between two and three hundred hogfheads. I am affured by a perfon, who ought to be a judge of the fubject, that there are fome few individuals, who will, this year, make five hundred hogfheads of liquor; including cider, perry, and their own family drink. This is the lefs incredible, when we confider that there are individual plantations—fingle orchards—in Herefordfhire, of thirty to forty acres each.

It

It is from thefe larger plantations that the markets are principally fupplied. Farmers, in general, have feldom more fruit than will fupply their own enormous drink houfes.

It is obfervable, however, that cottagers, from incroachments made from commons and larger waftes (paying perhaps the Lord of the Manor a fmall quit-rent) thrown in, collectively, no inconfiderable quantity of liquor. Some of them making perhaps in a plentiful year, eight or ten hogfheads; and having no thirfty work people to quench, the principal part of it goes of courfe to market.

THE PRODUCE OF THE COUNTRY, in a fruit year, muft be immenfe. Far exceeding the general conception. The produce of the four counties (of Glocefter, Monmouth, Hereford, and Worcefter) which has paffed through the dealer's hands, has been eftimated at fifteen thoufand hogfheads. And a quantity fuperior to that is, in a plentiful year, probably confumed within the diftrict. The produce of the four counties, on a par of years, may therefore be laid at thirty thoufand hogfheads.

GENERAL

GENERAL OBSERVATIONS ON FRUIT LIQUOR
AS AN OBJECT OF RURAL ECONOMY. Notwithstanding the extraordinary produce of
fruit, which this country affords, in a plentiful
year, it is a disputable point; especially between landlord and tenant; whether, upon
the whole, the liquor it yields be a good, or
an evil. This is a matter, which would be
difficult to determine, demonstrably.—I am
inclined to believe, from what I have seen,
that, every thing considered, it is, *under present circumstances*, the latter.

The damage done to the crops, by the
drip and shade of the trees, is annual, certain,
and, *at present*, excessive. Whereas a general
hit of fruit is most uncertain;—is not expected
oftener than every third year. This is the
fourth year from the last general fruitage.
Many trees, during this interval, not having,
perhaps, matured an apple: while this year,
though the produce be abundant, the price is
so low, that it little more than pays for labour,
carriage, and attention: yet the neat profits of
this year, small as they may be, have to stand
against the damage of four years; also against
a proportionate share of the cost of plants,

planting

planting, grafting, and defending the young trees; of the mill-houfe, and apparatus; of the wear and tear of cafks, and of cellar room; as well as as againft the evils of a habit of drinking; which, in a fruit year, is the caufe of much idlenefs; and, in a dearth of fruit, is the caufe of an unneceffary wafte of malt liquor; which, alfo, the neat profit of the fruit year, has to ftand againft.

Neverthelefs, it is fufficiently evident, from data interfperfed in the foregoing pages, though difficult to *prove*, that youthful, bearing trees, even of the common forts of fruit, and under their prefent neglect, produce, on a par of years, more than will repay their feveral encumbrances; and that the more valuable kinds are very advantageous to their occupiers.

THE EFFECT OF FRUIT TREES ON THE GROUNDS THEY GROW IN, depends much on the diftance they are planted from each other; as well as on the width of their heads, and the height of thefe from the ground. Low-fpreading trees, planted in clofe order; efpecially if full of wood; are ruinous to the crops, which are under them: drawing up corn

weak

weak and fpiritlefs; and, by deftroying or checking the better herbage, give grafs what is called a fournefs; entirely changing the quality of the herbage. On the contrary, tall-ftemmed lofty trees, kept within due bounds, thin of wood, and ftanding at fuit-able diftances, will admit of corn growing beneath them; efpecially while young; and, under thefe circumftances, are much lefs in-jurious to grafs (except in autumn with their leaves) than reafon may fuggeft. Befide, an advocate for fruit grounds might argue, that the trees feed, in part at leaft, below the corn mould, or vegetative ftratum; fo that the hufbandman might be faid to be reaping two crops, at the fame time, from the fame land: one the produce of the foil; the other of the fubftratum; whofe treafures, without the trees, would be loft to him. There is probably fome truth in this idea.

Upon the whole, I think, we may fairly conclude, that, by encreafing the better fruits, and, by purfuing proper management throughout, the fruit grounds and orchards of thefe counties, might be rendered a fource of riches to them; and, at the fame time, be a benefit to the nation at large. The

The particulars of improvement requifite to the acquifition of thefe advantages appear to be the following.

1. To clear the ground of fuch old and difeafed trees as encumber the foil, without making an adequate return ; due attention being paid, in this cafe, to the more valuable kinds of fruit. By this means, it is probable, the foil might be relieved from one fourth of its prefent encumbrance.

2. To clear away, while the wood remains of value, or to head down and graft with the better fruits, the wildings, kernels, and other inferior kinds of fruit, which encumber the ground, and croud better trees ; and which, by affording an inferior kind of liquor, bring difrepute on the whole. By this means much more than one fourth of the prefent encumbrance would be got rid of, without eventual injury ; *or* the ground would become productive of a fpecies of produce, which would, in a fhort time, be beneficial to the occupier and the community.

3. To fet up the low-headed, drooping trees, which remain ; thereby giving air to the crops growing beneath them ; and to free

the

the tops from all foulnefs and fuperfluity;
thereby giving health and vigour to the trees;
and, by leffening the darknefs of their fhad-
dows, at the fame time give health and vigour
to the crops: as well as by leffening the quantity of bearing wood, guard, as much perhaps
as human art can guard, againft an excefs of
fruit, in any one year; thereby doing as much
perhaps as can be done, towards obtaining,
what of all things is defireable to a fruit farmer, a crop of fruit every year*. But, as
there is no hope of obtaining this with full effect;

4. To

---

* PRUNING. The great danger to be guarded againft
in pruning fruit trees is that of *doing too much at once*. Taking away a large proportion of the top of a fruit tree injures, in all probability, its roots, eventually, by rendering part of them ufelefs; and the top, in the firft inftance,
by a glut of fap. On the contrary, taking away a fmall
proportion of the top, in equal probability, ftrengthens
the roots; by enabling them to fupply, with greater eafe,
the wood and foliage, that are left; as well as to throw out
a ftronger bloffom, and mature, with greater certainty,
the fruit which fucceeds.

Hence, the pruning of an orchard, whofe trees are in a
wild thick-wooded ftate, ought to be made the work of
three or four years: removing, the firft year, the moft offenfive boughs, only. Thus rendering the work progreffive
and pleafurable; in as much as it becomes, by thefe means,
light, yet moft effectual.

4. To erect, on the larger plantations at leaft, fuitable buildings, proportioned to the quantity of planting; for the purpofe of manufacturing, on the premifes, the liquors they refpectively produce.* Suffering dealers, from all quarters of the kingdom, to impofe, in open convoc tion, what prices they pleafe, in a plentiful year, is difgraceful to the country. Inftead of fourteen or fifteen fhillings a hogf-head, a grower might enfure with moral certainty, by keeping his liquors, perhaps, only one year, three times, perhaps four times, that price—perhaps ten times the *neat* profit which he now receives. It would be worth the tenants' while to pay doubly the intereft laid out on fuch erections. To fuffer the dealers from London, and other diftant markets, to fend agents into their neighbourhood, and make this profit out of them, perhaps within fight of their plantations, is an abfurdity, which ought not to efcape cenfure. The landed intereft of the diftrict is involved in the difcredit.†

5. To

* See note page 351 ; and page 323.

† The country dealers are likewife involved in the difgrace: to fuffer men, whom, in the regular courfe of bufinefs

5. To endeavour, by every deviſeable means, to propagate, in ſuitable ſoils, and well choſen ſituations, the "OLD FRUITS;"— which, if they can, by any art yet known, or by any, which ſtudy and application may hit upon, be continued only one *generation* longer, the advantage might, in my opinion, be of conſiderable magnitude.*

6. To

buſineſs, *they* ought to *ſupply*, to manufacture their own li-quors in the place of their growth, is at once a diſgrace and a diſadvantage to them.

* PROPAGATION OF THE OLD FRUITS. The ſtire apple, *it is ſaid*, is propagated with tolerable ſucceſs, upon the Foreſt of Dean (its favorite ſoil) by *ſuckers*; or rather young wood pulled out of the crown of the tree; in the ſame manner as the codlin is uſually propagated. *Layer-ing*, in tubs of earth elevated for that purpoſe, might be a ſtill better mode of propagation.

The ſquaſh pear has been *budded*; but with what degree of ſucceſs is yet to be tried.

The golden pippin, *it is ſaid*, is raiſed, with ſucceſs, by attending properly to its head, while young; preventing it from running too much to wood; keeping it within due bounds, by judicious *pruning*; eſpecially by taking off the *midſummer ſhoots*; which not only exhauſt the ſap, and thereby weaken the tree in the inſtant; but being tender, are liable to be froſt-nipped; decay; rot off; and leave a wound in the young branch which threw it out.

Be this as it may, nothing is more likely to keep the young trees in health, and preſerve them from the CANKER;

which

6. To fet about, with all fpeed, the raifing
of FRESH VARIETIES : for although it feems
poffible that, by proper exertions of art, the
old fruits may be kept in being fome fhort
time longer, it appears, in my mind, impoffible that they can, by any art, be rendered
perpetual. Befides, the old varieties are,
indifputably, the productions of human induftry: and it is highly probable, that by
greater exertion, or by greater fuccefs, new
varieties of ftill higher value may be produced.

A reform of this magnitude, however, muft
not, for various reafons, be expected from
the

which is fo fatal to the old fruits, than keeping the head
within due bounds ; thereby enabling the roots to give vigour to the whole plant.

I have been informed, however, by a Gentleman, who,
for amufement, prunes his own wall trees, that *nicking the
bark,* by drawing the edge of a fharp knife carefully down
it, will, by giving freedom to the fap veffels, ftop the
CANKER; and I was fhown trees, on which its effects was
fufficiently ftriking to warrant my mentioning it in this
place.

The reader, however, is requefted to receive the above
particulars as *hints,* which being in poffeffion of, without
having either leifure or opportunity to enable me to eftablifh the proof of their practicability, I deliver up to the
ufe of thofe, who, being in practice, may have both.

the *tenantry*. Fruit trees, as an object of rural economy, class with woodlands and hedges: they are *fixtures* belonging to the premises.— The tenant has only the use of them, perhaps for a time uncertain. His object, of course, is present profit. It, therefore, behoves the proprietor, who has a permanent interest in them, to look forward to future advantages.

The great objects of the reform would be, to free the estate from unprofitable encumberances. To stop the efflux of inferior liquors; which, by finding their way to market, bring general discredit on ENGLISH FRUIT LIQUORS: and, above all, to encrease the quantity of liquors of the *first quality*; that their richness, their flavor, and their generous disposition may be universally known;—that the demand may be in consequence enlarged; the prices be raised; the value of estates augmented; and the prosperity of these counties proportionally encreased.

THE END OF THE SECOND VOLUME.

INDEX.

Calves

INDEX.

C.

INDEX.

D d 3   Dimenfions

INDEX.

INDEX.

Hoing,

I N D E X.

Plan

INDEX.

Waggon

I N D E X.

T H E   E N D.